Business Despite Borders

Santiago Iñiguez de Onzoño
Kazuo Ichijo
Editors

Business Despite Borders

Companies in the Age of Populist
Anti-Globalization

Editors
Santiago Iñiguez de Onzoño
Instituto de Empresa
Madrid, Spain

Kazuo Ichijo
Graduate School of International Corporate
Strategy
Hitotsubashi University
Tokyo, Japan

ISBN 978-3-319-76305-7   ISBN 978-3-319-76306-4   (eBook)
https://doi.org/10.1007/978-3-319-76306-4

Library of Congress Control Number: 2018944600

Cover illustration: petekarici/E+/Getty

Printed on acid-free paper

This Palgrave Macmillan imprint is published by the registered company Springer International Publishing AG part of Springer Nature.
The registered company address is: Gewerbestrasse 11, 6330 Cham, Switzerland

Preface

Globalization, a process that has taken place through the economy and other areas of society across continents, has been one of the most important drivers in the development of business in recent decades. However, recent political developments in Europe, the United States and elsewhere, along with resentment toward globalization reflected, for example, in the upsurge of nationalism and populism, have raised questions about the evolution of global trade and international business.

In this challenging context, innovative companies must not only find new ways to operate across borders, but they can also contribute toward improving international relations and develop new forms of valuable relationships among people from different nations and cultures: as stated elsewhere, "the best antidote to bad international politics is good business".[1]

In fact, we believe that the current potential threats to globalization also provide opportunities for innovative companies to reinvent the way we carry out business across borders.

In the context of the ongoing challenges globalization faces, this book provides models and references for companies that plan to continue operating globally or to expand their presence internationally, along with a collection of case studies that illustrate how companies from different regions of the world are succeeding in reaching out to different, sometimes distant, territories.

This book also portrays a number of business leaders and CEOs who are actively developing imaginative strategies to build business bridges across continents.

Business Despite Borders provides a series of case studies portraying innovative companies that are setting new standards in internationalization at a time when globalization is being questioned, for example, in the aftermath of

Brexit or through the revived protectionism and nationalism sparked by some governments, even in developed countries.

This book also aims to show how new forms of business internationalization, by using new technologies or innovative strategies, can overcome obstacles to free trade and protectionism and how business leaders can develop imaginative strategies to strengthen ties across continents.

The reader may conclude that this book is based on an optimistic supposition: that globalization is, however, irreversible and that companies can contribute positively to achieve sustainable growth and a fair distribution of wealth across the world.

Business Despite Borders addresses the current challenging circumstances for globalization and provides models and guidance for companies operating globally or expanding internationally. It also offers a collection of case studies that illustrate how companies from different regions of the world are succeeding in reaching out to different, sometimes distant, geographies.

Finally, we would like to thank all the contributors to this book for their generous and prompt response to our invitation to participate. We hope this is the beginning of an ongoing conversation on other pressing issues over the future of management. Also, we would like to extend our gratitude to Stephen Partridge, our editor at Palgrave Macmillan, for all his support during the book production and his suggestions, including the book's title.

Madrid, Spain   Santiago Iñiguez de Onzoño
Tokyo, Japan   Kazuo Ichijo

Notes

1. S. Iñiguez de Onzoño, *The Learning Curve. How Business Schools Are Reinventing Higher Education* (London: Palgrave Macmillan, 2011); p. 25.

Contents

Notes on Contributors

Salvador Aragón is Head of Innovation and Professor of Information Systems and Innovation at IE Business School (Spain). From a research perspective, he defines innovation as an intersection between market, organization and technology. He holds a PhD in innovation governance, a master's degree in business administration (MBA) and a bachelor's degree in industrial engineering.

Jorge Ardiles is Professor of Management at Universidad del Desarrollo (Chile). He holds a PhD in management from IESE. He is a visiting professor at different universities in Latin America and Germany.

Maria Antonia OG Arroyo is a multi-awarded social entrepreneur, investor and Adjunct Professor of Innovation and Entrepreneurship at the Asian Institute of Management (AIM; Philippines). Maoi was selected as a Young Global Leader of the Word Economic Forum in 2015.

Paolo Boccardelli is the dean and Professor of Corporate Strategy and Management of LUISS Business School (Italy). He has been appointed Expert of International Standing at the Australian Research Council and Chairman of the Scientific Committee of the Ericsson Foundation. His research interests focus on corporate and business strategy, creative and digital Industries, entrepreneurship and innovation.

Luiz Artur Ledur Brito is the dean of Fundaçao Getulio Vargas EASP in Sao Paulo (Brazil), where he is also Professor of Operations Management. He has combined his academic work with positions at companies including Sanbra, Santista Alimentos and Dixie Toga. His research interests focus on the relations between operations management and strategy as well as operational factors that affect business performance.

Gabriela Alvarado Cabrera is the director of the Business Intelligence Center and Professor of Marketing at ITAM, Mexico, where she is also the past associate dean of MBA programs. She holds a doctor in business administration degree from IE Business School. Her research examines the effects of organizational reputation on business schools' strategic choices and her next book deals with the future of management education in Latin America.

Salvador Carmona is Professor of Accounting and Management Control at IE University (Spain), where he serves as Rector. Salvador has conducted extensive consultancy and empirical research in the car industry as well as in high-tech startups. Salvador's areas of interest are the role of management control systems in strategy implementation and the organizational and social aspects of accounting systems. He has served as the president of the European Accounting Association during 2015–2017.

Lilian Soares Pereira Carvalho is a researcher at the Brazilian Small Business Bureau. She is also Professor of Marketing at the Saint Paul Business School (Brazil), and she has been a visiting professor at Concordia University (Canada). She holds a PhD in marketing from Fundaçao Getulio Vargas EASP (Brazil), and her research interests focus mostly on the behavior of consumers.

Fernando A. D'Alessio DBA, Eng D., was the founder and first director general of CENTRUM Catolica Graduate Business School (Peru), where he is also a full professor and researcher. D'Alessio achieved the rank of Vice Admiral at the Peruvian Navy and was awarded its Sword of Honor. For the production of this volume's case he was assisted by CENTRUM International MBA students Omar Eusebio, Renato Salarrayán, Paul Tupayachi and Pablo Zúñiga.

Celia de Anca is the director of the Center for Diversity in Global Management and Professor of Diversity and Islamic Finances at IE Business School (Spain). She is the author of *Beyond Tribalism* (Palgrave Macmillan 2012) and co-author of *Managing Diversity in the Global Organization* (Palgrave Macmillan 2007). She was recognized as Women Executive of the year (ASEME, 2008) and has been listed among the *Top 50* thinkers, the global management influencers list.

Santiago Iñiguez de Onzoño is the president of IE University (Spain), where he is Professor of Strategic Management. His two most recent books *The Learning Curve: How Business Schools Are Reinventing Education* (Palgrave Macmillan 2011) and *Cosmopolitan Managers: Executive Education That Works* (Palgrave Macmillan 2016) are focused on business education and executive development. He is a LinkedIn Global Influencer and past Chair of AACSB International.

Ziliang Deng is Associate Professor of International Business at the Renmin Business School, Renmin University of China (China). His main research interests are international entrepreneurship, international knowledge management and international non-market strategies in emerging markets.

Kazuo Ichijo is the dean and a professor at Graduate School of International Corporate Strategy, Hitotsubashi University in Tokyo (Japan). He received a PhD in business administration from the University of Michigan. His research interests are focused on organizational behavior (knowledge creation theory), leadership and change management.

Runtian Jing is Professor of Organizational Management at the Antai College of Economics and Management of Shanghai Jiao Tong University (China). His areas of interest are organizational change and leadership behavior. He is the vice president of the International Association for Chinese Management Research.

Jikyeong Kang is the president and dean of the Asian Institute of Management (AIM, Philippines). She has been a professor of marketing at Manchester Business School, IE Business School, CEIBS and ESSEC, among others. She serves on the boards of AACSB and EFMD. She also serves as an independent director on the Board of Security Bank.

Cristian Larroulet is one of the founders of Universidad del Desarrollo (Chile), where he is also Professor of Management and Vice President of Graduate Studies. He has been a professor at Universidad Católica de Chile and Universidad Adolfo Ibáñez. He held several positions in public office and he is a former Minister of the Presidency of Chile (2000–2014).

Daniel R. LeClair is Executive Vice President and Chief Strategy and Innovation Officer at AACSB International (USA). His work is focused on strategy and innovation in business education. He was the principal architect of AACSB's data and research services and spearheaded its development as an industry thought leader. Previously, Dan was an academic economist and business school administrator.

Ariel T Lopez is a senior consultant at Hybridigm Consulting Inc. (Philippines), specializing in strategy creation and implementation, idea design and marketing.

Peter Lorange is a renowned global scholar in international strategy and management. He is a former president of IMD and the President Emeritus of the Zurich/CEIBS Institute of Business Education. He has been affiliated to the Wharton School, University of Pennsylvania, The Sloan School of Management (MIT) and the Stockholm School of Economics, among others. He has published more than 20 books and 120 articles related to multinational management, strategic planning processes, strategic control and alliances, and internally generated growth processes.

Ji-Ye Mao is a professor and the dean of the Renmin Business School, Renmin University of China (China), and previously a tenured professor at the University of Waterloo, Canada. His areas of research include managerial and behavioral issues in the adoption of information systems in general, and IT outsourcing management and digital transformation in particular. He is the Chair of the China association for information systems (CNAIS).

Manuel Muñiz is the dean of the School of International Relations at IE University (Spain) and the founding director of its Center for the Governance of Change. He is also a senior associate at Harvard's Belfer Center for Science and International Affairs as well as one of the co-founders of its Transatlantic Relations Initiative. A PhD graduate from the University of Oxford, his research focuses on innovation and disruption, geopolitics, and regional and global governance.

John C Orlina is the COO of Hybridigm Consulting Inc. (Philippines), where he has worked with all sectors in the Philippine innovation ecosystem in commercializing locally developed technologies.

Germán Pérez-Casanova is an adjunct faculty member at IE Business School (Spain). He has developed his professional career in the car industry, where he has held positions in a wide range of areas: comptroller, operations manager, managing director and leader of cost improvement programs. Germán is interested in the role of accounting and management control systems in processes of organizational forgetting.

Enzo Peruffo is Senior Assistant Professor of Strategy at LUISS University, (Italy), where he is also the head of Specialized Masters and director of part-time MBA. Enzo's areas of interest are corporate strategy and corporate governance, family business and innovation, and digital turnaround in the SMEs.

Eileen M. Rogers is an adjunct faculty member of the Villanova University (USA) and teaches a course entitled "Leading Positive Change" in the MBA program there. She is Founder and CEO of LeadershipSigma®, a company dedicated to developing leadership globally. She is co-author with Nick van Dam of their ground-breaking book *YOU! The Positive Force in Change*. Eileen consults in strategic leadership development, facilitates leadership learning programs and also works as an executive coach.

Henry Bradford Sicard is the president of the CESA School of Business (Colombia), where he is also Professor of Leadership and Strategy. He has held financial management and corporate positions at Citibank (Colombia and Spain), BBVA, Banco Colpatria and Porvenir Pension Funds. He is a doctor in business administration candidate at IE Business School. He is currently a member of several boards of directors of various institutions.

Nick van Dam is Visiting Professor of Learning and Leadership Development at Nyenrode Business University (Netherlands), the University of Pennsylvania and IE Business School. He is a partner, Global Chief Learning Officer and Client advisor at McKinsey & Co. He is keenly interested in the emerging insights from the fields of positive psychology, cognitive neuroscience and philosophy. Nick is also founder and chairman of the e-Learning for Kids Foundation.

Lin Zhou has been the dean of the Antai College of Economics and Management of Shanghai Jiao Tong University (SJTU, China) since 2010, where he is also Professor of Economics. Before joining SJTU, he taught for more than 20 years in various universities, including Yale, Duke and ASU in the United States. He specializes in microeconomics and game theory. He is a fellow of the Econometric Society.

Yufeng Zou is an assistant dean and director of EMBA and Executive Education programs at the Renmin Business School, Renmin University of China (China). He is an expert in China's executive education market. He is currently pursuing a doctor in business administration degree at IE Business School. His research interests are the internationalization of Chinese businesses and human resources.

List of Figures

List of Tables

1

Business Globalization: The Nightmare of Populism and the Hopes Brought by Technology

Peter Lorange, Kazuo Ichijo, and Santiago Iñiguez de Onzoño

Abstract Despite the recent spread of populism and nationalism, particularly in developed countries, the globalization of business is an unstoppable and irreversible process. Some major drivers of this global integration of business include the impact of technology and the international orientation of millennials and younger generations as well as the diffusion of entrepreneurship. This chapter describes the major avenues used by companies to internationalize their activities as well as the major threats posed to global trade.

Is Globalization Irreversible?

The Populist Time Bomb

The year 2016 will go down in history as a turning point in the globalization of the economy and business. The UK's decision in a referendum (Brexit) to leave the European Union (EU) was the first in a series of unforeseen events

P. Lorange
Zurich/CEIBS Institute of Business Education, Zurich, Switzerland

K. Ichijo
Graduate School of International Corporate Strategy, Hitotsubashi University, Tokyo, Japan

S. Iñiguez de Onzoño (✉)
IE University, Madrid, Spain
e-mail: santiago.iniguez@ie.edu

© The Author(s) 2018
S. Iñiguez de Onzoño, K. Ichijo (eds.), *Business Despite Borders*,
https://doi.org/10.1007/978-3-319-76306-4_1

1

that called into question the process of global integration, previously taken for granted by most experts.

Soon after, in 2017, the announcement of protectionist policies by the US Presidency amid questions over the practice of free trade and the decision to exit certain international bodies and initiatives, such as the Pacific Alliance, confirmed an antiglobalization drift in the world's most advanced economy, prompting probable reciprocal reactions from other, developed and emerging, nations.

At the same time, the rise of populism and nationalism on several continents has sharpened antiglobal tendencies. According to MacDonald, "The globalization backlash has moved from anarchist rioters at G8 summits into the political mainstream" (MacDonald 2017).

In spite of these outbreaks of populism and a welter of pessimistic forecasts, populist candidates failed to take power in French presidential elections and a general election in the Netherlands, results that calmed many economic agents and constituted a fillip for the project of European renewal. In the face of doommongering, the Old Continent had recovered its economic and political drive.

Populism is by no means confined to one continent. It has taken root in several Latin American countries, most notably in Venezuela, and stirrings of nationalism can be detected in Asia, where North Korea persists as a powerful black hole, besides unresolved tensions between China and Japan, and some eccentric speechifying on the part of leaders such as the president of the Philippines.

And so the world's political and economic context changed in less than a year. As Livesey explains, three generally accepted basic precepts have been shattered: globalization will become consolidated; free trade generated prosperity and development; and that the geo-political center of gravity was moving from West to East. As of today, those three suppositions are clearly in some doubt. A common expression used to define today's context is the "post-world". We are post-global, post-truth, and post-certain (Livesey 2017).

What seems undeniable is that globalization does not have many friends these days.

The Process of Globalizing Business

Belief in the irreversible nature of globalization began to form in the 1980s, with the transcontinental development of multinational companies, not only from the US, but also from Japan, Europe, and Korea. The fall of the Berlin Wall and the collapse of communism also served to confirm the consolidation of capitalism and liberal democracy as the dominant and preferred economic and political models. China's gradual process of opening up to global trade as well as development in emerging countries, in particular the BRICS

(Brazil, Russia, India, China, South Africa) nations, encouraged the idea of a multipolar world supported by permanent growth.

But prior to this, the thinking and theory that underpinned the global development of companies had been nurtured in business schools, the cradle of so many leaders who piloted the globalization of business process over the last four decades. A 1983 article by Theodore Levitt entitled "The Global Village" (1983) is considered a seminal watermark in the globalization of business process. The author explained that "Technological, Social Political and Economic changes drive the World toward a 'Global Village' or 'converging commonality'. The main beneficiaries of this are global companies that offer standardized products and have costs advantage." Time would show, however, that companies' international expansion may not necessarily bring with it the achievement of economies of scale, but could actually multiply costs arising from complexity and coordination, and require the decentralization of some activities from the value chain. This correction of the initial approach to globalization is encapsulated in the formula "think globally, act locally".

A key contribution to theory relating to the development of multinationals was made by Christopher Bartlett and Sumantra Goshal in 1989, with their concept of transnational companies. The authors described the process of geographical expansion by corporations with a global presence. They identified two distinct models, one of which was that of traditional multinationals that operated with complete organizations in each country, comprising all business functions and business units. These were the multidomestic corporations.

A classic example of the multidomestic model in the 1950s was Philips, a company founded in the Netherlands that had factories in all of the large countries in which it operated, with subsidiaries that were self-sufficient in terms of management and operations. Essentially, this way of working was a result of the existence of tariffs on cross-border trade, plus various technical specifications regarding products in each country, and non-tariff barriers against imports. With the passage of time and the advancing of regional integration initiatives, especially the EU, these barriers were gradually lowered or disappeared altogether, a situation that justified companies like Philips splitting their business units between various countries with the aim of achieving economies of scale and exploiting synergies in different business areas. Then, companies with matrix structures appeared, with two organizational hubs: business units and geographical divisions. One of the corporative challenges for the top management of these companies was how to balance the geographical and business hubs, and knowing which part of the matrix to favor in the result of conflicts, which were frequent.

Apart from the traditional multinational model, another kind of corporation emerged and consolidated in Japan: the *keiretsu*, a business model with a global vocation that operated most of its processes in a centralized manner, from R&D to production, and which distributed its products on a global scale. Toyota and Honda are two examples from the automotive sector that followed this approach, as did Matsushita (currently named as Panasonic) and Sony in consumer electronics. In these cases, the economies of scale were clearly evident through the concentration of activities within headquarters, allowing the corporations to cope with higher logistics and transportation costs in delivering their products to distant parts of the world.

Faced by these two corporative models—multidomestic and global—Bartlett and Goshal (1989) put forward the transnational company model. In the authors' view, the two fundamental forces determining the structure and configuration of a multinational corporation are pressure for local responsiveness, as seen in the case of Philips in 1950, and pressure for local integration, as with Toyota, for example. Considering such extreme cases, the authors proposed a model that combined the two forces to determine the location of activities from the value chain, while establishing the necessary mechanisms of coordination to function effectively.

An analogous approach to corporate internationalization strategies was made by George Yip in his book "Total Global Strategy" (1992). In Yip's view, international development was also based on two models: the "multilocal", under which companies operate in each country or region on a standalone basis; and "global", where activities and strategies are integrated across the world. Interestingly, Yip explains that the globalization of companies is not questionable, but rather a continuum of differing scales, both in its formulation and implementation through the various activities in the value chain. The globalization of a product or service consists in standardizing its "core" element and localizing the "peripheral" parts.

Perhaps the next significant contribution to the theory of the internalization of companies came with the 1990 publication of Michael Porter's "*The Competitive Advantage of Nations*", a work in which the author explores the factors that make a country or region potentially more successful through the formulation of his "Diamond model". These determining factors for a region's success include education and access to raw materials, to pick two examples, but also companies' structures and the advantages therein, government involvement, and the luck factor—not the first time it had appeared in a scientific essay by an economist. A positive conjunction of these various elements dictates that certain geographical locations become the site of hubs or clusters for a given sector, as has happened, for example, with the concentration of tech startups in Silicon Valley, the fashion and design industry in Milan, or pharmaceuticals in central Switzerland.

As corporations with a global presence grew and became more sophisticated, while the economy was reconfigured toward the generation of value through innovation and knowledge creation, new management models and tools emerged in consonance. An example of this is the proposal by Jeffrey Rayport and John Sviokla (1995), known as the Virtual Value Change. According to this model, the generation of value takes place in the "extended enterprise", a broad space that includes interrelations with suppliers, sometimes in distant geographical locations, as well as the channels employed in the distribution of products and services. In such organizations, the use of information, in particular the strategic management of knowledge, becomes a key competitive advantage.

This new business framework with virtual value chains coincided with the development of a previously unknown level of connectivity and interconnectedness arising from the development of information technology. Today, more than two decades later, we are able to calibrate the decisive impact that these technologies, and, in general, the digitalization of business activities, have had on the economy, looking at technological platforms, applications, and social networks, among others.

With the arrival of a new millennium and with the globalization of business already consolidated, one of the most-repeated quotes that contributed to create the image of an integrated and continually expanding global economy was the warning by Gary Hamel, an international strategy guru: "Out there in some garage is an entrepreneur who's forging a bullet with your company's name on it. You've got one option now – to shoot first. You've got to out-innovate the innovators" (Schumpeter 2012). It was now possible to bring down a multinational from any location, even from a remote corner of the planet that had previously been an impossible place from where to conduct business. It was a warning to stagnating multinationals, those elephants who had to learn to dance, in the words of Moss Kanter (1989); but it was also an invitation to the most innovative entrepreneurs to design their start-ups with a global vocation and slant right from the very moment of their conception.

In a world advancing toward a commercial integration, in which technological advances were generating robust interconnection, "the world is flat" maxim put forward by Thomas Friedman in 2005 quickly gained popularity and became a slogan repeated over and over. Friedman's point was that the world had become a level playing field in trading terms, where all potential competitors enjoyed equal access, independent of their location, size, or background. His work was among the most commented on and garlanded of that year, widely disseminated and engaged with by the business world and academia.

"The world is flat" was so oft-repeated in business speeches that it was taken for granted as a statement of fact that could be applied to all kinds of sectors.

As De Kluyver concluded, this globalization of the business world meant that "the question is not: *Is* my Industry Global? But rather: *How* Global is my Industry?" (De Kluyver, 2010). The challenge facing all company executives was how to ensure that their products and services reached external markets; how to design global supply value chains with international presence and reach; and how to take the greatest possible advantage of the global stage.

Globalization was an accepted fact that was growing and irreversible.

Populism's Reaction and Possible Consequences for Business Strategy

In fact, while globalization may have appeared to be consolidated, its basis and sustainability were still weak. This was clearly demonstrated by the impact and consequences of the financial crisis sparked in 2008, and whose effects continue to be felt in the economies of many countries.

Moreover, despite the possible perception of a continual lowering of trade barriers, World Trade Alert, an initiative coordinated by the Centre for Economic Policy Research in London, issued a warning in 2012 about the introduction of more than 6000 measures of a protectionist nature. That same year, the director general of the WTO stated: "The accumulation of trade restrictions is now a matter of serious concern. Trade coverage of the restrictive measures put in place since October 2008, excluding those that were terminated, is estimated to be almost 3% of world merchandise trade, and almost 4% of G-20 trade. The discrepancy between the commitments taken and the actions on the ground add to credibility concerns."[1] (Lamy, 2012) It would appear that the journey toward free trade was not going to be so speedy.

In general terms, it is considered that the process of globalization has lacked a global institutional architecture that could foment sustainable and balanced development. Self-regulation by global industry players, especially in the financial services sector, has not worked for guaranteeing an equilibrated growth either. It is felt that globalization has widened the gaps between countries and between developed and emerging nations.

As far as the internal impact on individual countries, it is argued that globalization has increased fractures within societies and economic inequality, especially in those with greater levels of growth. One cause is the outsourcing of factories and other economic activities toward territories with more competitive labor costs; for example, from the US to Mexico and China.

Actually, the negative effects of globalization on employment grew worse still during the financial crisis between 2004 and 2012. Employees' salaries took a serious dip, with 80% of US homes reporting a fall or leveling out in their income (Pinkus et al. 2017).

On the other hand, globalization is also associated with phenomena that have occurred in parallel, such as technological advances, automatization, and the "robotization" of many activities, together with the development of solutions using artificial intelligence (AI), all of which have a major impact on low-added-value employment, constituting a growing threat to many workers and exacerbating labor precariousness (Lesser et al. 2017).

In circumstances of relative impoverishment of the middle classes in many developed countries, globalization has become an easy target for criticism by politicians, be they populists or moderates. A prime example is how the impact of disruptive companies such as Uber and Airbnb, which provide traditional services in a cheaper and more agile manner using digital technologies, is seen by many as an effect of globalization. The arrival of these new international competitors from the digital economy in some countries has been used to stir up nationalist sentiment. In the campaign that preceded the Brexit referendum, for example, it was even argued that Uber was a consequence of membership of the EU.

As Ghemawat (2016) has explained, nationalism generates a kind of superiority complex in a nation. Among other causes, this nationalism is the consequence of ignorance concerning the international context, and produces a belligerent attitude toward free trade owing to a belief that national products are better and that the protection of domestic industry leads to higher quality employment.

Nationalism and populism create trade barriers and mistrust in economic and business investors. In the medium and long term, they lead to economic decline, social inequality, and political instability in the countries that breed these tendencies.

Nationalism and populism also foment an emotional, antiscientific movement, one which rejects empirical evidence as the manifestation of mere opinion from a given academic or professional elite. A remarkable aspect of the Brexit referendum campaign was the way in which the majority of the UK's universities and economic bodies, not to mention the most prestigious specialist media outlets, explained in painstaking detail the potentially negative long-term effects of exiting the EU—only for these arguments to be drowned out by slogans and emotional arguments. Campaigns against the Paris Agreement on climate change follow a similar pattern.

Nevertheless, any endeavor to build a fairer future society also depends on the recognition of globalization's errors and negative effects, and trying to correct them. Indeed, the neglect suffered by the middle classes, their relative impoverishment, and loss of influence in social initiatives is one of the causes behind the rise of populism and political extremism, as well as the unexpected rupturist directions we have been taken in since 2016.

Among the initiatives being debated today are several ideas that go way beyond traditional redistributive approaches. Examples include the creation of an annual universal income to compensate for long periods of unemployment or the structural impact of robotization on some sectors, and the possibility of taxing new forms of value generation, such as Bill Gates' proposal of taxing robots.

International Growth Avenues for Companies

Companies are organizations with a vocation for growth, meaning that the expansion of sales and markets is a strategic option from the outset. Indeed, the origin of limited liability corporations stems from the founding of large organizations such as the Honourable East India Company (HEIC), chartered by Queen Elizabeth I in 1600, and the *Vereenigde Oostindische Compagnie*, recognized by the Netherlands' States General, both operating as trade monopolies in Asia.

One of the tenets of this collective book is that businesses are beneficial institutions for international relations and the integration of society. Even during periods of conflict or one of negative reactions toward international trade—and we can consider the present day to be such a period—multinationals have fulfilled their role by serving as a bridge between peoples and balancing out negativity arising from political tensions among nations. We repeatedly tell our students a maxim that we consider to be true: "Good business is the best antidote to bad international politics."

Analogies from biology are often imported to explain how businesses grow and the development of industry sectors. The Darwinian phrase "survival of the fittest", and not necessarily the strongest, has been useful to illustrate the reasons that certain companies have been successful in the competitive international environment.

The alternative avenues that companies wishing to grow internationally can consider are listed in Fig. 1.1.

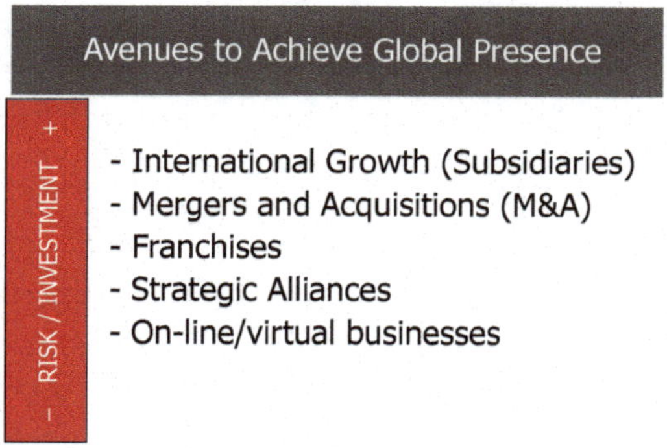

Avenues to Achieve Global Presence

RISK / INVESTMENT   +

- International Growth (Subsidiaries)
- Mergers and Acquisitions (M&A)
- Franchises
- Strategic Alliances
- On-line/virtual businesses

−

Fig. 1.1 Avenues for international growth

So we can see that companies are able to systematically examine various other ways of entering external markets besides direct exports from origin. These options, or alternative avenues, are listed in Fig. 1.1 for the necessary investment required and the concomitant level of risk involved in the operation.

There is also an intuitive association between the intensive nature of the resources involved and the speed of execution in any given strategy. For example, organic growth via subsidiaries—greenhouse investments—takes longer to implement than an approach using franchises or strategic alliances. Sometimes, this may be due to legal barriers, regulatory issues, or the need for authorization to operate in a country or in order to execute mergers and acquisitions (M&As). Slower implementation speed in the case of M&As could be down to the need to integrate different organizations, the search for synergies, and other economies of scope, elements which do not fit into place automatically, but require time and a learning curve process. For these reasons, when the resources for a great investment are not available or there is a desire to act quickly to take advantage of a temporarily held advantage or be a pioneer, those options that allow a rapid entry into international markets are preferable. This is the case even though they offer less control over the direction of the resulting business and possibly even the risk of failure due to dependence on the continued agreement of external partners. In any case, it is important to bear in mind at all times that winning strategies are not produced at a particular moment, but rather as a result of extended processes. A well-articulated strategic alliance, developed over a long period of time, can generate better results than organic growth or an M&A process. Given time, it may even end up as an acquisition, something which occurs with great frequency.

The Role of Global Corporations and Their CEOs

Multinational companies have changed, in their very nature as well as their perception by the global society. It is possible to identify certain key characteristics to better understand their recent evolution:

- *Today global corporations are a multipolar phenomenon.* Traditionally, global meant US. However, this association has been weakened over the past two decades. For example, among the top ten on the 2016 Global Fortune 500 list,[2] there were three Chinese corporations, where a decade ago there were none. In this book, two cases of Chinese corporations with a global presence are presented: Huawei and Haier, both of which compete directly in terms of innovation with Western companies that are well established in their sectors. We have seen multinationals emerge across the breadth of the world, such as the "multilatinas" from Latin America, which occupy leading positions in their home region and have growing degrees of global presence. Some examples are included in this book, including Televisa and Latam.
- In fact, even going back a decade, US companies were not the most globalized. Some analysts have explained that of three million registered companies, fewer than 1% exported, and most of these did so to a single other country. Companies that export experience greater levels of growth and productivity, and their workers earn higher salaries (Pinkus et alii. 2017).
- *Any proper assessment of global corporations' activity goes beyond the merely economic and commercial aspects.* The presence and impact can be evaluated by social agents, with more and more participation in social innovation projects. Through foundations, corporations undertake significant activity of genuine scope in the diverse communities in which they are present. On the other hand, the growth in corporate social responsibility initiatives and increased awareness of the importance of non-market strategies means this approach has become a priority among the roles of top-level executives. Many corporations with a global presence now report on their triple bottom line and take part in initiatives or evaluation schemes referring to various facets of their sustainability and social impact. We are reaching a point where the assessment of modern multinationals is not to be done purely on economic and commercial grounds, but rather in terms of compliance and ethical criteria.
- One example of this is the debate in recent years over the legal and fiscal configurations used by large multinationals, and whether their meeting of

tax requirements also fulfills ethical standards, even if what they are doing is legal.
- *Tensions between global integration and local adaptation.* However, benefits from global connections cannot be gained easily. There is always a tension between the forces for global integration and the forces for local adaptation. This tension requires a creative solution and this solution might be different contingent on the CAGE conditions: the Cultural, Administrative, Geographic, and Economic differences between countries at the industry level must be assessed.
- As a consequence of this social function held by global corporations, *the role of a CEO is transformed*, while his or her relationship with a broad array of stakeholders, and not just company shareholders, takes on special significance. These stakeholders include governments, both on national and local levels, as well as the representatives of social and special interest groups, and, undoubtedly, the traditional media and social media influencers. This new kind of company requires, in turn, a new style of leadership from their CEOs.

In a 1993 article about the search for the next CEO of IBM, at times when the Big Blue was already a leading multinational company, but confronting a leadership as well as a business crisis, the *Financial Times* invented a job advertisement that read: "Executive willing to take on the most challenging management job in the World. Must be a natural leader, able to make tough decisions, boost the morale of 300,000 employees and win the confidence of millions of shareholders and customers worldwide. Knowledge of 'computer-speak' helpful. Salary high and negotiable. Benefits include worldwide instant recognition. Wearers of white shirts need not apply." (Financial Times, 1993)

As this fictitious ad shows, the ideal profile of the CEO of multinationals has more to do with their political skills rather than their technical ability. To inspire the confidence of millions of shareholders, or to run an organization with hundreds of thousands of employees with a budget exceeding that of many nations, is comparable with, or indeed more difficult than, the work of many senior politicians. As the advertisement suggests, a CEO is as visible as many world leaders, and, in the same way, his or her decisions and actions are subject to the same kind of public scrutiny.

There have been references elsewhere to the model of cosmopolitan manager, the model of leader who is competent, cultivated, and committed— managers who are knowledgeable of the latest management models and consider lifelong education as permanent reference. Cosmopolitan because they realize how diverse today's world is and know how to make the best of this in terms of social innovation and transformation. They are versed in the cultural contributions of different civilizations. In the long run, these managers exercise a more effective leadership than those who rely purely on charisma or passion, because they are able to motivate others more on rational grounds, thus securing a more sustainable commitment from them.

Recently, new roles of global CEOs are being required because of the digital transformations, which have dramatically changed business and management.

The Impact of Big Data in Business Strategy and Marketing

The recent rapid growth of AI and digital technologies has been casting new challenges to CEOs. One of their top concerns is how to adapt their companies to digital disruption and adopt new business practices and managerial skills. (Siegler, 2010) In addition, companies may need to develop new corporate cultures to accommodate "new collar" workers such as data analysts, programmers, social network facilitators, and related jobs. All this may result in major corporate transformations, which can only be led by the CEO.

The availability of so-called Big Data analysis has dramatically transformed many aspects of management practice including the way retailers and producers have been running their businesses, such as improving inventory management, supply chain efficiency, sales forecasting, and price management. In many instances, it also helps in predicting shopper behavior including improving the offering in order to maximize the return on each transaction in a store, at a specific location. The fundamentals of Big Data are based on the technological innovations (Internet of Things, cloud computing), socio-cultural evolutions (private information sharing), and opportunistic usage of business innovations (loyalty schemes). In summary, there are many examples of Big Data applications that affect all business processes. Above all, perhaps, these effects might be particularly profound when it comes to impacting the discipline of marketing, including finding new routes-to-market (Eevells et al. 2016; Laenzliger and Lorange 2017).[3]

There are perhaps above all three areas of evolving new insights that have reshaped the field of marketing:

- *Customer Centric*: How can consumer preferences lead to the identification of new route-to-markets?
- *Process Centric*: How can the implementation of marketing campaigns be more accurately monitored so as to detect potential frauds, potential new shippers in logistics potentials, and so on?

– *Business Model Diversification*: How can one identify different specific segments which might lend themselves to different promotional optimizations (e.g. regarding price, packaging, and the assessment of quality)?

Cloud Computing and Big Data Analysis

As we have alluded to, we now have at our disposal entirely new analytics that can help revolutionize our understanding. While the relevant algorithms in general have been developed for some time, it is the availability of the capacity to analyze large sets of data that represents the breakthrough (Bodrev and Kamsaev 2015).

With the infinite storage capacity with cloud computing, there are no limits to what companies can sort and share. Every two days we create as much information as we did from the dawn of civilization up until 2003, according to Eric Schmidt, Executive Chairman of Alphabet Inc. Today's data centers occupy an area of land equal in size to almost 6000 football fields. The areas of application seem to be endless. For instance, Microsoft Cloud features the analysis of large sets of golf shots data, to gain new insights regarding what might constitute optimal golf shots under various circumstances (Duchesel and Laurin 2013). Large sets of DNA data from mosquitos are being analyzed to identify possibly dangerous infectious viruses, such as the recent Zika virus, in order to develop vaccines for prevention. And, in finance, new patterns of investment are being developed to stay away from too risky approaches, and so on. We see other applications in such diverse areas as pharma and health, automation, investments, banking, retailing, and so on.

But how is the rise of Big Data affecting the way we manage our business? Are we in a position to make use of this new extraordinary flow of information and make it a simple, efficient tool to improve our business results? Can we make it sufficiently focused? Can we, for instance, evolve from *Big Data Analysis* to *Smart Data Analysis*? Can smart targeting yield better results, say for banks, when it comes to finding better categories of investments (categories, regions, or specific firms)?

Cloud computing is leading to the so-called *deep learning*. While the relevant algorithms have been available for some time, as already noticed, Big Data are now applied analytically. Statistical distribution problems are also avoided, due to the abundance of data.

With the growth of Omni channel, Big Data analytics is a key element in understanding shopper behavior at many touch points, thus multiplying the chances to sell products and services. Big Data analytics is becoming a key and essential element in the search for better route to market. Revenue growth management (RGM) is becoming key, at least where it is available. So, how are these analytical processes affecting our capability to manage price, promotions, shopper marketing, and what are also the limits in some key sectors?

Let us now first discuss in some more detail two areas of applications within the field of marketing, namely *Pricing* as well as *Campaign Optimizing*, for us then to be able to point out briefly some limitations regarding Big Data analysis.

Pricing

Price management is the essential part of RGM. The capability to generate margins is the real oxygen for growth. Margins are a consequence of costs and revenue management, and in our specific case Big Data helps in increasing sustainable revenues, through prices management in a very spectacular way. Many are familiar with the notion of Dynamic Marketing. Dynamic Marketing would imply, in many ways, the end of strategic planning, as today's world offers the capability to correct and change our plans and actions very quickly: from grabbing attention to holding attention, from price promoting to instant price management. The notion of dynamic pricing is one that is very exciting today in order to optimize sales and margins. Based on Big Data analytics, it helps companies to simultaneously target different prices for different customers or shoppers. In fact, dynamic pricing is based on customer perceptions of values. Machine-learning algorithms automatically spot prices that on average can bring a 7% total margin compared to manual price selection.

Airlines represent an excellent example regarding this. They are able to segment an airplane accurately not only to extract different price offers based on where you sit or which class you are booked in, but also based on the timing of your booking, your personal profile, competitor's offers, and many other relevant criteria. The objective is of course to maximize margins per seat, and optimize overall results of a plane as a business model.

Amazon is another good example. Amazon changes its prices more than 2.5 million times a day, in order to capture more transactions and to optimize margins. And the fashion industry has become highly performing in retailing in managing prices in matrix model combining timing and shopper segments (fashion fans, regular customers, and price sensitive customers). Here, Zara (Inditex) has built its entire business model with a capacity to entirely renew its offer every month. Big retailers are the champions of predictive consumer behavior and price management.

Campaign Optimizing

Data analytics might help here, in three critical domains: predicting, understanding, and optimizing. A leading beer company started using Big Data to perform better with retailers. This effort clearly had an RGM focus. Data analysis allowed for the review of past experience in promoted volumes, and to predict future results more accurately. This was essential for a better understanding of price/promotions activities, optimizing brands and packages offerings, and taking correcting actions when and where necessary. Data analytics helped also in predicting competitor's reactions and its potential effects on the brewer. For the purists, a conjoint analysis was done on a big scale.

Today shopper behavior represents a very important element in marketing. The main focus of marketing in the past was perhaps on the consumers. Shopper behavior, to be more specific, is about creating a very pragmatic decision: a purchase at a point of sales. Thus, how can we sell products and services at a particular moment in time, in the right location and at the right price? Here data analytics will be critical in three essential moments: to better understand the pre-purchase, the purchase, and the post-purchase.

These three steps are characterized by a vast number of touch points, or "moments of truth". We might demonstrate, for example, that in pharmaceutical industry the numbers of touch points for any medicine during the key moments of the path to purchase were at least double digits! Each of these touch points will have to be understood, analyzed, and managed. Predictive analytics will help to fundamentally understand the pre-purchase element. Big Data analysis would be key.

Data analytics will thus help in responding to at least three important questions: why do shoppers shop, where do they shop, and how do they shop? Retailers will use techniques such as eye tracing, purchase decisions analytics, traffic analytics, and so on to better understand the shopper's behavior in stores. In the case of a producer, the key will be to better understand the shopping occasions, evaluate their size and potential business impact, and prepare the right offer to be captured. Key questions might include: what key drivers started the shopping process? What sources of information or influence were consulted? What was the structure of the purchase trip (shopper mission)? Who influenced the shopper in store? What did the shopper do after the purchase? And so on. Analytics will be essential to understand traffic builders (advertising, digital), basket builders (displays, packaging, on pack promotion), and the loyalty builders (coupons, loyalty cards, rebates).

Some Limitations and Conclusions on the Impact of Big Data

So, what about the places where Big Data analytics might not be applicable? Ones that come to mind might be about more traditional sectors, often with more fragmented channels—small retail, mom and dad stores, bars, restaurants, pharmacies, and so on. These sectors are of course, still very important and generally tend to generate more margins than when it comes to the main retailers. While data may not readily be available, there may be methods to capture them. The name of the game here is to combine several pieces of Big Data, to better understand paths to purchase, pre-purchase, and the post-purchase, and to combine them with more traditional data collection methods in store (small data). The finality is the same, while the method will differ because of the lack of data availability.

Clearly Big Data is affecting the business lives of many of us in a massive way today and we may just have touched the surface of what it will bring to business. In retail, we are likely to see the rise of AI as shopping assistants, of innovative screens and services and the development of store analytics in real time. Stores will be completely "datafied", meaning intelligent, spaces will be interactive and responsive. The traditional economy may also be affected.

Today, techniques are being developed to merge Big Data and small data in order to offer producers and traditional outlets a good capacity to manage their future and optimize their operations. Geo-localization and social network data are essential for these traditional sectors. All of this for one key purpose as far as I am concerned: generating oxygen for growth.

Big Data provides both opportunities and challenges to companies and global CEOs recognize the urgency of adapting all business processes at their companies. As regard talent management, they may hire "new collar" employees as well as instill the newly required digital skills among traditional blue- and white-collar employees. Large companies may also need to develop new management styles and renovated corporate cultures, in order to attract the new collar employees and digital natives, since they will be otherwise inclined to join startups or create their own companies.

We may also expect that organizational boundaries become disrupted by phenomena such as Blockchain, affecting logistics, manufacturing, sales, and marketing. The fashion retail industry provides good examples of how Big Data can become integrated and managed across all the value chain activities, like the case of Inditex mentioned above.

Another reference of this transformation in the retail industry is provided by First Retailing, the Japanese company that owns the Uniqlo brand. Mr. Tadashi Yanai, its Chairman and CEO, has been fostering major changes to transform the company into a new digital consumer retail company. His initiatives include the construction of a big logistic facility, Uniqlo City Tokyo, which operates as their new global headquarters and center of its integrated operations.

We are just at the beginning of a fascinating evolution that will affect all industries. Even if change may not happen at the speed that some tech gurus predict, digital transformation is, and will remain, a key issue in the CEO's strategic agenda.

Business Schools as Trailblazers of Good Globalization

One of the consequences of populism is that business schools, along with other higher education institutions, have become a favorite target of critics who claim that we are the cradle of globalization and perpetuate elitism. Few can be unaware of such criticisms having been made—it is anything but novel; however, it would be naïve to think that given the current climate, it will dissolve as quickly as in the past.

What business schools face today is a historic opportunity to reinvent our mission and reposition our activities to influence the transformation of the global society. Business schools can contribute to the development and preparation of managers and entrepreneurs to be the architects of inclusive and fair societal structures. Our faculty can develop impactful research that addresses real problems in our communities. This is particularly important during times like the present when antiscientific attitudes are rampant. We can and should contribute to the design of a better society, one that is more just and equal.

It is very likely that all these changes will continue to create turbulence in the short term, turbulence that will affect our activity as business schools. We may witness a drop in the flow of cross-border talent (students, faculty, entrepreneurs, and recruiters) because of increased obstacles to mobility between countries. Or there may be a change in the nature and way that companies do business that will impact our graduates; for example, the configuration of supply chains or a move from offshoring to onshoring to confront trade tariffs.

Yet, there are two good reasons to nurture hope for the long term. First, given the unstoppable development of digitalization across all sectors, including education, it is very likely that the world will evolve toward further integration, despite the odds. Second, millennials and younger generations—our current and future students—have a distinctly cosmopolitan mindset with which they actively cultivate a feeling of global citizenship.

According to Cooper Ramo (2016), centuries from now, our great-great-grandchildren will look at our age and name it, as we have named the Enlightenment. Perhaps they will call this era the "Great Connection" or "Great Enmeshment" or some such. Without the "Great Connection", the economy in any region has no future and no chance of survival. Nobody can ignore the benefits of global great connections.

New global specifies must be identified, and new insights and knowledge for global companies and their management must be discovered. In this book, diverse authors set to work on this important new research agenda, describing and profiling new global species.

To paraphrase Charles Dickens, when he wrote about the French Revolution, and bearing in mind the Industrial Revolution he was living through, these may be the worst of times, but also the best of times.[4] There are many opportunities to be seized by business schools, reclaiming their role as trailblazers of the future global society.

Notes

1. See: http://cepr.org/content/reports
2. See: http://fortune.com/global500/2016/
3. For a good general discussion on Big Data analysis, see B. Brown, M. Chui, and J. Manzika, "Are You Ready for the Era of "Big Data"?", *McKinsey Quarterly*, 4 (1) (2011), pp. 24–35.
4. Opening lines of C. Dickens, *A Tale of Two Cities*, http://www.gutenberg.org/ebooks/98

References

S. MacDonald, "Businesses Can No Longer Avoid Becoming Political", *Harvard Business Review*, April 19, 2017.

F. Livesey, *Form Global To Local. The Making of Things And The End of Globalization*, (London: Profile Books Ltd., 2017), Ch. 1.

T. Leavitt, "The Globalization of Markets", *Harvard Business Review, May 1983*.

C.A. Bartlett, S. Goshal, *Managing Across Borders: The Transnational Solution*, (Boston: Harvard University Press, 1989).

G. Yip, *Total Global Strategy: Managing for Worldwide Competitive Advantage* Englewood Cliffs, NJ: Prentice Hall, 1992).

M. Porter, *The Competitive Advantage of Nations* (New York, NY: Simon and Schuster, 1990).

J.F. Rayport and J. Sviokla, "Exploiting The Virtual Value Chain", *Harvard Business Review,* November-December 1995.

Schumpeter, "An A-Z Business Quotations: Innovation", *The Economist,* August 17, 2012 https://www.economist.com/blogs/schumpeter/2012/08/z-business-quotations-1

R. Moss Kanter, *When Giants Learn to Dance* (New York, NY: Simon and Schuster, 1989).

T. Friedman, "*The Wolrd Is Flat: A Brief Histroy of The Twenty-first Century*", (New York, NY: Picador, 2005).

C. A. De Kluyver: *Fundamentals of Global Strategy 2: The Globalization of Companies and Industries',*(Boston: Harvard Business Publishing, 2010).

C.A. De Kluyver, "Fundamentals of Global Strategy: A Business Model Approach" (Business Expert Press: New York, 2011).

G. Pinkus, J. Manyika and Sree Ramaswamy, "We Can't Undo Globalization, but We Can Improve It", *Harvard Business Review, January 10, 2017.*

See the interesting article by R. Lesser, M. Reeves and J. Harnoss, "Tackling Inequality: The Challenge for Corporate Leaders", Rotman Management, Winter 2017, pp. 21-25.

P. Ghemawat, "People Are Angry About Globalization. Here's What to Do About It", *Harvard Business Review,* November 2016.

http://fortune.com/global500/2016/

G. Pinkus, J. Manyika and Sree Ramaswamy, op. cit.

'IBM Needs a New Boss: Who's got the Right Stuff'. *Financial Times,* 29/3/93.

S. Eevells, N. Fukawa, and L. Swayne "Big Data Consumer Analytics and the Transformation of Marketing", Journal of Business Research (2016), pp 899–904.

A. Bodrev and V.M. Kamsaev, "Modern Big Data Analysis Technology", Fundamental Research (2015), pp 5295–5299.

M.G. Siegler, "Eric Schmidt: Every 2 Days We Create As Much Information As We Did Up To 2003", August 10 2010. Retrieved from: https://techcrunch.com/2010/08/04/schmidt-data/

P. Duchesel and E.J.M. Laurin, "Decision Tree Models in Profiting Ski Resorts", Expert Systems with Applications (2013), pp 5822–5829.

J. Cooper Ramo, *The Seventh Sense: Power, Fortune, and Survival in the Age of Networks* (New York, NY: Little Brown and Company, 2016).

M. Laenzliger, and P. Lorange, "New Routes-to-Market at Migrolino", unpublished working paper (2017).

P. Lamy "Rise in trade restrictions now 'alarming', Lamy tells WTO ambassadors" 7 June 2012. Retrieved from https://www.wto.org/english/news_e/sppl_e/sppl234_e.htm

Further Bibliography

B. Emmot, *The Fate of the West: The Battle to Safe the World's Most Successful Political Idea* (London: The Economist books, 2017).

V. Govindarajan and A. K. Gupta, *The Quest for Global Dominance. Transforming Global Presence into Global Competitive Advantage,* (San Francisco, CA: Jossey Bass, 2001).

S. Iñiguez de Onzoño, *Cosmopolitan Managers. Executive Education That Works,* (London: Palgrave Macmillan, 2016).

S. King, *Grave New World: The End of Globalization, The Return of History* (New Haven, CT: Yale University Press, 2017).

P. Lorange, *Leading in Turbulent Times. Lessons Learnt and Implications for The Future* (Bingley: Emerald Books, 2010).

G. Stonehouse, D. Campbell, J. Hamill and Tony Purdie, *Global and Transnational Business. Strategy and Management,* (Chichester: John Wiley & Sons, 2004).

2

The Governance of Change: How Companies and Governments Should Adapt to Technological Disruption

Manuel Muñiz

Abstract Technological change brings with it many opportunities and some daunting challenges. Global corporations can now successfully do business around the world thanks to a large extent to the way in which technology enhances their ability to govern complexity and conduct operations across time zones, national borders and cultural and political environments. One of the greatest challenges, however, will be to govern the externalities of the generalized pick up of advanced technologies such as artificial intelligence and others. Perhaps the most significant of these challenges will be the erosion of our middle class produced by automation. This dynamic is behind the deep political convulsion being experienced in Europe and the US, and which is already affecting how corporations do business around the world. Finding a solution to some of the challenges brought about by technological disruption will require a new business paradigm that emphasizes long-term business sustainability and takes into account the broader political dynamics unleashed by the widespread implementation of technology. Innovative companies will have to take this issue head on if they wish to become responsible stakeholders in the communities they operate.

M. Muñiz (✉)
Dean, IE School of International Relations, Madrid, Spain
e-mail: manuel.muniz@ie.edu

© The Author(s) 2018
S. Iñiguez de Onzoño, K. Ichijo (eds.), *Business Despite Borders*,
https://doi.org/10.1007/978-3-319-76306-4_2

The Macro Perspective: The Governance of Emerging Technologies

As stated by colleagues throughout this book, technology and innovation are radically changing how private corporations do business. In recent decades, developments such as the emergence of big data, complex operations management software, advanced artificial intelligence (AI), deep learning and others have provided companies around the world with extremely powerful tools to grow their business and to operate across borders. As this edited volume shows, our knowledge of these processes of transformation at the micro/company level is considerable and although companies struggle to adapt to the rapid rate of change, many do so with great success.

The picture, however, is very different at the aggregate or macro level. What are the consequences of rapid digitalization of productive processes for how wealth is generated and distributed within our societies? What sort of transformation will the advent of advanced AI produce in our labor markets? Or what will be the impact of the generalized use of smart machines in productive processes on the types of skills and abilities that are demanded by employers? How can governments and companies both foster innovation but at the same time manage some of the externalities produced by the generalized pick up and implementation of technological advances? These sorts of macro questions, despite their evident importance, remain to a large extent unanswered. That this is the case is a major source of risk for corporations themselves as some of these changes are unleashing unexpected political forces that will ultimately impact private enterprises around the world. This chapter is an attempt to provide a backdrop to the many micro case studies of innovation addressed by colleagues, and in the process outline the macro challenges faced by governments and corporations when it comes to the management of emerging technologies.

A New Reality: Exponential Change

In order to understand the extraordinary rate at which the world is changing, it is useful to go back and look at the development of measures of prosperity over the last 200 years. If one takes, for example, total world population, the rate of change since the 1800s has been exponential. World population reached the one billion figure in the very early nineteenth century. It took over 100 years before that figure was doubled. A century after that, by around 2037, the UN estimates that world population will have surpassed the nine billion barrier; close to a 500% increase in a century. Even more radical has been the increase in our capacity to generate material wealth. According to the World Bank, global GDP at the turn of the twentieth century was around one trillion United States Dollars (USD). By 2016 that figure had reached 78 trillion USD (both figures in constant 1990 USD). The average American earned ten times less in 1960 than today. In the case of the author's country, Spain, progress was even more pronounced. GDP per capita in Spain was 396 USD in 1960 and 35,580 in 2008 (both in current USD). These gains in material wealth are very much connected to processes of technological innovation such as the ones studied in other chapters of this book.

Progress has not been limited to the economic realm. Life expectancy around the world has skyrocketed in recent decades. So much so that life expectancy gains made over the last 30 years average three months of additional expectancy per year lived. The explosion of data gives us yet another measure of change. In the last two years alone, humanity produced more data than in the previous 20,000. These trends of exponential change have led many around the world, including thinkers such as Ray Kurzweil, to state that human technological progress of the next century will equal that of the last 20 millennia. Table 2.1 captures the nature and velocity of the transformation we face.

There are multiple causes for this accelerated rate of change but technological advancement and, in particular, the application of technology to productive processes are certainly the most important. According to the McKinsey Global Institute there are at least 12 areas where rapid change is occurring today: mobile internet, automation of knowledge work, the Internet of Things, cloud technology, advanced robotics, autonomous vehicles, next-generation genomics, advanced oil and gas exploration and recovery, 3D printing, advanced materials, energy storage and renewable energy. On top of truly impactful advances in each of these fields, one has to add the effect of the convergence of progress across areas and technologies. It is that convergence of technological advancement that makes change exponential and hard to predict.

The Challenge: The Great Decoupling

Living on a curve of accelerated transformation brings with it many benefits, from the eradication of scarcity to the enabling of numerous human endeavors. For example, just in the last two decades alone over 600 million people have been lifted out of poverty.

Table 2.1 World Per Capita GDP—10,000 BCE—2003 CE (1990 International Dollars). (Source: DeLong 1998)

AVERAGE WORLD GDP PER CAPITA	
YEAR	1990 International USD
-1000000	92
-300000	92
-25000	92
-10000	93
-8000	96
-5000	103
-4000	109
-3000	113
-2000	112
-1600	121
-1000	127
-800	143
-500	137
-400	130
-200	113
14	102
200	98
350	94
400	97
500	102
600	104
700	112
800	116
900	131
1000	133
1100	124
1200	104
1250	99
1300	89
1340	109
1400	128
1500	138
1600	141
1650	150
1700	164
1750	178
1800	195
1850	300
1875	429
1900	679
1920	956
1925	1108
1930	1134
1940	1356
1950	1622
1955	1968
1960	2270
1965	2736
1970	3282
1975	3714
1980	4231
1985	4634
1990	5204
1995	5840
2000	6539

It also brings with it, however, numerous challenges. One such challenge is the transformation brought to labor markets. We have witnessed over the last two centuries major changes in the types of jobs available within our societies. From 1860 to 1960, for example, the percentage of the US labor force employed in agriculture collapsed from around 60% to single digits. In that same period, US primary sector productivity skyrocketed due to the application of technology to agriculture. The US employs today less than 5% of its population in agricultural tasks and is yet a net exporter of agricultural products. A similar process has been taking place in the industrial sector. Since 1980, the number of Americans working in industry has halved while industrial output has increased by around 250%. According to data from the Brookings Institution, it took 24.6 Americans to produce one million dollars of industrial output in 1980. By 2015 that figure had come down to 6.4.

As the primary and secondary sectors were automated, more and more of our labor force shifted to jobs in services. What seems to be occurring today, however, is that automation is reaching the tertiary sector as well. According to Professors Frey and Osborne from the University of Oxford, 47% of current jobs are in high risk of computerization (i.e. automation) in the next two decades. Most of those jobs are in the services sector. Tasks such as those performed by secretaries, translators, truck or cab drivers and many others could soon be automated. In many instances, automation has already affected the most routine elements of those jobs. In order to understand the significance of this change, one has to remember that just in the US there are over three million jobs in the transportation sector. These are all in risk of automation due to the development of autonomous vehicles.

One could of course assume that technological change will follow a similar path to that seen in the historical cases cited above and that jobs destroyed in one sector will be compensated by new jobs in other areas of the economy or, perhaps, by the emergence of an entirely new employment category. There are reasons to believe, however, that this time it could be different. The first is related to the nature of the task substitution occurring today. For the first time since the advent of technology, gains in productivity are not a product of the substitution of human or animal physical force for that of machines but rather due to the substitution of information processing capacity. We are, in effect, substituting brains with thinking machines. This suggests that the new job categories that could emerge will probably take longer to be configured and be detached from tasks linked to the performance of cognitive tasks. It is hard to imagine how those jobs might look like but a consensus is emerging that the empathy and creativity components will almost certainly be central.

The second factor that suggests that this time things could be different is the evolving relationship between returns on capital and labor. For the last 200 years, increases in productivity led to increases in labor wages. Although it sometimes took some time for this process to fully play out, productivity would eventually trickle down to wages and help sustain a growing middle class. Since the 1970s, however, productivity of goods and services increased by over 250% in the US while labor wages remained stagnant. Some like Andre McAfee and Erik Brynjolfsson at the Massachusetts Institute of Technology (MIT) have referred to this as the "Great Decoupling". Others, including the author, have spoken of these trends as a breach of our social contract because they put into question the sustainability of our current economic development model. Additionally, they also tell us that there is something truly unique about the current process of economic disruption. We seem to have unlocked the capability of increasing productivity without the need to create employment or to remunerate better the employment already in existence.

The two fundamental consequences of this decoupling are the stagnation of income at the middle of advance economies' income distribution and, ultimately, growing levels of inequality. From 2005 to 2014, over 90% of Italian households saw their income stagnate or decline. That was also the case for over 80% of US households or 70% of UK ones. Stagnation has also had an inter-generational component with socio-economic progress being frozen across generations. According to Raj Chetty from Stanford, the probability of an American born in the 1940s earning more than his parents throughout his lifetime was of around 92%. For an American born in the 1980s that probability had fallen to 50%. This is, in effect, the death of the American dream.

Inequality has, in turn, increased markedly in the US and Europe. According to research conducted by Thomas Piketty the top 1% of income earners in the US saw the percentage of pre-tax US income accruing to them increase from around 10% in 1970 to over 20% in 2015. By the mid-1990s, the top 1% of earners in the US were capturing a larger proportion of the total US pre-tax income than the bottom 50% of earners. The top 1% of Americans now collectively possess close to 50% of the total wealth in the country meaning the US is reaching levels of inequality not seen since the 1920s.

The Perverse Politics of Disruption

Why should the trends described above be of concern to private companies and corporate leaders? The answer is simple: the political dynamics unleashed by the process of erosion of the middle class is producing an ever more hostile environment within which to conduct business.

Since the political earthquakes of 2016, fundamentally the decision made by the British electorate to have the UK leave the European Union (EU) and the election of Donald J. Trump as the President of the United States, we have learned more about the drivers and dynamics behind the rise of discontent with the established order. We know, for example, that the way in which this discontent is operationalized, or the process by which it affects political behavior, is through pessimism about the future and a strong anti-elite sentiment.

A survey conducted by Pew two weeks before the US presidential elections revealed that over 80% of Trump supporters believed their lives and those of people like them were worse than 50 years before. Close to 60% of Hilary supporters thought exactly the opposite: the last 50 years had seen their living standards rise. Overall, however, Westerners have become pessimistic about the future. Over 60% of Europeans and Americans believe today that their children will be worse off than them in the future. This pessimism is correlated with anti-elite sentiment. According to YouGov data released before the Brexit referendum, Britons who supported leaving the EU (i.e. supporting "Brexit") had negative net levels of trust in academics, economists, the Bank of England and other "elite" bodies and institutions. Those elites, as a matter of fact, expressed strong opposition to the UK leaving the EU with little effect. See Table 2.2 for a visual representation of this.

In parallel to these trends, we have seen rising support for extreme left and extreme right parties in Europe and falling levels of trust in the EU and other supra-national institutions. In fact, the new political movements emerging in Europe and the US share a strong anti-liberal streak. Many are anti-free trade, anti-cosmopolitanism, and in some instances, particularly in the European setting, openly anti-capitalist. So much so that some, including the author, have termed this period the Anti Elite and Anti Liberal Era.

Anti-liberalism is a consequence of at least two factors. The first is that these new political movements emerge in large part due to the failings of the pre-

Table 2.2 Anti-Elitism 101

Thinking about the EU referendum, how much do you trust what the following types of people say whether we should leave or remain in the European Union?		
	Net trust (%)	
	Remain supporters	Leave supporters
People from well-known businesses	25	−28
Think tanks	18	−49
Economists	41	−36
People from international organizations	40	−58
People from the Bank of England	34	−45
Academics	49	−28

Source: YouGov (2016)

ponderant liberal order of the last seven decades. The second is that the liberal order is particularly vulnerable to anti-elite sentiment. If one looks at the mechanisms by which free trade agreements are established and sustained or regional integration processes are pushed forward, one sees that the role of elites is central. It is business, political and intellectual elites that are aware of the benefits of free trade or of regional integration. They are also the ones that are most aware of the costs or externalities of disintegration. It is unlikely that anyone not fully dedicated to negotiating free trade agreements will, for example, understand the complexity that goes into their configuration. If trust between elites and those they represent is severed, the entire edifice collapses as a house of cards. It is therefore not surprising that the populist upheaval is causing intense damage to institutions and arrangements that are so dependent on high levels of trust in elites and technocrats to be sustainable.

The Precariat

Surprisingly, all the developments described above are occurring at a time of great economic prosperity in most of the advanced economies. The US returned to pre-financial-crisis GDP levels in 2012. The UK did in 2014. Truly radical political options prevailed in these countries at a time of record economic performance. The liberal order is quite evidently a great generator of wealth but due to a structural change in how wealth is distributed within our societies and, in particular, due to the undermining of the redistributive role played by labor wages, it is the equity of the distribution of that wealth that is failing. Not being capable of managing this is for all intents and purposes a failure of intelligence or, to put it differently, a failure in the management of abundance.

The collective that is driving the response to these trends has sometimes been referred to as the "precariat". This large group is not just made up of the unemployed, who are sometimes small in number due to accounting norms and others, but also the underemployed, people who are working but would like to work more, the sub-employed, those who perform tasks that are below their skill and education level, and, importantly, the precariously employed, people who work full time but live in economic precariousness.

Days after the 2016 US presidential elections, data were released on the voting patterns in counties in the US with high levels of unemployment and in those with high proportions of routine jobs. Unemployment levels did not correlate with any particular voting preference. Counties with a high percentage of routine jobs, however, were won by Donald Trump by a margin of, on average, 35 percentage points. It seems, therefore, that crude unemployment figures obfuscate part of the challenges brought about by automation and sometimes prevent policymakers from detecting the underlying precariousness and fear about the future that is driving political behavior.

A New Paradigm: The Future Corporation

Finding a solution to the challenge of growing inequality within our societies and to the decreasing importance of labor wages will require the implementation of a complex set of policies. Many of these are linked to the transformation of our education system that needs to adapt with more agility to the changing demands of our labor market. Others pertain to how income and wealth are taxed within our societies and some form of shift from labor taxation to capital taxation is bound to occur. Fiscal traction over capital might also adopt a "participatory" character and be implemented through the creation of public venture capital funds or other financial platforms that provide the state with a source of income connected to returns on capital. Additionally, it is easy to imagine new forms of wealth redistribution being implemented and complementing the decreasing role played by labor wages.

Be that as it may, what is evident is that one entire set of transformations will pertain to the role played by corporations in the economy. The fundamental driver of the need for this change is the decoupling of productivity and hourly wages discussed above. In an environment, where corporations can grow and be profitable without creating jobs or remunerating existing jobs better, the simple principle of maximizing profits and shareholder value becomes insufficient. Or, to put it differently, if all corporations across our economy apply a narrow rule of shareholder value maximization and in the process implement as much technology as is needed to gain productivity and reduce costs, the end result will be a deep erosion of the middle class, political radicalization and, ultimately, the collapse of the liberal order upon which much of corporate success and wealth depends. This is particularly true of the well-being of global corporations like the ones studied in this edited volume. The global corporation is nothing but a product of the globalized world that populists are calling into question today.

We face, therefore, a major dilemma and a collective action problem of the first order. Private companies around the world are designed to procure efficiency and to maximize profits. This is how leadership and employee performance is assessed within them. It is how they compete with one another when accessing financial markets. And, ultimately, and in particular in the US case, it is how the relationship between shareholders and company managers is legally structured. US corporations have a fiduciary duty to shareholders that very much drives management behavior; this relationship is enshrined in the US corporate law and is protected by US courts. And yet, if companies are to truly build sustainability into their business model they should also think in broader terms and incorporate into their strategic thinking the aggregate effects of the use of advanced technologies. This new notion of business sustainability should be accompanied by a redefinition of the idea of company stakeholder to include not just shareholders, employees and providers, but also the company's non-workers or all those that are made redundant by the implementation of job-saving technologies.

The ideas outlined above are in some instances radical, difficult to implement and will require changes to how corporations do business around the world. They will, however, be necessary if companies do not want to operate in a growingly hostile social and political environment. As outlined above, we know that if the erosion of our middle class continues, anti-elite sentiment will deepen. Included in the elites being questioned today are CEOs and corporate leaders, as well as institutions that are very much needed if the private sector is to do well such as business associations, central banks or international organizations like the EU or the World Trade Organization. The collapse in trust in these elites and in the institutions they help build and sustain will be followed by policies that will be extremely costly to corporations. It is private businesses and their bottom line that would be hit the hardest if trade agreements collapse, or there are strong currency fluctuations or currency risk. If anti-capitalist movements do begin to populate Western parliaments and perhaps governments, it is evident that the policies they will implement will be anti-business and highly costly for corporations and all of their stakeholders. The stakes are therefore high and the writing is now on the wall.

There are examples of how a different kind of way of doing business could emerge. The concept of the fourth sector or the "for social benefit" corporation is perhaps a good example. Also, the idea of investing while seeking social impact is also gaining ground with social impact indexes emerging in Europe and the US. There are also now long-term investors that seek to deploy their resources in companies that seek to "do good" and that take into account the broad impact of their actions on the communities where they operate. A plethora of changes will have to be implemented and in many instances they will be country and sector specific. What is evident is that a new way of doing business will have to emerge if global corporations are to become responsible stakeholders in the countries and communities where they operate.

Conclusions and Takeaways

If the diagnosis outlined above is an accurate one then what is producing our current political turmoil is a structural change in the economy and, in particular, a shift in how wealth is created and distributed within our societies. The point of contact of this transformation is the jobs market and the ultimate cause is the effect of advanced technologies on income distribution.

The political convulsion produced by these trends will only get worse as time progresses unless the underlying drivers of the erosion of the Western middle class are addressed. Part of the solution to the macro challenges faced by governments and corporations lies in the ability of the latter to adapt the way they do business to current technological trends and their impact on the communities they operate in. This will require an expansion of the concept of business sustainability to include broader social and economic trends. Should global corporates ignore this need they might well be some of the principal agents contributing to the weakening of the liberal order and of globalization; the very process that saw them emerge and grow in the first place.

References

YouGov, "YouGov / Today Programme Survey Results", *YouGov*, June 14 2016. Available on: https://d25d2506sfb94s.cloudfront.net/cumulus_uploads/document/x4iynd1mn7/TodayResults_160614_EUReferendum_W.pdf

B. Delong, "Estimates of World GDP, One Million B.C. – Present", Berkeley University, 1998. Available on: http://delong.typepad.com/print/20061012_LRWGDP.pdf

Further Bibliography

J. Barrat, *Artificial Intelligence and the End of the Human Era: Our Final Invention* (New York, NY: Martins Press, 2013).

M. Boehm, "Job Polarisation and the Decline of Middle-Class Workers' Wages", *VOX: CEPR's Policy Portal*, February 8, 2014.

N. Bostrom, *Superintelligence: Paths, Dangers, Strategies* (Oxford: Oxford University Press, 2014).

E. Brynjolfsson and A. Mcafee, *The Second Machine Age: Work, Progress, and Prosperity in a Time of Brilliant Technologies*, 1st edition (New York: W. W. Norton & Company, 2014).

R. Chetty et al., "Where is the Land of Opportunity? The Geography of Intergenerational Mobility in the United States", *Quarterly Journal of Economics,* 129(4), pp.1553–1623, 2014.

G. Church and E. Regis, *How Synthetic Biology Will Reinvent Nature and Ourselves* (Nueva York, NY: Basic Books, 2012).

B. Delong, "Making Do With More", *Project Syndicate*, February, 2015.

R. Dobbs et al., "Poorer than their parents? A new perspective on income inequality", *McKinsey Global Institute Report,* 2016.

R. Dornbusch and S. Edwards, "The Macroeconomics of Populism," in Dornbusch, Rudiger, and Sebastian Edwards (ed.), *The Macroeconomics of Populism in Latin America*, 7-13 (Chicago: University of Chicago Press, 1991).

P. Dunleavy et al., *Digital Era Governance: IT Corporations, The State and E-Government* (Oxford: Oxford University Press, 2016).

M. Feldstein, "An Interview with Paul Volcker." *Journal of Economic Perspectives*, 27(4): 105–20, 2013.

R.S. FOA and Y. Mounk, "The Democratic Disconnect", *Journal of Democracy*, 27(3), July, 2016.

C.B. Frey and M. Osborne, "The Future of Employment: How Susceptible are Jobs to Computerization?", *Oxford Martin School Publications,* Oxford, United Kingdom, September, 2013.

H. Gardner, *5 Minds For The Future* (Boston: Harvard Business Review Press, 2008).

R. Inglehart and P. Norris, "Trump, Brexit and the Rise of Populism: Economic Have-Nots and Cultural Backlash", *Faculty Research Working Paper Series*, Harvard Kennedy School of Government, 2016.

M. Kaku, *Physics of the Future: How Science Will Shape Human Destiny And Our Daily Lives By The Year 2100* (London: Penguin, 2011).

J.M. Keynes, "Economic Possibilities for our Grandchildren", *Essays in Persuation*, New York: W.W. Norton & Co., pp. 358–373, 1930.

P. Krugamn, "Trade and Manufacturing Employment: No Real Disagreement", 2016. Available on:https://www.gc.cuny.edu/CUNY_GC/media/LISCenter/pkrugman/Trade-and-Manufacturing-Employment.pdf

R. Kurzweil, *The Singularity is Near: When Humans Transcend Biology,* 2008 Edition (London: Duckworth Overlook, 2005).

A. Maddison, *Contours of the World Economy 1 – 2030 AD: Essays in Macroeconomic History* (New York, NY: Oxford University Press, 2007).

R. Meyer, "Donald Trump Is the First Demagogue of the Anthropocene", *The Atlantic*, October, 2016.

I. Morris, *Why the West rules – for now. The cyles of of history and what they tell us about the future,* 1st edition (New York, NY: Farrar, Straus and Giroux, 2010).

M. Muniz, and A. Perez, "Progreso Tecnológico y Orden Internacional: hacia una nueva economía y una mejor gobernanza" ("Technological Progress and the International Order: Towards a New Economy and a Better Governance"), *Revista Información Comercial Económica*, 880, pp. 39-55, October, 2014.

M. Muniz, "Brexit and the Anti Elite Era", *Europe's World*, June, 2016.

M. Muniz, "La Era Anti-Elites" ("The Anti Elite Era"), *Estudios de Política* Exterior. 172, pp. 46–52, July/August, 2016.

M. Muniz and B. Navazo, "Brexit and the Perverse Geopolitics of Leaving the European Union", *The New* Atlanticist, July, 2016.

M. Muniz, "Populism And The Need For A New Social Contract", *Social Europe*, October, 2016.

M. Muniz et al., "Technological Change, Inequality and the Collapse of the Liberal Order," *G20 Insights*, April, 2017.

N. Oreskes and E.M. Conway, *The Collapse of Western Civilization: A View From the Future* (New York, NY: Columbia University Press, 2014).

K. Picket and R. Wilkinson, *The Spirit Level: Why Equality is Better for Everybody* (London: Penguin, 2010).

T. Piketty, *Capital in the Twenty-First Century*, 1st edition (Cambridge. Harvard University Press, 2014).

J. Rifkin, *The Zero Marginal Cost Society. The Internet of Things, The Collaborative Commons, and The Eclipse of Capitalism*, 1st edition (New York, NY: Palgrave Macmillan, 2014).

D. Rodrik, "From Welfare State to Innovation State". *Project Syndicate*, January, 2015.

J. Savulescu and M. Bostrom, *Human Enhancement*, 1st edition (New York, NY: Oxford University Press, 2009).

E. Schmidt and J. Cohen, *The New Digital Age* (London: Hackette, 2013).

G. Soros, "The Capitalist Threat". *The Atlantic*, February, 1997.

L. Summers, "The Age of Secular Stagnation: What It Is and What to Do About It". *Foreign Affairs*, February, 2016.

R. Van Santen, J. Khoe and B. Vermee, *2030 Technology That Will Change The World* (New York, NY: Oxford University Press, 2010).

3

The Journey of Corporate Diversity in Tribal Times: Corporate Communities of Aspiration in MAPFRE

Celia de Anca and Salvador Aragón

Abstract Understanding diversity and its connection with identity in global organizations is particularly relevant at this moment in history, often described as tribal and whose driving force takes the form of a collective mindset, as illustrated by many terms that have recently entered into currency: co-creation, co-working, co-thinking or co-financing, along with working collectively, all key elements in the new forms of economic activity.

The first step to correctly manage diversity is to understand what it means, as well as understand the different types of diversity that can be found in global organizations. This is covered in the first part of this chapter.

We then move to the relationship between diversity and identity. Understanding identities helps us to use the existing tools correctly to effectively include diversity in corporate life.

Next, we define how diversity fits in the new tribal context and how companies can use the emerging collective mindset as a driving force. The concept of collective individualism can help companies balance our desire for community with our individual needs.

Finally, we describe the case of Spanish insurance company, MAPFRE, as an illustration of how corporate communities of aspiration can become a powerful tool for companies to channel the power of diversity into innovative energy.

C. de Anca (✉) • S. Aragón
IE Business School, Madrid, UK
e-mail: Celia.deanca@ie.edu

© The Author(s) 2018
S. Iñiguez de Onzoño, K. Ichijo (eds.), *Business Despite Borders*,
https://doi.org/10.1007/978-3-319-76306-4_3

Introduction

> If action as beginning corresponds to the fact of birth, if it is the actualization of the human condition of natality, then speech corresponds to the fact of distinctness and is the actualization of the human condition of plurality, that is, of living as a distinct and unique being among equals (Arendt 1958, 1998 p. 178).

Imagine you are applying for the job of your dreams. You understand the requirements and are sure you will fit perfectly in the organization and its project.

The day of the final interview goes as planned and you have a good feeling that the job is yours.

The following day, you receive a call from Mr Casterman, the head of human resources: "Congratulations"—he says—"the job is yours," and just when you are about to jump for joy, he adds, "We have decided to give you the position, because YOU ARE A WOMAN, and we really believe in women's talent in this organization."

How would that make you feel? Not too good, right?

Most women we know, would be offended by that explanation. Not because we reject our identity, but because we want to be recognized as individuals, not by what we share with half of the world's population!

Now imagine the same situation, the same interview, the same good feeling followed by the happy call. But this time Mr Casterman, after congratulating you for the job, adds, "We decided to give you the position, because we love your ideas, and the way you see our business. We need you to contribute to our project!"

That makes you feel a lot better, right?

Most people, women and men alike, would be happy to work in such an organization, because we want to be recognized by our uniqueness and contribute with our ideas alongside other individuals to jointly make a project move forward.

The example above helps to illustrate the diversity journey in the corporate world, which frames the content of this chapter: companies that manage diversity, helping their employees move from their demographic diversity to their cognitive diversity. Good corporate diversity management helps us to navigate from our identities of origin to our identities of aspiration.

Diversity: The Journey in Our Human Condition of Plurality

Diversity can mean different things to different people, as Lu and Page note:

> *In the common understanding, diversity in a group of people refers to differences in their demographic characteristics, cultural identities and ethnicity, and training and*

expertise. Advocates of diversity in problem-solving groups claim a linkage among these sorts of diversity (which we will refer to as identity diversity) and what we might call functional diversity, differences in how people represent problems and how they go about solving them. (Lu and Page 2004, p. 16385)

In a recent study of 180 Spanish corporate managers, we explored diversity perceptions in two departments: human resources and innovation (de Anca and Aragón 2018).

The results indicated that the majority of human resources managers perceived diversity as the differences between individuals in terms of gender, culture, age, sexual orientation or disabilities.

Most respondents from the innovation unit perceived diversity as the differences between individuals in terms of ideas.

Some of the participants in both groups also included in their diversity perception differences among people due to their professional backgrounds and work experiences.

Following the research findings, we classify organizational diversity in three categories.

Demographic Diversity: It is defined as the characteristics that are given to us by our *human condition of natality* (Arendt 1998). We come into this world in different shapes, sizes and colors, and often the first thing that is said about us, even before having a name, is whether we are a boy or a girl. We are then given a nationality and some rights and obligations, as well as specific cultural traits and traditions. So, before our first birthday, and without having any say in the matter, we already have a number of characteristics that classify us and that we will carry around with us for the rest of our lives.

Experiential Diversity: In our journey *of becoming distinct and unique beings* (Arendt 1998), most of us keep on adding new characteristics and abilities based on the experiences gained by our education, workplace, hobby, organization, friends and so on. Life experiences shape our emotional universe. Our likes make us curious about certain disciplines and push us to dig deeper into them, and our dislikes make us avoid certain activities and individuals. Affinity bonds us to people with whom we share some of our likes and dislikes, building emotional communities. (Bauman 2001, p. 1). And in today's connected world, we can form emotional communities across the world.

Cognitive Diversity: Diversity literature defines cognitive diversity as differences in thinking styles, knowledge, skills, values and beliefs (Shin et al. 2012; Wang et al. 2016).

The integration of our demographic diversities and real-life experiences shapes our cognition, making us unique beings with a distinct individual mental map that helps us interpret reality, respond to intellectual stimuli, solve problems, develop ideas and create, fulfilling thus our human condition of living as a distinct and unique being among equals (Arendt 1998).

All three diversities are connected, but it is important to remember that categories only serve the purpose of classification. Often, this kind of compartmentalized classification does not stand analysis, since differences are blurred and we often have traits, the origins of which are unclear.

Corporate Diversity Management: Navigating Our Different Identities

Our individual diversity does not exist in isolation. For diversity to happen, we need numbers (Page 2011). We need a group to share our diversities with, the people around with whom we conform our different social identities, which is defined as the internalization of collective identifications (Jenkings 2008, p. 120).

Identification is rooted in basic and generic human processes, and it is meaningful to individuals because it allows self-evaluation (Jenkings 2008). The word identity comes from the Latin *Idem* meaning same, and *Entis* meaning entity. It is the movement of becoming identical to some entity, implying a two-way process. I might decide, consciously or unconsciously, that I do belong to a certain group, and thus *identify* with it, meaning that I follow certain patterns of that group's behavior (Jenkings 2008 p. 158). Equally, the process can be external: *Others that are not me* decide to *categorize* me into a certain group, which implies a certain pattern of behavior which people expect me to conform with, which I may or may not identify with.

Social identities, with their interplay between identification of similarity and difference, can be found in every aspect of our life, including the organizations we work in. And those identities are directly linked to our different diversity types.

- Demographic diversity connects us with our identities of origin.
- Experiential diversity makes us share likes and dislikes over time, what we might call identities of growth.
- Cognitive diversity makes us look for other minds to complement our thinking: what we might call identities of aspiration.

Classifying diversities helps corporations establish policies to solve specific diversity challenges. We will now look at the different strategies corporations can adopt to deal with diversity.

Corporate Strategies to Manage Identities of Origin

Identities of origin are our connection with the past. Whether we identify with them (through a self-identification process) or not, other people will often categorize us on the basis of the characteristics of our origin, race, gender and culture. Therefore, we might encounter both internal as well as external barriers preventing us from developing our organizational capabilities to their full potential.

Some of the external barriers that minorities often run into in organizations include stereotyping, cultural pressure, lack of opportunities, lack of minority role models, a hostile corporate culture, or in extreme cases, discriminatory practices and legislation. In terms of internal barriers, internal cultural models or low self-confidence are identified among the most frequent for women and minority groups (De Anca and Aragon 2018).

Since the 1980s, most global companies have developed diversity and inclusion policies to effectively include individuals in their organizations led by human resources, reinforced by top management. The most frequent include, assessment tools (climate surveys, statistics monitoring and minority targets), human resources programs (flexible policies, mentoring or coaching), communication campaigns to give voice to the diversity strategy, and specific training programs.

Some of those policies have become increasingly effective. However, companies still need to be alert, since many of the barriers individuals from minorities face are still in place, and holding onto talent requires continued surveillance and proactive measures. Recent cases, such as discrimination at Uber (Timberg and Dwoskin 2017), show that diversity policies of inclusion are not some old-fashioned twentieth century strategy, but something all companies should take seriously, including new emerging tech ventures.

Corporate experience shows that the most adequate strategy for companies to manage communities of origin is to eliminate barriers to inclusion and development.

We can find a good example in managing identities of origin in the Sodexho Diversity unit.

Sodexho is considered one of the pioneers in developing diversity and inclusion policies. One of the triggers may have been a 2001 lawsuit alleging *discrimination in promotion practices after the* 1998 merger of Marriott International food services and the US division of Sodexho.

In 2002 the company hired a chief diversity officer, Anand Rohini, to make diversity a priority at Sodexho. Some of the diversity priorities at Sodexho focused on gender, ethnicity disabilities or age. And the diversity strategy included a series of systems and processes including:

1. Human resources policies, including flexibility measures, training, selection processes and career services
2. Diversity scorecards
3. Quantitative targets of diversity

By 2005, Sodexho was widely recognized as a diversity champion and for more than a decade has been consistently ranked among the top in the diversityinc top 50 list (Diversity inc 2017) and Anand Rohini has been widely recognized as a global diversity champion. The diversity at Sodexho has been looked at in a famous Harvard Business School (HBS) case study (Thomas and Creary 2011).

Corporate Strategies to Manage Identities of Growth

Identities of growth often provide us with a feeling of security. Our likes and dislikes change over time, and so our affinity groups change. Identities of growth dictate who we spend time with.

Many companies have developed friendship-based communities among employees, typically organizing activities such as weekends away, departmental Christmas parties and so on, in a bid to create emotional ties between workers and the company. But because emotional communities are held together as much by the likes as by the dislikes of members, they can be unpredictable and difficult to manage in the long term. As a result, these emotional communities can sometimes work to the benefit of organizations, but they can just as often end up having the opposite effect, particularly when people share a dislike for certain policies, boss or what they consider to be an unfair situation.

Our diversity research suggests that the best policy for dealing with communities of growth is through minimum intervention. Emotional communities will emerge in organizations, whether management likes it or not, and will have a life of their own. For that reason, it is best to take a neutral position. Creating affinity groups is positive for the company. But these groups should always be voluntary and develop at their own pace, without management interference.

Corporate experience shows that the most adequate strategy for companies to manage experiential communities is neutrality.

We can find a good example in managing identities of growth in the IBM Resource Groups initiative.

IBM is another pioneer in diversity management. IBM Business Resource Groups (BRGs) are volunteer employee-driven groups focused on a common area of interest or a certain constituency such as race, gender or emerging issues like cross-generational differences, veteran or work/life integration. The company allows for different groups to emerge, without taking positions or preferences for any of the constituted groups. By 2016, there were 250 BRGs registered globally in 45 countries which support 13 different constituencies or interest areas (Frydensberg 2016).

Corporate Strategies to Manage Identities of Aspiration

Our cognitive differences find their place in a community of aspiration where equals among equals can share their different ideas to contribute to a common project. In these communities, we are valued not by what makes us equal or by our affinities, but by our unique way of understanding and interpreting the world. Rather than a particular community, a community of aspiration is a space of interest that people share, where our ideas are valued for their contribution to a common project, regardless of our different traits and individual likes or dislikes beyond the task in hand.

Innovative organizations are shifting from managing units to managing challenges or projects, asking employees to voluntarily join projects, creating structures where employees can move out of their comfort zones to join temporary communities of aspiration that strengthen cross-organizational ties and help the company achieve its strategic goals. People join in to co-create or co-execute a solution for an existing problem or to co-develop a new initiative or a new product.

Corporate experience shows that the most adequate strategy for companies to manage communities of aspiration is to create the contexts and the project for them to emerge.

We can find a good example in managing identities of aspiration at Valve Corporation.

Valve Corporation, a videogame developer, has defined a unique corporate structure with no bosses or managers at all. Each member of the company is

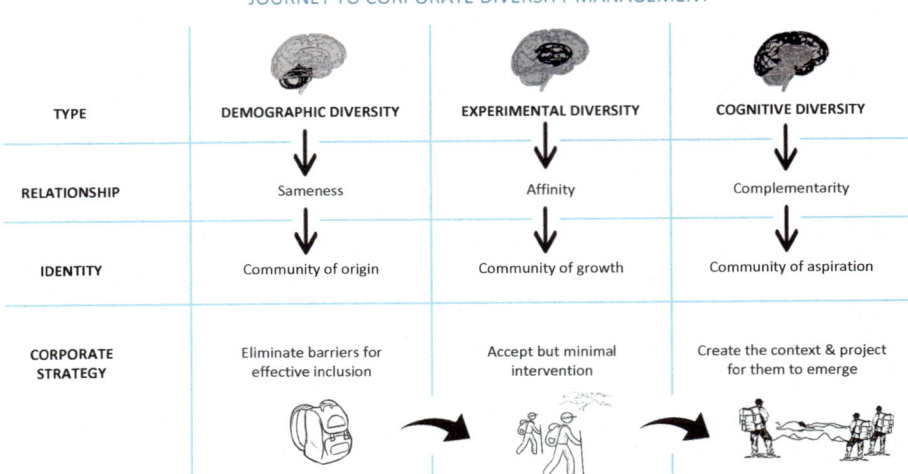

Fig. 3.1 Journey to corporate diversity management

invited to define her/his contribution to the company according to their choices and preferences. A highly talented developer specialized in graphics animation might choose to work on a game by assuming a *group contributor role*, becoming part of the group developing that game. (On the other hand, after finishing this *group contribution*, the same person might choose to work in a more individualistic fashion on the next task.) This *free to choose* approach is mirrored in the firm's office design. Valve Corporation offices incorporate wheeled desks to foster mobility and allow the fast configuration and reconfiguration of groups as well as individual work (Valve 2017).

Collective Individualism in Tribal Times

Understanding the corporate navigation from communities of origin to communities of aspiration is particularly relevant in our tribal times, with a shift from a longing for independence in a society made up of communities, to a longing for belonging in a society made up of individuals (De Anca 2012).

There have been periods in human evolution when the individual stands above the community, and periods in which community is more important. But every philosophy and religion agrees that a healthy society needs both, individuals developed to their fullest, in healthy communities in which individuals can contribute. The Sumak Kawsay of the Andean Ancestors, or the Civitate Dei, of

Agustin of Hipo, as well as the symbol of the hero fighting the dragon rising above himself to then go back to the community to help them evolve, present in most cultural traditions, are only a few of multitude of cultural examples of the urge for developing oneself individually and in community.

The individual was at the center of Western culture from the seventeenth century until the last decade of the twentieth century, when a collective energy emerged in a phenomena labeled by sociologists as new tribalism (Maffesoli 1988). Maffesoli described a society shifting from one built around the individual to a world populated by *affective communities*. Today this *being together* has been dramatically incremented by technology. Wherever we look, everyone is staring into their phone. And if we get closer, we will probably realize that the conversation is not with just one person, but with a group via the social networks. Group-talk is now part of everyday life and often spread across different time zones, with friends and family connecting whenever they want. Our individuality is expressed within different groups.

Is this really just a response to technology? Some sociologists think that we have been looking for tools to shape a new collective emerging energy, reflecting a deep-rooted desire to connect and live our daily lives in small communities. This new form of *being together* is labeled *sociality*, in which the person (persona), instead of having a function, plays a role (Maffesoli 1988). In these new identities, individuals seek to transcend their individualities by playing a role in tribes that provide them with temporary identification. Castells, describing the networking society (1997), describes the new forms of communal identity as projected identities.

Individuals now choose identities consciously. We want to play with a multiplicity of identities and use them in as many different roles as their different affiliations allow. This is why initiatives such as *lean in* are so popular.

Corporate Communities of Aspiration and Innovation. The Case of MAPFRE

MAPFRE is a publicly owned multinational Spanish insurance company, the biggest in Spain and the largest non-life insurance company in Latin America. It is present in 49 countries and in 2016 had turnover of €27 billon.

Traditionally, its growth has been based on the deployment of local companies in internal markets called Local Entities (LEs), which enjoy significant managerial autonomy. This *federal model* has provided a solid foundation for the geographical expansion of the company, built on growth through group synergies and efficiency.

Since 2013, this federal approach has been refined by the introduction of a functional corporate-level layer which crosses all the LEs. This layer includes Operations, Information Technologies and Innovation.

Responding to the changing environment in the insurance industry as well as the transformation of closely related Industries (automotive, information technology, etc.), MAPFRE defined an innovation strategy built around three components mirroring its existing structure: a Corporate Innovation Unit (CIU), a number of local Innovation and Development Offices (IDOs) and finally a number of Innovation Agents (IAs).

The CIU's mission is to coordinate all innovation, manage the innovation project portfolio, lead the implementation of innovation projects, provide common methodologies (design thinking and lean startup) and create a shared innovation culture.

The IDOs operate on a local basis, with dual dependence: each IDO has a hierarchical dependence on its LE Steering Committee and a functional one on the CIU. All of the current 14 IDOs are focused on translating the main LE's strategic challenges into specific innovation projects that could be locally managed (see chart in Fig. 3.2).

The IAs provide a less formal way to generate innovation in the company by taking advantage of communities and informal networks. The IAs are all MAPFRE employees able to allocate part of their working time into a given innovation challenge of their choice.

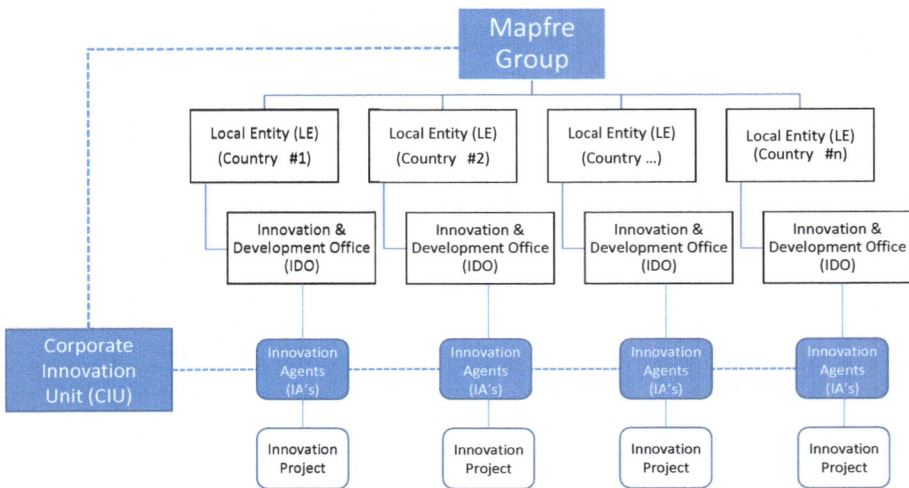

Fig. 3.2 Mapfre: organization of innovation

A real-life example we identified that illustrates the innovation model and the use of Corporate Communities of Aspiration (CCA) by MAPFRE through this organizational role is that of a talented employee working in the reinsurance part of the business who shows interest in satellite-based valuation and appraisal.

This employee would be invited to share his/her interest to the local IDO. After this, the IDO qualifies him/her as an IA by providing basic training in methodologies such as design thinking and lean startup, guaranteeing some basic prototyping capabilities.

Once recognized as an IA this person would be invited to participate in two other projects as a member of the team under the leadership of other IAs. This preliminary experience guarantees both the development of innovation leadership capabilities and commitment.

Once this training period is completed, the new IA begins his/her innovation project. The most relevant task would be to find additional team members. To accomplish this, a direct invitation mechanism is used: the IA takes advantage of his/her informal network within the organization, a mechanism that has been proven as very successful. To quote the Corporate Head of Innovation: "the most dynamic employees are very efficient at identifying other dynamic employees."

In the case of our satellite-based valuation IA, he was able to gather a team of seven highly motivated workmates. The project has been recognized as very promising by the company.

From the CCA perspective, these factors have been seen as crucial in order to guarantee their success: the training process provides the right filter in terms of capabilities and motivation, the use of collaborative tools (groupware) allows both physical and virtual interaction among team members and the usage of identity-based tokens make the IA visible to the rest of the organization. This allows an IA buddy to receive proper recognition through internal communication channels.

The Journey of Corporate Diversity in Tribal Times: Conclusions

The current collective meme risks regression, as can be seen from the many current political and social movements harking back to older political and tribal models, taking away individual freedoms to retain the essence of group. Those regressive movements are based on *sameness*: similarities that bind the group together. However, in the new forms of collective individualism, the communities of aspirations, *difference* is what binds the group. Aspirational communities are formed by independent and free thinkers that want to build a common project enriched by the large cognitive diversity of the group, thus providing robustness to the system, innovation and productivity and, most importantly, as Page suggests, making the process more interesting to all (Page 2011, p. 10).

The new tribalism is a place to work and act, not a place to live; it embraces community without renouncing universality. Communities of aspiration, whether in companies or the collaborative economy, are open, voluntary, flexible and interlinked with other communities.

Organizations cannot force motivation upon individuals, nor engineer creativity; what they can and should do, as shown in the MAPFRE example, is capture the collective energy of the times in their understanding of diversity, create contexts of possibility and adapt their management styles accordingly to be able to foster innovation and efficiency.

References

H. Arendt, *The Human Condition* (*Chicago, IL:* University of Chicago Press, *1958, ed 1998).*

Z. Bauman, *Community; seeking safety in an insecure world* (Cambridge, UK: Polity Press, 2001, ed. 2008).

M. Castells, *The Power of Identity, The Information Age: Economy, Society and Culture Vol. II.* (Cambridge, MA: Blackwell, 1997 ed. 2004).

C. de Anca, C, *Beyond Tribalism, Managing Identities in a Diverse World* (*London, UK: Palgrave Mcmillan, 2012).*

C. de Anca, and S. Aragón, "Diversidad e Innovación dos extraños destinados a encontrarse", http://centerfordiversity.ie.edu/wp-content/uploads/2016/10/ULTIMA-VERSION-Informe-Innovacion_Diversidad-26sept.pdf, (last entered March 10, 2018).

Diversity inc http://www.diversityinc.com/about-the-diversityinc-top-50/, (last entered July 10, 2017).

A. R Frydensberg, https://blog.ibm.jobs/2016/06/01/meet-ibms-all-volunteer-business-resource-groups/, (last entered July 14, 2017).

R. Jenkings, *Social identity* (New York, NY: Routledge, 1996 ed. 2008).

H. LU, and S. Page, "Groups of diverse problem solvers can outperform groups of high-ability problem solvers", *PNAS,* November 16, vol. 101 no. 46 pp. 16385–16389, September 17, 2004.

M. Maffesoli, *Le temps des tribus* (Paris, FR : Le Livre de Poche, 1988).

S. Page, *Diversity and Complexity* (Princeton, NJ: Princeton University Press, 2011).

S.J. Shin, J.Y. Lee and, L. Bian, "Cognitive team diversity and individual team member creativity: A cross-level interaction", Academy of Management Journal, 55(1), pp. 197–212, February 1, 2012.

C. Timberg, and E. Dwoskin, "Uber fires 20 employees as part of harassment investigation" *Washington Post, June 6, 2017.* https://www.washingtonpost.com/news/the-switch/wp/2017/06/06/uber-fires-more-than-20-employees-as-part-of-sexual-harassment-investigation/?utm_term=.9f1382183996. (Last entered, June 29 2017).

D. Thomas, and S.J. Creary, "Shifting the Diversity Climate; the Sodexho Solution*", Harvard Business School, Case Study,* pp. 9-412-020 *Harvard Business School,* July 25, 2011.

Valve Corporation http://www.valvesoftware.com/ (Last entered July 2017).

X.H.F. Wang, T.Y. Kim and D.R. Lee, "Cognitive diversity and team creativity: Effects of team intrinsic motivation and transformational leadership", *Journal of Business Research* 69 pp. 3231–3239, September, 2016.

4

The Global Expansion of Televisa

Gabriela Alvarado Cabrera

Abstract Based in Mexico, Televisa is a leading media company in the Spanish-speaking world. Over the last 20 years—since Emilio Azcárraga Jean became the president of Televisa in 1997 and until he stepped down as its CEO at the end of 2017—the company has followed different foreign entry strategies, such as strategic alliances, joint ventures, and international acquisitions to expand the reach of its content to new markets. Currently, the company distributes the audiovisual content it produces to over 80 countries through several pay-television brands, television networks, cable operators, and over-the-top services via the Internet. In addition, Televisa's international activities include publishing and feature-film distribution in Latin America. Nowadays, Mexico, Latin America, and the US Hispanic community are Televisa's most important media marketplaces. However, in recent years, the pace of economic growth in Latin America has slowed down, while Mexico's prospects might be seriously affected in the upcoming future by Donald Trump's protectionist policies. Further, the constitutional reform in the telecommunications sector enacted by President Enrique Peña Nieto has brought about increased competition in the Mexican telecommunications and broadcasting sectors. Hence, Televisa must strengthen its presence globally and develop innovative ways to reach more international audiences.

G. Alvarado Cabrera (✉)
Department of Business, ITAM, Mexico
e-mail: galvar@itam.mx

© The Author(s) 2018
S. Iñiguez de Onzoño, K. Ichijo (eds.), *Business Despite Borders*,
https://doi.org/10.1007/978-3-319-76306-4_4

Company Overview

Televisa is a leading media company in the Spanish-speaking world, an important cable operator in Mexico, and a leading direct-to-home (DTH) satellite pay-television (pay-TV) system. The company's strategic focus has ensured its continued industry leadership and growth. Televisa is constantly anticipating new market trends, adapting its business strategy, innovating and diversifying its content offering, formats, and services to meet the needs of customers. It was judged the third most valuable Mexican brand by the BrandZ and Kantar ranking released in February 2017. Today, the company is divided into four business segments: Content, Cable, Sky (DTH satellite television system), and other businesses.

Televisa Segments

A brief description of each business segment, along with its size and growth, is provided below.

Content

In 2016, Televisa produced more than 90,000 hours of content for free-to-air and pay-TV, representing 36.9% of the segment's net sales and 37.9% of operating segment income (OSI). Compared with the previous year, content net sales increased by 6.9%, while the OSI margin was 40.2%. Sales in this segment come from three major areas: advertising, licensing and syndication, and network subscription revenue (Grupo Televisa 2017b).

As regard advertising, with four free-to-air channels in Mexico City that the company operates in combination with owned and affiliated stations throughout the country, a strong portfolio of pay-TV networks, and new media platforms, Televisa is one of the largest providers of advertising alternatives in the Mexican market. Advertising revenue accounted for 23.4% of the segment's net sales in 2016, but it reached only a modest growth of 0.8%.

In terms of licensing and syndication, Televisa remains committed to creating innovative content that reaches audiences worldwide. The company exports its programs and formats to television networks around the world with an approximate outreach of more than 80 countries. During 2016, Televisa exported over 93,473 hours of its original programming and by the end of the year it had 264,671 half-hours of television programming in its library available for licensing. Revenue from this area was 9.1% of the segment's net sales and it grew by 17.6% over 2015. This increase is mainly explained by a positive translation effect on foreign-currency-denominated revenues. In the United States, Televisa distributes its content through Univision, the leading media company serving the Hispanic market, under a programming license agreement (PLA). Royalties from Univision reached US$324.6 million in 2016, equivalent to a growth of 4.3% on 2015.

With regard to network subscription revenue, Televisa is one of the world's leading producers of the original Spanish-language content for pay-TV platforms. It commercializes 26 pay-TV brands through 52 domestic and international feeds, which reach over 44 million subscribers around the world. In the United States, Televisa distributes its pay-TV channels through Univision. During 2016, Televisa produced more than 27,000 hours of content for pay-TV networks and the business constituted 4.4% of the segment's net sales. Network subscription revenue expanded by 22.4%, partially helped by the depreciation of the peso.

Cable

Televisa is an important player in the cable industry in Mexico and offers video, fixed voice, and high-speed data services. Televisa's network consists of more than 80,000 kilometers of coaxial cable and more than 33,000 kilometers of fiber optic. In 2016, the cable business generated 32.1% of the segment's net sales and 34% of the OSI. The same year, this segment's revenues grew 11.9% and the OSI margin reached 41.5%—the highest on record.

Sky

Televisa owns a 58.7% interest in Sky, a leading DTH satellite television system that operates in Mexico, Central America, and the Dominican Republic. Sky offers pay-TV packages, including exclusive content that includes sports, concerts, and special events. During 2016, Sky added more than 742,000 subscribers, reaching over eight million pay-TV subscribers and becoming one of the most competitive DTH pay-TV companies in the continent. Its contribution to the segment's net sales was 22.1%, and to the OSI, 25.4%. Sky's net sales increased 14.0% and the OSI margin reached 45.1%.

Other Businesses

Televisa's other businesses serve as important complements to its core businesses, while providing further diversification opportunities. This segment includes publishing—Editorial Televisa publishes 136 magazine titles in 15 countries, some aiming to capitalize on the success of Televisa's audiovisual content and to engage with its audiences at a deeper level—gaming, radio, soccer, feature-film distribution in Mexico and Latin America, and publishing distribution through Intermex, Televisa's company engaged in the continental distribution of its publications. Intermex has a network of more than 25,000 points of sale in Mexico and over 80,000 abroad. It owns the leading publications distributors in Argentina, Chile, Colombia, Ecuador, Panama, and Peru. In 2016, these other businesses represented 8.9% of the segment's net sales and 2.7% of the OSI. Revenues increased 8.7% over the previous year.

In addition, among its unconsolidated businesses, Televisa holds a 40% equity interest in OCESA, a live-entertainment company in Mexico, Central America, and Colombia. OCESA organized 2969 events in Mexico and Colombia during 2016.

In 2016, Televisa's four business segments jointly reached net sales and OSI of 96,287.4 and 38,923.2 million pesos, respectively. This meant a growth in consolidated revenues of 9.4% and an OSI of 9.0% over 2015. Table 4.1 displays these figures by the business segments (Grupo Televisa 2017a). Further, the growth in revenues was accompanied by growth in profitability. For the second consecutive year, Televisa's three core businesses, Content, Cable, and Sky, posted OSI margins in excess of 40%.

The Path Toward Internationalization

The beginning of Televisa's international activities dates back to 1961 when Emilio Azcárraga Milmo (appointed as the president of the company in 1972 after his father, Emilio Azcárraga Vidaurreta, passed away) had begun to realize his vision for Televisa with the launch of the Spanish International Network in the United States, which later became Univision.

Twenty years ago, Emilio Azcárraga Jean became the president of Televisa, after his father passed away in 1997, and was also its CEO until the end of 2017 when he left this second role and remained as the Executive Chairman of the Board to focus on the firm's long-term strategy, as well as on the soccer business and Televisa foundation. Under Azcárraga Jean's leadership, a new

Table 4.1 Operating segment results

(Millions of Mexican Pesos)	Year ended December 31		
	2016	2015	Change %
Segment net sales			
Content	36,686.7	34,332.6	6.9
Advertising	23,223.2	23,029.3	0.8
Licensing and syndication	9064.2	7707.9	17.6
Network subscription revenue	4399.3	3595.4	22.4
Cable	31,891.6	28,488.3	11.9
Sky	21,941.2	19,253.5	14.0
Other businesses	8828.3	8124.3	8.7
Segment net sales	99,347.8	90,198.7	10.1
Intersegment operations[a]	(3060.4)	(2146.9)	(42.5)
Net sales	96,287.4	88,051.8	9.4
Operating segment income			
Content	14,748.0	14,564.2	1.3
Cable	13,236.1	11,405.6	16.0
Sky	9898.5	8972.3	10.3
Other businesses	1040.6	753.2	38.2
Operating segment income (OSI)[b]	38,923.2	35,695.3	9.0

[a]For segment reporting purposes, intersegment revenues are included in each of the segment operations

[b]OSI is defined as operating income before corporate expenses, depreciation and amortization, and other expense, net

wave of innovation and internationalization began. Since then, various foreign entry strategies, such as strategic alliances, joint ventures, and international acquisitions have been followed by the company to expand the reach of the content it produces to new markets.

Strategic Alliances

During the last two decades, Televisa has developed different strategic alliance agreements to expand its most important business segment—content—into new markets. Through these agreements, Televisa and its partners have enhanced their respective business potential and value creation opportunities at a faster rate by getting access to additional knowledge and resources, while remaining autonomous in nature.

In 2001, Univision, Televisa, and Venevision reached a multi-faceted strategic alliance to further penetrate the rapidly growing US Hispanic market by aligning the resources of the three leading Spanish-language media companies. Under the agreement, Univision's three networks—Univision, Galavision, and Telefutura—secured exclusive US broadcast rights to Televisa and Venevision programming in exchange for a royalty payment through 2017. As part of the agreement, Televisa also made an equity investment in Univision, increasing Televisa's fully diluted ownership stake in Univision to about 15%. In addition, Emilio Azcárraga Jean joined Univision's board of directors as vice-chairman. This agreement was the most important and broad-reaching alliance in Spanish-language media at that time, and enabled all three companies to significantly accelerate their growth by capitalizing on the opportunities in the US Hispanic market.

Nine years later, Univision and Televisa strengthened their strategic partnership through an agreement in which Televisa invested $1.2 billion in Univision, while their PLA was expanded to include digital media platforms and extended to 2025. In connection with the investment, three Televisa representatives joined the Univision board of directors and under the new PLA, Univision received exclusive Spanish-language broadcast and digital rights to use Televisa online, network and pay-TV programming on its three existing television networks, any future Spanish-language networks, and on existing and future Univision interactive platforms (Univision.com, Univision Móvil, and Video on Demand) in the United States. In exchange for the expanded rights and content, Televisa would receive increased royalties from Univision.

Furthermore, in 2011, Televisa reached a multi-year content licensing agreement with Netflix, the world's leading Internet subscription service for movies and TV shows. Under the agreement, Televisa made around 3000 hours annually of telenovelas, series, and other general entertainment programming of its extensive library available to Netflix on a non-exclusive basis until June 2016. This agreement increased the availability of Televisa programming in Latin America and the Caribbean, but did not include the United States. The content licensing agreement with Netflix was an important first step in the company's plan to monetize its library of over 50,000 hours of content via digital distribution.

Joint Ventures

To further penetrate foreign markets, Televisa has also partnered with local firms to pool their resources and set up new companies through joint venture arrangements. Under these agreements, Televisa and its partners have shared the ownership, governance, returns, and risks, associated with the new ventures, which have included not only Televisa's content business segment but also its other businesses.

On top of the 2001 strategic alliance between Univision, Televisa, and Venevision, Televisa and Univision agreed to create a 50/50 joint venture to introduce Televisa's satellite and cable pay-TV programming in the United States and create future channels.

In 2004, Televisa and Hispanic Publishing Group, a leading publishing company in the US Hispanic market, formed a joint venture under which Televisa acquired 51% of a new company, which was called Hispanic Publishing Associates, while Hispanic Publishing Group retained a 49% equity stake. With this alliance, Editorial Televisa acquired its first two English-written magazines for Hispanics in the United States: *Hispanic Magazine*, with a 280,000 circulation, and *Hispanic Trends*, with a 75,000 circulation. These two titles complemented Televisa's US strategy by permitting access to new general market advertisers interested in the US Hispanic community.

The following year, Televisa and EMI, the world's largest independent music company, combined their respective strengths in music, distribution, and media, forming a new 50/50 joint venture record company in Mexico (Televisa EMI Music), along with Televisa's partnership in EMI's US Latin operations (EMI Televisa Music). Both ventures, Televisa EMI Music in Mexico and EMI Televisa Music in the United States, were headed by the Director of Televisa Music and ended in 2009.

Also in 2005, Televisa participated in a public bid to obtain a concession for a free-to-air television channel in Spain as the Spanish market presented an attractive investment opportunity for Televisa given its size, growth potential, and content-production synergies. The Spanish government granted the concession to a consortium formed by Televisa, Globomedia (formerly Grupo Árbol), and Mediapro. At that time, Globomedia and Mediapro, the leading suppliers of prime-time content in Spain, were merging. The new company resulting from the merger, Imagina Media Audiovisual, became the largest television content production company in Spain and second largest in Europe, bringing an experienced management team in Spanish television to lead the project. The new channel, La Sexta, features original programs, mainly produced by Globomedia and Mediapro, incorporating the latest technologies to offer viewers the most advanced interactive services available through digital television. Televisa held a 40% participation interest in La Sexta and Imagina Media Audiovisual, 60%.

International Acquisition

As part of Televisa's international expansion strategy in its other businesses segments, in 2007 it acquired 99.9% of the shares of Editorial Atlántida, the leading magazine publishing company in Argentina, which published a total of 11 magazines and operated a book publishing business, interactive websites, and numerous brand-extension projects. Editorial Televisa had had presence in Argentina since 1978, distributing 22 magazines with a total annual circulation of 3.2 million copies. With the acquisition of Atlántida, Editorial

Televisa strengthened its activities in Argentina and its position as the world's leading Spanish-language publishing company. The grandson of Atlántida's founder remained an active member of the board and strategic counsel for Editorial Televisa.

The Hispanic Market in the United States

At present, the Hispanic community in the United States represents Televisa's most important media marketplace outside Mexico, given the size and rapid growth of this market and its demographic similarity to Mexico and Latin America.

Indeed, according to the 2014 Population Estimates of the United States Census Bureau, the Hispanic population of the United States was more than 55 million, representing 17% of the nation's total population and making people of Hispanic origin the largest ethnic or racial minority in the United States. Furthermore, the projected Hispanic population of the United States for 2060 is 119 million people. Based upon this projection, the Hispanic community will constitute over 28% of the nation's population by that date (United States Census Bureau 2014).

Televisa content has reached US Hispanic audiences through its PLA with Univision for many years. The PLA grants Univision exclusive access to most of Televisa's audiovisual content in any format for distribution in the United States and Televisa gets a royalty payment of 11.84% from Univision on all its audiovisual revenues. The PLA has also set an increase in the royalty rate to 16.13% in January 2018 and 16.45% in June 2018. In addition, Televisa has equity and warrants, which upon exercise would represent approximately 36% on a fully diluted, as-converted basis of the equity capital in Univision Holdings Inc., the controlling company of Univision.

The US market is an integral part of Televisa strategy to keep on expanding its global reach, and the partnership and alignment with Univision is the key to success of this expansion as Univision has continued to serve Hispanic audiences like no other company. In 2016, for the 24th consecutive year, Univision's flagship network was the number one network in the United States among Hispanics, including newscasts, cable entertainment networks, and cable sports networks. Besides, Univision reported, for the first time ever, revenues in excess of US$3 billion. As a result, royalties to Televisa reached US$324.6 million in the year. This is twice the amount of royalties received by Televisa in 2010.

Other International Markets

Televisa's content has been exported globally for many decades through different foreign entry strategies, and it enjoys an enduring base of followers beyond Mexico and the United States.

The company distributes the audiovisual content it produces to over 80 countries in Central America and the Caribbean, South America, Western and Eastern Europe, West and East Africa, the Middle East, Asia, and Australia. This endeavor is carried out through several pay-TV brands, television networks, cable operators, and over-the-top services via the Internet.

During 2016, Televisa reached more than 44 million pay-TV subscribers worldwide. Moreover, Sky, Televisa's DTH satellite television system, which launched operations in Spanish-speaking Central America and the Caribbean in 2007, has added close to five million customers in the last six years, closing 2016 with 8,026,519 net active subscribers. Of these, 206,814 subscribers were from Central America and the Dominican Republic. Over the last ten years, Sky revenue and OSI have expanded at a compounded annual growth rate of 11% and 10%, respectively, being one of the most successful pay-TV operations in the region.

In addition, Televisa publishes magazine titles in 15 countries, distributes its publications in Latin America through a network of more than 80,000 points of sale outside Mexico, and is engaged in the feature-film distribution business in Latin America.

The successful global expansion of Televisa's content beyond the US Hispanic market and Latin America, where people not only share a language but also values and beliefs due to their common historical and cultural past, can be spelled out to some extent by national cultural similarities. In particular, analyzing the power distance and individualism scores of Hofstede's national culture model from countries where Televisa has successfully distributed its content reveals meaningful similarities with those in Latin American countries.

Power distance is the extent to which the less powerful members of a society accept and expect that power is distributed unequally (Hofstede et al. 2010). High values in power distance are associated with hierarchical societies, whereas low values correspond to cultures in which people question authority and try to distribute power. Mexico ranks among the top ten countries with highest power distance scores in the world, while Latin American nations are predominantly high on power distance, akin to countries in Southeast Asia, Eastern Europe, the Middle East, and Africa, places where Televisa content has been exported. Available power distance scores for some of these countries are shown in Table 4.2.

Table 4.2 Power distance scores of some countries where Televisa content has been exported

Rank	Country	Score	Rank	Country	Score
1–2	Malaysia	104	22–25	Morocco	70
1–2	Slovakia	104	22–25	Switzerland Fr	70
3–4	Guatemala	95	22–25	Vietnam	70
3–4	Panama	95	26	Brazil	69
5	Philippines	94	27–29	France	68
6	Russia	93	27–29	Hong Kong	68
7	Romania	90	27–29	Poland	68
8	Serbia	86	30–31	Belgium Fr	67
9	Suriname	85	30–31	Colombia	67
10–11	Mexico	81	32–33	El Salvador	66
10–11	Venezuela	81	32–33	Turkey	66
12–14	Arab countries	80	34–36	East Africa	64
12–14	China	80	34–36	Peru	64
15–16	Ecuador	78	34–36	Thailand	64
15–16	Indonesia	78	37–38	Chile	63
17–18	India	77	37–38	Portugal	63
17–18	West Africa	77	39–40	Belgium Nl	61
19	Singapore	74	39–40	Uruguay	61
20	Croatia	73	41–42	Greece	60
21	Slovenia	71	41–42	South Korea	60
22–25	Bulgaria	70			

Source: Hofstede et al. (2010)

While individualism refers to societies in which the ties between individuals are loose, collectivism relates to societies in which people are integrated into strong, cohesive in-groups that protect them in exchange for unquestioning loyalty (Hofstede et al. 2010). In this case, scores above 50 correspond to individualist cultures and scores below to collectivist ones. All nations in Latin America, including Mexico, are mainly collectivist cultures, yet again similar to countries in Southeast Asia, Eastern Europe, the Middle East, and Africa, where Televisa content has been distributed. Table 4.3 displays available individualism scores for some of these countries.

In summary, the choice of the appropriate foreign entry strategy, along with a clear understanding of national cultural similarities among countries, has strongly contributed to expanding Televisa's presence globally while building connections among people from different nations and cultures.

Current Challenges

Mexico, Latin America, and the Hispanic community in the United States have been so far the most important media marketplaces for Televisa. However, in recent years, the pace of the economic growth in virtually all Latin American

Table 4.3 Individualism scores of some countries where Televisa content has been distributed

Rank	Country	Score	Rank	Country	Score
39–40	Jamaica	39	57	Chile	23
39–40	Russia	39	58–63	China	20
41–42	Arab countries	38	58–63	Singapore	20
41–42	Brazil	38	58–63	Thailand	20
43	Turkey	37	58–63	Vietnam	20
44	Uruguay	36	58–63	West Africa	20
45	Greece	35	64	El Salvador	19
46	Croatia	33	65	South Korea	18
47	Philippines	32	67–68	Peru	16
48–50	Bulgaria	30	67–68	Trinidad	16
48–50	Mexico	30	69	Costa Rica	15
48–50	Romania	30	70–71	Indonesia	14
51–53	East Africa	27	72	Colombia	13
51–53	Portugal	27	73	Venezuela	12
51–53	Slovenia	27	74	Panama	11
54	Malaysia	26	75	Ecuador	8
55–56	Hong Kong	25	76	Guatemala	6
55–56	Serbia	25			

Source: Hofstede et al. (2010)

countries has slowed down due to weak external demand, further declines in commodity prices, volatile financial conditions, and large exchange rate depreciations. The only two nations whose economies grew during 2015 and 2016 were Peru and Costa Rica. At the present time, economic growth in Latin America faces two consecutive years of negative growth for the first time in over three decades (IMF 2016).

In particular, the Mexican economy slowed down toward the end of 2016 and the peso depreciated even further after an already steep decline in 2015. In these circumstances, it has been very important and valuable for Televisa to have close to US\$1 billion in revenues that are either US dollar-denominated or dollar-linked, and over US\$4 billion in US dollar-denominated assets. Yet, the growing macroeconomic uncertainty was clearly felt by the Cable and Sky business segments in the pace of net additions during the fourth quarter of 2016.

In addition, Televisa is facing an environment characterized by increased competition in the Mexican telecommunications and broadcasting sectors. The constitutional reform in telecommunications matters enacted by President Enrique Peña Nieto gave rise to the new Federal Telecommunications and Broadcasting Law that was published in July 2014 and whose principal objectives are the creation of more rights for the users and audiences, the promotion of competition, and the provision of better services at lower prices (Mexico Gobierno de la República 2014).

As part of the reform, the Federal Telecommunications Institute (the IFT) was created to guarantee economic competition and content plurality, and to encourage universal coverage, interconnectedness, convergence, quality, free access, and continuity. The IFT has the authority to sanction or even split up companies engaged in monopolistic practices, and to establish ad hoc restrictions to minimize market advantages of preponderant economic agents in the industry—companies that capture over 50% market share through their number of users, capacity, or network infrastructure.

Under the constitutional reform, foreign direct investment is permitted to the extent of 100% in telecommunications and 49% in broadcasting to strengthen competition. Also, the IFT was entrusted with conducting the processes of bidding for two new digital free-to-air television channels with national coverage. According to the new law, in the area of broadcasting, the concessionaires of broadcast television services shall allow the retransmission of their signal for free, without discrimination, and simultaneously, in the same geographic area, without modifications and with the same quality to the concessionaires of pay-TV services (must offer). On the other hand, the concessionaires of pay-TV services shall transmit those signals of free-to-air television (must carry) under the same rules.

With regard to the rights of the users and audiences, the law allows the providers of telecommunications services to set prices freely, except in the case of preponderant economic agents or those with substantial power. Besides, the IFT will monitor and sanction the compliance of the maximum amount of time for the transmission of advertising. A balance shall be maintained between advertising and programming, and advertising shall not exceed 18%, in open television, of the total time per channel and six minutes per hour of pay-TV.

In March 2017, Televisa was declared by the IFT to be an economic agent with substantial power in the market of pay-TV services, imposing additional obligations on Televisa and some of its subsidiaries under the new preponderance measures. These new measures were determined at a time when the broadcasting sector was experiencing greater competition not only from new technologies and other audiovisual platforms but also when a new national broadcasting network is competing in the market and gaining market share, and in the middle of a new auction of broadcasting stations in several geographical markets nationwide. Such increased competition, together with the regulatory measures imposed on Televisa, has resulted in a decline in the operating margins of its content business segment in addition to the effects derived from the must-offer rules.

On top of these challenging contexts for Televisa in a country with a slower economy and a weaker peso, the prospects of Mexico's economic growth might be seriously affected in the upcoming future by Donald Trump's protectionist policies given that current economic ties with the United States are strong, owing largely to North American Free Trade Agreement (NAFTA).

Due to the importance of the US marketplace to Televisa's international expansion strategy, on January 17, 2017, just three days before Donald Trump became the President of the United States, Televisa and Univision announced a strengthened and expanded relationship between the two companies by unifying both of their content development and production efforts for the distribution on multiple platforms in Mexico and the United States. Both companies will benefit from a single, integrated focus on the Hispanic audience in the United States and the domestic Mexican audience, as well as from potential cost synergies from aligned content initiatives as Mexico and the US Hispanic market together represent a combined audience of more than 175 million viewers.

The Chief News, Entertainment and Digital Officer for Univision and CEO for Fusion—a 24-hour English-language news and lifestyle TV and digital network—will assume the role of Chief Content Officer of both Televisa and Univision to unify the leadership and strategic direction of the production of content for audiences in both markets. This initiative will allow both companies to compete more effectively in their respective markets in an environment where the viewing habits of consumers are evolving rapidly and where competition is increasing, both from new content offerings and from traditional and emerging platforms.

In addition, as the US Federal Communications Commission recently approved an increase in the authorized aggregate foreign ownership of Univision's issued and outstanding shares of common stock from 25% to 49%, Televisa will increase its current equity stake in Univision.

As Table 4.4 shows, even though Televisa's export net sales reached 13,947.1 million pesos in 2016, equivalent to a growth of 15% over 2015, and have increased for three consecutive years, they still represent only 14.5% of the company's net sales.

Given the prevailing macroeconomic uncertainty and the changing competitive landscape in Mexico's telecommunications and broadcasting sectors, there is a huge need and opportunity for Televisa to strengthen its presence beyond its current main markets, while expanding its content franchise globally and diversifying its sources of income.

Table 4.4 Televisa export net sales

(Millions of Mexican Pesos)	2016	2015	2014
Segment net sales			
Mexico	82,340.3	75,926.6	69,163.4
Other countries	13,947.1	12,125.2	10,955.0
Net sales	96,287.4	88,051.8	80,118.4

Besides choosing the right market entry strategy and identifying national cultural similarities with Mexico, key to the success of this endeavor will be expanding local production initiatives and the development of more and innovative multi-platforms strategies to increase the international reach of its content. Televisa has exported programs and some of its most popular formats to television networks around the world, assisting local production companies in bringing them to life. Some of its most popular shows, locally produced, have entertained audiences in countries in Latin America, Eastern Europe, and Asia.

In addition, by leveraging all of the company's assets to transform its television content into rich multimedia experiences for its audiences, Televisa has already drawn higher ratings and increasing revenues in all of its business segments. In the publishing business, Televisa has restructured its operations in Mexico, moving from an organization based on titles and brands to an organization that creates teams dedicated to provide best services to its clients and fulfill their needs by offering a wide range of segmented audiences through different media. Its facilities now include the required technology to develop online videos, which complement Televisa contents and have opened a new way of offering advertising inventory to its clients. Further, Televisa has now started to carry out similar initiatives throughout the rest of its operations in Latin America.

As Emilio Azcárraga said in the company's press release of October 26, 2017 (Grupo Televisa 2017a):

> Our industry is undergoing a massive transformation, presenting us with big challenges, but even bigger opportunities…I am confident that Televisa will continue to strengthen its presence as one of Mexico's fastest growing telecom providers and as the leading Spanish-language content producer worldwide…

Conclusions

During the last two decades, Televisa has consolidated its position as a leading media company in the Spanish-speaking world. In particular, over the last decade, Televisa has delivered solid growth every year, posting an average growth in consolidated revenues of 9.4%, and in the last two, OSI margins in all its core businesses of above 40%.

As to the company's international activities, the content it produces has successfully reached international audiences and currently it has presence in more than 80 countries, covering all continents.

The successful international expansion of Televisa has been achieved through a combination of different foreign entry strategies, along with a proper understanding of the media markets where it participates. In terms of entry strategies, Televisa has carefully chosen between developing either horizontal or vertical strategic alliances, setting up joint ventures with foreign partner companies, or performing international acquisitions, depending on the particular business segment. This has granted Televisa access to valuable knowledge and resources, allowing it to tap market opportunities in foreign countries at a faster pace. In addition, identifying the right local partner has been crucial, like in the case of Univision in the US Hispanic market.

Media and telecommunications continue to converge, and viewing habits, content preferences, and the way people communicate are evolving very rapidly. In this regard, Televisa needs to embrace the challenges the current context is posing and develop even more fully integrated media and content distribution platforms.

Overall, companies looking for expanding their presence globally must be aware of and prepared for changes in the international, political, economic, and business environments, and at the market level. With regard to the latter, the understanding of cultural and demographic similarities among countries should be complemented with a deep knowledge on how the behavior of international customers is evolving, allowing them to develop innovative strategies to successfully enter and settle in foreign markets.

References

Grupo Televisa, S.A.B., "Grupo Televisa appoints Bernardo Gomez and Alfonso de Angoitia co-Chief Executive Officers effective January 1, 2018", October 26, 2017a.

Grupo Televisa, S.A.B., 2016 Annual Report, Mexico City, April 28 2017b.

G. Hofstede, G. J. Hofstede and M. Minkov, Cultures and Organizations: Software of the Mind, USA: McGraw-Hill, 2010.

International Monetary Fund, Regional Economic Outlook: Western Hemisphere. Managing Transitions and Risks, Washington, DC, April 2016.

México Gobierno de la República, Reforma en Materia de Telecomunicaciones. Resumen Ejecutivo, Mexico, 2014.

United States Census Bureau, U. S. Population Projections: 2014–2060, USA, 2014.

5

How Technogym Created the Wellness Industry

Paolo Boccardelli and Enzo Peruffo

Abstract Based on the philosophy *mens sana in corpore sano*, Technogym is considered by some analysts to be the leading global promoter of wellness. A common expression used to define Technogym stakeholders is "The Wellness Company." Its founder, the Italian entrepreneur Nerio Alessandri, has transformed a startup based on fitness equipment into an international and competitive business, always convinced that "dream, vision, work, desire and effort have been the fundamental ingredients to succeed."

In recent years, the digital transformation has begun to affect the health and fitness industry and, to use this disruption properly, the Wellness Company needed to redefine its business model, providing end users and companies with a range of smart and connected products.

The growth has already begun and Technogym aims at spreading the "Italian Quality of Life" worldwide, reinforcing its presence in mature markets and further developing its business in emerging ones.

The authors are grateful to Chiara Acciarini for her valuable assistance on this business case and Vanessa Krause and Martina Binacci for the final revision.

P. Boccardelli (✉) • E. Peruffo
LUISS Guido Carli, Rome, Italy
e-mail: pboccard@luiss.it; eperuffo@luiss.it

© The Author(s) 2018
S. Iñiguez de Onzoño, K. Ichijo (eds.), *Business Despite Borders*,
https://doi.org/10.1007/978-3-319-76306-4_5

The Rise of Technogym: The "Wellness Ecosystem"

Set up in 1983 in Cesena, Emilia-Romagna, Technogym is nowadays recognized as a worldwide leader in the wellness and fitness industry. Since its first products, internationalization and innovation have been at the heart of its DNA. Technogym combines two things: TECHNO for technology and planning, and GYM for fitness and movement. Nerio Alessandri, who founded Technogym at the age of 22, has developed a "wellness ecosystem," a blend of technology, digital strategy, and product innovation, opening new market opportunities in the insurance and pharmaceutical industries. The digital network is based on the Internet of Things: all the machines are connected to an open *cloud* platform where the *apps* communicate with every kind of device (Visentini 2016a, b).

The Wellness Company distributes its products and services in four specific segments: fitness and wellness clubs, hospitality residential, HCP (health, corporate, and performance), and the home. Manufacturing is focused on two product lines: the *professional line* offers a complete range of products and services for fitness training, while the *biomedical line* is related to prevention, evaluation, and physical therapy.

The company is a leading player in the health and fitness market and has a presence in more than 100 countries worldwide, with branches in the United States, Brazil, Japan, United Kingdom, Germany, France, Spain, and Switzerland, as well as through exclusive distributors. This international presence accounts for more than 90% of total turnover, worth about €400 million, while just 10% of the total amount is achieved in Italy. Technogym, Life Fitness, Johnson Health Tech, Precor, and Cybex are the key players in the industry and account for about 72% of the global market (Hollasch 2016). This substantial presence in the global market resulted in the initial public offering (IPO) of 2016 after a ten-day roadshow that started in Milan and took in London, New York, Boston, Paris, and Frankfurt. The company now has a global community of over 40 million people who are trained each day on its products in 65,000 fitness centers and over 200,000 private homes, making Technogym the benchmark for fitness, wellness, and sports. With approximately 40 million daily active users and more than 2000 employees, its mission is to provide people with innovative, engaging, and high-quality solutions to help them to achieve and maintain a healthy lifestyle.

Thirty years on from the foundation, the company has consolidated a leadership position in its segment with some diversified products offering cardio, strength and functional equipment, training and consultancy, and a digital cloud platform (Cesena Today 2017).

The mission of the founder is to differentiate the company from competitors through the creation of integrated and original systems, because, "Technogym is not just fitness equipment; it's a symbol of a lifestyle, a combination of design and technology, a cultural and social icon."

The Health and Fitness Industry: Market Size and Emerging Trends

Over the past few years, there has been major growth in health clubs and gyms in cities and towns. In fact, according to the *Fitness Equipment Market Size, Share, Global Report – 2023*, the fitness equipment market in 2015 was over $10 billion and is estimated to grow at 3.8% from 2016 to 2023. Moreover, from 2009 to 2016, the total growth of fitness clubs worldwide was considerable. "The US is one of the biggest markets in the world in terms of number of clubs and memberships, while Europe is the second-largest market in the fitness equipment segment, with more than 50,000 fitness centers," Zion Market Research reports. According to the research company, nearly 8000 are in Germany, more than 6000 in Italy, and about 6000 are in the United Kingdom. The Asia Pacific segment is expected to grow quickly in the coming years.

The wellness sector is expected to continue growing throughout the world: with consumer demand for wellness services and products higher than ever, the global market was worth $10 billion dollars in 2015 and is expected to reach $12.5 billion by 2021. Deloitte's 2016 *European Health & Fitness Market* survey listed the top five European countries by revenue: United Kingdom (more than €5 billion); Germany (€4.8 billion); and France, Italy, and Spain (more than €2 billion). These five countries represent about 65% of the total European market.

The Impact of Connected Systems

Strong market demand, market competition, the increasing number of Internet users, and the development of innovative and connected devices are the major factors driving the global fitness equipment market. In this digital and transforming context, both users and organizations can access data about fitness activities in real time, allowing businesses to collect information to create new products and solutions. Therefore, companies need to reorient their businesses to attract new clients in innovative and engaging ways (Van Belleghem 2015).

The growing number of smart and connected products is disrupting value chains, increasing the amount of data that can be analyzed. Connectivity requires new technology infrastructures that include modified hardware and software, operating systems integrated in the products, and a platform that contains the information (Porter and Heppelmann 2014).

The *2016 Worldwide Survey* analyzed the new top fitness trends of the year: wearable technology, *apps* for smartphone exercises, and mobility rollers have impacted the industry (Thomson 2016). Wearable technology such as the Apple Watch increases customization and monitors users' activities (Coorevitis and Coenen 2016). Some studies have shown that monitoring employees through wearable equipment can increase their health and well-being, encouraging them to achieve determined fitness goals (Giddens et al. 2016). Fitness *apps* are being used in medicine: *MyFitnessPal* is a nutritional and calorie-counting database that is used by millions of people to track food intake and to monitor lifestyle, as well as weight loss. Accenture Consulting estimates that by the end of 2017, 1.7 billion smartphones and tablets will have a health *app* installed (Accenture Consulting 2013). The evaluation of most *apps* can be based on different principles such as usefulness, accuracy, objectivity, functionally, design, security, and value (Hanrahan et al. 2014).

The outcomes of the same global survey affirmed the results of previous years, identifying new trends such as group training and the global health initiative, *Exercise is Medicine*, managed by the American College of Sports Medicine (ACSM) (Thomson 2016). Group exercises are useful to motivate and guide people at different fitness levels, while *Exercise is Medicine* encourages health-care providers to include physical activity when designing treatment plans for patients.

The impact of digital fitness products and services on the fitness industry has been investigated through an online survey conducted on 157 participants. It suggests that people who adopt digital technologies can benefit from the collection and analysis of more extended data (heart rate, calorie consumption, or GPS data) over conventional gyms (Jung 2016). The digital transformation is reshaping the health and fitness industry, and the redefinition of the business models should consider the advent of technological changes that ensure on-demand experiences for customers who can access the services they want anytime, anywhere. Innovation is changing the way businesses compete; furthermore, the creation of digital networks encourages the exchange of information between structures and individuals, creating value-added systems. In this context, the challenge is how to evolve businesses into more dynamic operating models characterized by flexible and cost-effective supply chains to deliver innovative seamless customer experiences: How is Technogym reacting to these disruptive transformations to compete in the global arena?

Technogym's Background and Product Range: Launch and Development of the Startup

In 1983, Nerio Alessandri created the *Hack Squat* for bodybuilding exercises in his garage in Cesena. After a year, he had produced 150 units. The founder and president of the company immediately understood the business potential and decided to resign from his previous job and rent 100 square meters of warehouse, later extending this to 2000 square meters. Technogym was funded through bootstrapping, using some capital from Alessandri's savings.

In 1997, "Mr. Technogym" was named the entrepreneur of the year in the field of innovation, and in 2002, he unveiled *Wellness Valley* to create a network in the territory between organizations and individuals who promote wellness as a lifestyle. The Cesena facility, designed to guarantee both maximum productive efficiency and a work environment inspired by the principles of wellness, covers around 40,000 square meters. The Technogym Village is "the workshop for the new era" and is considered a landmark for research, innovation, and wellness.

In 2003, Alessandri launched the *Wellness Foundation*, a non-profit organization that works with universities, schools, and research centers to improve the quality of people's lives. The organization promotes wellness by emphasizing the importance of a healthy and active lifestyle. The *Wellness Foundation* is in the Palazzo Romagnoli, one of the most important historical buildings in the Romagna region.

The company's commitment to sports has always been marked, proven by exclusive partnerships with the Olympic Games. In 2010, Technogym provided 16 out of 32 participating teams of the South Africa World Cup with training equipment, and in the same year was a supplier to the Singapore Youth Games. In addition, it has been a sports consultant and supporter to many national and international football clubs such as Real Madrid, Juventus, Chelsea, Liverpool, and Manchester United.

Key Financial Data

Despite a market dominated by uncertainty, Technogym continues to out-grow its competitors, achieving revenues of €511 million in 2015 and more than €550 million in 2016—more than 8.5% compared to the previous year (Technogym 2016).

The Wellness Company has continued to boost growth with €124 million of consolidated profits in the first quarter of 2017—more than 7% up in the same period in 2016—and turnover is expected to continue to grow in the coming years.

Global expansion has been a major growth driver: in the first quarter of 2017, sales in Asia Pacific rose 23.2%, and 18.7% in North America, where Technogym saw revenue of more than $4.5 billion in 2015 (Global Market Insights 2016). In mature markets such as Italy, it grew by15.2%, and more than 7.3% in Europe overall. The Wellness Company is also doing well in emerging markets like Brazil and India where less than 3% of people work on their fitness, but that are characterized by a fast growing fitness culture (Shah and Suresh 2009).

The Digital Strategy of Technogym

Technogym has created the global online campaign, "Let's Move for a Better World" to promote wellness and a healthy lifestyle. Innovation, design, and product development represent the core of a business model that aims to capture value through the digital transformation of its activities. The wide range of fitness solutions serves B2C (Business to Client) and mainly B2B (Business to Business) market segments. The implementation of the "wellness on the go" strategy encourages the creation of programs that are available wherever and whenever the users want them (Il Sole 24 Ore 2015). As Alessandri says, "the idea of "wellness on the go" is not just about going to the gym three times a week—it's physical activity 24 hours a day, seven days a week. It is a mental approach, something that is continually practiced, at work, at home."

The Wellness solution includes a series of complete and personalized services, "in addition to a wider and more diversified range of tools for professional operators who want to expand and retain the customer base." Technogym is carrying out an "incremental innovation strategy," based on the integration of optional and additional services and machines able to respond to a range of needs. Technogym's main goal is to help everyone enjoy customized experiences, offering a package of connected equipment that enable access to contents and training programs anywhere. For instance, the so-called *home fitness line*, composed of products such as *UNICA*, *Multipla*, and *Pratica*, offers professional training exercises directly at home. This cloud modality—able to connect products, a large customer base, and fitness centers—allows customers to experience wellness directly from their smartphone, tablet, smart TV, PC, and *mywellness* key (Vesentini 2016a, b).

Product Lines and Customer Experience

Products are the central element of the innovation strategy and the steady innovative process is focused on the opportunity to adapt product lines to new market segments. During 2016, Technogym has launched many solutions like *Skillmill*, dedicated to athletes who want to focus on strength, resistance, and speed: *Power Personal*. Technogym has also launched *MyRun*, the treadmill for home, created to offer the best running experience with personalized programs and feedbacks; the device is integrated with a dedicated app and tablet. The revolutionary CPR (constant pulse rate) system was patented by Technogym in 1988 to monitor heart rate and adapt cardiovascular training. In 1992, after five years of research collaboration with the Massachusetts Institute of Technology, Technogym launched an isokinetic tool for functional rehabilitation called *REV 9000*. These continuous investments in technology have led to the first TV screen integrated in a piece of fitness equipment, called *Wellness TV* and launched in 2002.

In 2015, at EXPO Milan, Technogym launched "Let's move for a better world," in line with the event's theme: "Feeding the planet, energy for life." The idea, thanks to the equipment connected to the *mywellness cloud* technological platform, allowed visitors to turn performed movement into meals donated to countries affected by malnutrition. In the same year, the startup acceleration program—called *Wellness Accelerator Program*—was launched in cooperation with H-Farm in order to find European startups able to present innovative projects capable of revolutionizing and improving the fitness industry (Technogym 2015a, b). The initiative has encouraged the digital transformation of the businesses, especially in relation to wearable devices, new *apps* and tools, big data, and analytics (Comini 2015). During the following year, Technogym bought Exerp, a Danish firm that makes fitness management software, highlighting its digitization strategy.

As part of its diversification strategy, Technogym has acquired 31.77% of Enervit S.p.A., a leader in the sector of sports nutrition. This transaction consolidated the partnership through the Wellness Foundation to promote a healthy lifestyle and to support scientific research. In 2016, the company announced a partnership with the National Strength and Conditioning Association (NSCA), the worldwide authority on strength and conditioning research and education. The collaboration created a series of innovative contents in the fields of health and wellness (National Strength and Conditioning Association 2016). In March 2017, Technogym announced an initiative with IBM to develop a new generation of fitness platforms able to communicate with people; these technologies can offer different customized programs that take into account user's goals and other parameters such as weather and nutrition, to maintain a healthy lifestyle (La Repubblica 2017). Thanks to the combination of digital and cloud-computing technologies between Technogym and IBM, these innovative platforms can be integrated with a virtual coach. Further digital integrations for the updated *MyWellness App* and new products such as *skillrow*, the groundbreaking solution for indoor rowing, and *mycicling*, a new indoor training solution for cyclists, were presented in April 2017 at FIBO, the most important European tradeshow dedicated to fitness and wellness.

Alessandri continues to look to the long term, investing in research and development: about 10% of Technogym's 2000 employees work in the research center, including engineers, doctors, and technicians who make renewable and safe materials, reflecting Technogym's commitment to social responsibility and environmental sustainability.

Going Global

During the second year of business activity, Technogym has started to export its products abroad and now it is present in various market segments, thanks to an "omni-channel" distribution strategy that includes retail, field sales, wholesale, and inside sale. The company's growth is due in large part to a *glocal* international strategy: it is global in terms of brand promotion and innovative processes application, and local for the customization of products and services. Technogym has acquired the leadership in the international market of fitness equipment through innovative machines characterized by design and creativity—wearable devices, *apps*, audiovisual technologies, and so on. Hermann Simon, arguably the most influential management thinker after Peter Drucker, defined the Wellness Company as a "hidden champion that remains a virtually unexplored source of knowledge": its secretiveness is in contrast with its dominant position in the international markets (Simon 2009).

The implementation of a global strategy is fundamental to understanding the competitive scenario in terms of cultural, administrative, geographic, and economic distance. The *CAGE Distance Framework* is based on these four dimensions that, respectively, refer to interaction between the individuals of a society; the relationships between diverse countries and related trade agreements; the physical distance between countries (borders, access to the ocean, and so on); and finally, economic factors such as resources, infrastructure, and labor costs (Ghemawat 2010). Market selection represents a strategic decision related to the globalization of the business, and Technogym aims at maintaining the United States as the preferred market for future growth. The coverage of the premium market in the United States allows Technogym to differentiate its offering, achieving $41.9 million profits in 2016. For example, companies such as Google, Facebook, Cisco, Goldman Sachs, and the University of Stanford have opted for Technogym (Techonogym 2017a, b, c). The US fitness market is the world's largest—accounting for about 15% of revenue—and it is the place where the largest equipment maker, *Life Fitness*, is based (Tagliabue 2008).

Technogym has faced different challenges, depending on the markets. For instance, the Chinese fitness market is more complex than those in the West: over 16% of people in the United States take part in some form of exercise every day, compared to 0.6% in China. Moreover, the costs for sport infrastructure are heavy (Daxue Consulting 2016). However, Technogym has understood the rapid development of the Chinese fitness market, which has shown an annual growth of 11.8% from 2011 to 2016—as IBISWorld shows. Nevertheless, the company has been in the Chinese market for over 15 years, and a marketing research study made by Daxue Consulting in 2013 shows that there were already over 1000 gyms in China using Technogym's products and, meanwhile, the business provides products and services for some hotels (Daxue Consulting 2013). The challenges of the Chinese market have not stopped the rapid expansion of the company.

In 2007, Technogym expanded its boundaries to the Emirates, thanks to a joint venture with Wellness Solution, the Dubai-based company already working alongside Technogym as a local distributor (Technogym 2007). In October 2016, the Wellness Company opened a new showroom of 600 square meters in Mexico City, in one of the most dynamic areas in the city; this move has confirmed the intention of investing in the Mexican market and includes a new indoor solution—*Group Cycle Connect*—that allows users to perform customized connected trainings.

When an organization is looking to expand, among the concerns are legal risks, related to ensuring compliance with different laws and regulations, intellectual property, due to weak protection in other countries, and direct and indirect taxation (Thomson Reuters 2015). In addition, possible risk factors related to globalization strategy have been underlined in an international study conducted by the London School of Economics that has found a link between globalization strategy and obesity: individuals who use innovative and highly interconnected devices (smartphones, TV, etc.) lack motivation to leave their desks or sofas (Costa-I-Font 2017). The analysis, based on 26 countries and focused on the period 1989–2005, shows that the lifestyle changes connected to sedentary activities have impacts on overall health. However, such market risks are mitigated by the group's geographically diverse operations and product diversification across market segments. Exposure to interest rate risks is lower because the Wellness Company does not use derivative instruments, while there are fewer internal risks, thanks to the application of well-structured procedures that ensure the correct development of processes (Technogym 2016).

Conclusions and Takeaways

This case provides a lesson about Technogym's successful internationalization strategy, which in turn illustrates how to take advantage of digital transformation. International expansion has given the Wellness Company the opportunity to increase its customer base and to enlarge the business by engaging users in a global community, where trainers and professionals are able to exchange information and data anytime and anywhere. Generally, the identification of international markets should take into consideration questions about the type of segment being sought, the opportunity to adapt businesses to local environments, and the possibility of creating chances and value-added activities from the evolution of the business models; the selection of stakeholders is also essential (Khanna and Palepu 2010).

This case offers many takeaways in terms of a company's ability to successfully reinvent its range of products and services, bearing in mind the need to digitize, as well as taking advantage of new markets. Technogym successfully seized three major opportunities generated by the digital transformation that has allowed it to shape a new form of international value chain:

- Connectivity has spread wellness culture via the mass dissemination of user-friendly tools and apps that everyone can use to monitor physical activity. Technogym took up the trend, introducing unique wellness and training experiences that increased both consumer loyalty and market share.

- Wearable devices and apps make it possible to collect and exploit daily information on consumers' lifestyles, making it possible to map their needs and to offer tailored wellness solutions, shortening cultural and geographical distances.
- Technology has been used as a means to detect, interpret, and exploit different countries' societal changes, building a continuously monitored community based on the evolution in real time of habits. The principle of the 1997 Wellness Valley has been displayed at a global level, establishing a fruitful environment to stimulate innovation and speed up the go-to-market through an incremental response to various geographically distributed needs.

To seize these opportunities in a global environment, Technogym has successfully conducted a *glocal* strategy, which led the company to become global as a brand and to deploy its offer locally in a customized way, thanks to a network of local subsidiaries and partners.

References

Accenture Consulting, "Consumer Health & Wellness Industry Trends, Health conscious consumers demand more from the wellness industry. That could grow the consumer health market by over $200 billion", 2013.

Cesena Today, "Il colosso cesenate del wellness Technogym cresce ancora: fatturato al +8,5%", 2017.

S. Comini, "Technogym ed H-Farm, insieme per le startup del wellness", *Il Sole 24 Ore*, 2015.

L. Coorevits and T. Coenen, "The Rise and Fall of Wearable Fitness Trackers", Academy of Management, 2016.

J. Costa-i-Font, "Globesity'? The effects of globalization on obesity and caloric intake", London School of Economics, 2017.

Daxue Consulting, "Fitness Industry in China: What are the Trends?", 2016.

Daxue Consulting, "Market Report: Technogym in China", 2013.

P. Ghemawat, *Strategy and the Business Landscape, Developing a Global Strategy* (Boston, MA: Pearson 2010).

L. Giddens, E. Gonzalez, D. Leidner, "I Track, Therefore I Am: Exploring the Impact of Wearable Fitness Devices on Employee Identity and Well-being", 2016, https://www.researchgate.net/publication/305701617_I_Track_Therefore_I_Am_Exploring_the_Impact_of_Wearable_Fitness_Devices_on_Employee_Identity_and_Well-being.

Global Market Insights, Fitness Equipment Market Size by Application (Gym/Health Clubs, Home/Individuals, Hospitals, Offices, Hotels), By Product (Strength Training Equipment, Cardiovascular Training Equipment, Activity Monitors, Body Analyzers), *Industry Analysis Report, Regional Outlook, Application Potential, Price Trends, Competitive Market Share & Forecast*, 2016–2023.

C. Hanrahan, T. Aungst, S. Cole, "Evaluating Mobile Medical Applications", *American Society of Health-System Pharmacists*, 2014.

K. Hollasch, "European Health & Fitness Market Study", Deloitte, 2016.

H. H. Jung, "The Effect of Digital Transformation on the Fitness Industry", Munich Business School Insights, 2016.

National Strength and Conditioning Association, "Industry Leaders Support Fitness Industry Through Educational Content", *Resources and Certification*, 2016.

R. Shah, K. Suresh, "Technogym, the Italian Fitness Brand: Tapping Global Markets", IBS Research Center, 2009.

H. Simon, *Hidden champions of the twenty-first century: The success strategies of unknown world market leaders, Who are they? A selection of hidden champions around the world*, (Bonn: Simon-Kucher & Partners, 2009).

J. Tagliabue, "Technogym, the Italian maker of fitness machines, turns to luxury markets", New York Times, 2008.

Technogym, *Annual Report 2016.*

Technogym, "Technogym *brings Innovation at FIBO 2017*", https://www.technogym.com/it, 2017a.

Technogym, "Technogym con H-Farm lancia il primo Wellness Accelerator Program rivolto ai giovani", in www.technogym.it, 2015a.

Technogym, "Technogym e IBM, nel wellness adesso arriva l'intelligenza artificiale di Watson", La Repubblica, 2017.

Technogym, "Technogym opens Dubai branch", in Trade Arabia, 2007.

Technogym, "Technogym punta sul fitness americano", in Il Sole 24 Ore, 2017c.

Technogym, "Technogym spinge sul Retail e porta il wellness a Expo", in Il Sole 24 Ore, 2015b.

W. Thomson, "Worldwide survey of fitness trends for 2016: 10th Anniversary Edition", *ACSM'S Health & Fitness Journal*, December 2015.

W. Thomson, "Worldwide Survey of Fitness Trends For 2017", *ACSM'S Health & Fitness Journal*, December 2016.

S. VAN Belleghem, *When Digital Becomes Human: The Transformation of Customer Relationships*, 2015.

I. Vesentini, *Italy's Technogym plays its new card, offers clients a new, digital fitness "ecosystem"*, Il Sole 24 Ore, 2016a.

I. Vesentini., *Technogym lancia un nuovo «ecosistema» digitale del benessere*, in Il Sole 24 Ore, 2016b.

6

Leadership, Global Mindset and Internationalization of Sempertex: From One Country to Ninety-five Countries and Five Continents

Henry Bradford Sicard

Abstract This chapter highlights the relevance of leaders' characteristics in the internationalization process of family firms. Specifically, it stresses the influence of the global mindset of a second-generation CEO who took Sempertex from a small local family firm in Colombia to a global competitor manufacturing high-quality latex balloons with a presence in almost ninety-five countries on five continents and an approximate 30 percent market share in the global market of high-quality latex balloons for professional use.

Introduction

Globalization and internationalization have been deeply researched and discussed in the business arena. Globalization is a phenomenon that has led to an increasingly integrated world economy through a constant flow of knowledge, people and technology across borders. Internationalization represents the response that people, firms and countries develop to face the challenges and advantages derived from globalization (Bradford et al. 2017). While some people see globalization as a scenario with plenty of opportunities for businesses, others consider it a huge threat and demand policies and programs to protect local enterprises and family businesses and shield them from global competitors. Hence, individual mindsets perceive globalization as either an

H. Bradford Sicard (✉)
CESA Business School, Bogota, Colombia
e-mail: henry.bradford@cesa.edu.co

© The Author(s) 2018
S. Iñiguez de Onzoño, K. Ichijo (eds.), *Business Despite Borders*,
https://doi.org/10.1007/978-3-319-76306-4_6

opportunity or a problem, which should lead us to concentrate our efforts in understanding leaders' mindset, its determinants and the relationship between it and a firm's approach to internationalization.

The values, beliefs, goals, and expectations of owner/managers in small- and medium-sized family businesses should have a direct impact on firms' behavior. Miller and Toulouse (1986) find a strong relationship between CEOs' personalities and the organizational characteristics in small firms. Kotey and Meredith (1997) highlight a relationship between owner/manager personal values, business strategies and firm performance. According to these authors, strategies are different in above-average and below-average performing firms, and owners/managers of firms performing above average show different personal values from those of below-average performing firms. Kyvik et al. (2013) argue that CEOs' attitudes, international orientation and mindset should explain differences in firms' strategic behavior regarding internationalization.

A leader with a global mindset will foster the firm's internationalization. However, what explains the global mindset? Does effective global leadership require having lived in more than one country, having traveled to other countries or speaking more than one language fluently? According to Cohen (2010), most people would say yes to these questions, but are these global experiences necessary, desirable or perhaps insufficient? In this chapter I highlight the relevance of a leader's characteristics in the internationalization process of family firms. I first consider factors that the literature finds important in shaping a global mindset and then use the case of Sempertex, a Colombian manufacturer of high-quality latex balloons and one of the most relevant firms in its market segment in the global arena, to show the relevance of these factors for small family businesses' internationalization behavior.

Leaders, Global Mindset and Business Across Borders

Different contextual factors suggest the need for a global perspective in managing and leading firms. According to Cohen (2010), an aging population worldwide and low birth rates, particularly in developed economies, have resulted in changes in population distribution, with the most increases in emerging economies. The expansion of some organizations into these markets, free trade agreements, a global workforce and advances in technology and transportation are facts that organizations and their leaders have to deal with, and an important attribute for effective global leadership is a global mindset.

But what is and what determines a global mindset? For Cseh et al. (2013), a global mindset is a concept that encompasses all the competences needed for leadership and strategic business decisions in a global context. After an exhaustive literature review of cultural, strategic and multidimensional perspectives, Levy et al. define a global mindset as: "a highly complex cognitive structure characterized by an openness to and articulation of multiple cultural and strategic realities on both global and local levels, and the cognitive ability to mediate and integrate across this multiplicity" (2007, pg. 244). In Cohen's words, it is the ability to "think and act both globally and locally at the same time" (2010, pg. 5). From their definition, Levy et al. (2007) highlight three complementary aspects of the global mindset: first, openness to and awareness of multiple spheres of meaning and action; second, complex representation and articulation of cultural and strategic dynamics; and third, mediation and integration of ideals and actions oriented both to the global and the local.

Hence, a CEO with a global mindset encompassing global leadership will influence the firm's internationalization behavior. Kyvik et al. (2013) assert that internationalization was traditionally viewed as a gradual process, but that recently international markets have been explained in terms of innovation and as an outcome of the CEOs' strategic search for opportunities (Liesch and Knight 1999; Knight 2000). Studies now recognize internationalization as an intersection of entrepreneurship and internationalization theory (McDougall and Oviatt 2000; Jones and Nummela 2008), and hence "the role of the entrepreneur as an innovator, broker, and facilitator remains crucial as the form perceives and explores opportunities for driving further expansion overseas" (Kyvik et al. 2013, pg. 175). A global mindset allows CEOs to explore global business opportunities and can be the main driver of success in global markets (Gupta and Govindarajan 2002; Felício et al. 2012).

Entrepreneurs' characteristics are relevant and are linked to the global mindset they reflect. According to Felício et al., "global mindset is explained by decision style, childhood, valuation of international experience, international background, technical expertise, international experience, global orientation of the firm, global orientation of the entrepreneur, firm characteristics and firm activities in the global market" (2012, pg. 470). This definition comes after a literature review of different contributors. For example, Gupta and Govindarajan assert that "curiosity and openness about how the world works reflect an attitude, an element of the individual's personality make-up. Like other elements of personality, it is shaped heavily by early childhood experiences and becomes more resistant to change with age" (2002, pg. 120). International experience (living and working abroad for a certain time) gives managers a broader perception and ability to adapt the competences of the company to situations of global change (Osland and Osland 2005; Hotho and Champion 2011). Individuals' background, including nationality, formal education, language skills and international management training, among other elements, shape the global mindset (Gupta and Govindarajan 2002; Clapp-Smith and Hughes 2007). In addition, the level of education and being part of a family from a foreign country contribute to the development of a global mindset (Arora et al. 2004).

The relevance of owners/managers or CEOs for the internationalization of small family businesses leads some authors to talk about the global leadership mindset, a combination of global mindset and global leadership (Cohen 2010; Cseh et al. 2013). According to Cohen (2010), a global leadership mindset implies balancing three overall dichotomies: global formalization versus local flexibility, global standardization versus local customization and global dictate versus local delegation. Davis et al. (2008) present the global leadership mindset model with three dimensions integrated by the learning process: orientation (way of being, including openness, collaboration, awareness, flexibility and cosmopolitanism, among other characteristics), knowledge (cognitive structure consisting, among other elements, of thinking, selection, analysis, imagination, reasoning, intuition, perception and judgment), and behavior (enactment of orientation and knowledge, which includes propensity to engage, be curious, be able to build emotional connections and demonstrate global business savvy, among other traits).

In the following two sections I describe the case of Sempertex as an illustration of the theory reviewed here. This successful internationalized Colombian company has a second-generation family CEO, Oswald Loewy, with a global mindset linked to the internationalization behavior of Sempertex.

Sempertex: A Family Firm with Global Presence

Sempertex S.A. is a well-known example of Colombian family-owned companies that have entered, performed and remained on the highly competitive international market scene. Due to its high standards, Sempertex has become a world leader in latex balloons for decoration and entertainment. CEO Oswald Loewy describes the company's main product, balloons, as "visual delights"[1] and has focused the company's strategy on innovation in quality and color. The company has been devoted to manufacturing latex products since 1938; however, it has only operated under the name Sempertex since 1964. The name is a fusion of the Latin word *semper*, which means always, and *tex*, for latex.

About the Company

Sempertex is located in Barranquilla, a city known as the golden door of Colombia for its access to the Magdalena River and the Caribbean Sea. As mentioned on the Sempertex website, its privileged geographical position permits the firm to import the best materials available in the world market to produce the best latex balloons under a promise of quality, price and service.

This family-owned company has a daily production of four million balloons, employs almost 1200 workers, exports to 95 countries on five continents and has a turnover of US$35 million annually. All of these features have established Sempertex as the second-ranked balloon company in terms of sales and as a worldwide leader in its sector in terms of high quality and high-performance balloons.

Sempertex is among the largest manufacturers of latex balloons in the world and its products have been featured in the events of several transnational brands (Victoria's Secret and Coca-Cola, among others). Currently, seven out of ten balloons that it manufactures are sold overseas, with Asia the most successful market, and where more than 30 percent of production is shipped. This area, with China in the lead, represents almost 20 percent of Sempertex's business.

In October 2015, Xavier Serbia from CNN interviewed CEO Oswald Loewy as representing one of the most successful family-owned companies in Colombia. Transparency and established rules are key factors in Sempertex's development. Other components are innovation, high-quality products, world class suppliers, human talent and 100 percent committed shareholders, as well as distributors who share and transmit the company's ideas and values.

Family, History and the Second Generation

At the beginning of World War II, many European families looked for a way to escape from the danger, persecutions and fear they were living in. The Loewy family, originally from Austria, was one of many Jewish families who fled their native land for South America. After a failed attempt in Argentina, engineer Emil Loewy, the patriarch of the family, decided to relocate to Barranquilla, Colombia. There, he founded a company dedicated to rubber manufacturing, taking advantage of his expertise, industry knowledge and experience with this raw material. Being a visionary, Mr. Loewy contributed his knowledge to start rubber plantations in a specific region in Colombia and established his first latex processing company in 1938.[2]

Around 40 years after the founding of the company, the second generation started to actively participate in its management. In 1978, due to their father's health issues, Oswald, Amalia, Kenneth, Lawrence and their other three siblings[3] became involved in the family business directly or indirectly. The eldest son, Oswald, interrupted his studies in chemical engineering to join the company at that time, taking evening classes in business administration at the Universidad Autonoma del Caribe. His studies were further complemented with top management programs inside and outside the country. In 1980 when his father passed away, Oswald Loewy took control of the top management job as CEO of Sempertex, pursuing the successful path his father had initiated.

Among the family members known to the public are Amalia, Kenneth and Lawrence Loewy. Amalia holds a bachelor's degree in Finance from Universidad del Norte, located in Barranquilla, and was the vice president of Sempertex. Kenneth holds a master's degree in economics from the University of Vienna, Austria; he was Project Manager from 1993 to 2006 and became operations vice president until 2006 when he left the firm. Lawrence was Utilities Manager of Sempertex from May 1993 to October 2006, then Manager of INDUCOL S.A. for five years. He is currently the CEO of Industrias de Refrigeración Hiver S.A.S., a different economic sector than that of his family's.

Current Sempertex CEO: Second Generation

Known for his strong leadership and personality, Oswald Loewy is a firm believer in the key role of integrity and is considered one of the best leaders among family-owned companies in Colombia. He is also known for leading Sempertex's technology development, which makes it unique in terms of production chain in the sector. A further innovation is extensive employment of women to guarantee careful attention to details. Since 1984, 80 percent of his workforce is composed of women.

Born in Barranquilla, Loewy began participating in company strategy at the age of 20. Achieving high levels of technological development, the company was able to acquire its own facilities and equipment. Fluent in Spanish, English and German, Loewy travels around the world seeking new markets and establishing important international connections. He claims it is easier to name countries where the company has no presence than to name those where it has. He is not afraid of regional integrations; rather, he is convinced other markets are good opportunities to consolidate Sempertex. Oswald Loewy was chosen as Colombia's Entrepreneur of the Year by Ernst & Young in 2015 and represented the country in a world competition in Monaco in 2016.[4]

Internationalization

Early in the 1990s, Loewy considered expanding Sempertex overseas as part of a strategy of getting closer to international markets through taking part in the best international fairs. These provided opportunities to demonstrate Sempertex products around the world. After analyzing the global market and identifying advantages and disadvantages, Loewy first expanded Sempertex beyond Colombia to Peru and Ecuador. Later came Costa Rica.[5]

The first main decision following the new opening strategy was to reinvest 100 percent of the profits to improve Sempertex's technology and become competitive internationally. Loewy affirms that the economic opening in 1990 showed the company's potential to compete in this new scenario. The main toy fairs around the world, in cities like New York, Nürnberg, Shanghai, Guadalajara, Chicago and Milan, attracted Sempertex's participation and were the key channel for reaching new international clients in multiple countries. Not long after, in 1999, Sempertex's exports to Europe exceeded US$1 million and in 2005 reached US$4.4 million worldwide.

Initially, exports were directed to Europe, Asia and Austria, partly because of the alliances established with those parts of the world. Nevertheless, the North American market continued to figure in the line of expansion. By the end of the 1990s, the process of establishing ties with China began with impressive positive results. By 1999, Sempertex had arrived in Japan and continued expanding in Asia. Among the countries that are part of the European market for Sempertex are Spain, Portugal, Ireland, the UK, Germany, Belgium, France, Italy, Greece, Cyprus, Albania, Romania, Bulgaria, Sweden, Finland, Norway and Russia. On the African continent, the firm has operations in South Africa, Egypt and Nigeria.[6]

Despite its international success, with distributors in almost 95 countries, the company has lately put a hold on its geographical expansion. "Our strategy is to delve into the markets we are already in," explains Loewy.[7] In 2014, the company was carrying out a new expansion with a bigger distribution center and an increase in its productive capacity to 5000 tons of latex per year.[8] In 2016, Sempertex acquired Disney's exclusive license in party supplies for the wholesale channel, specialty stores and party decoration stores (piñaterías) in Colombia. With this agreement, Sempertex was expecting its licensed character segment to grow by 20 percent in sales.

Discussion: Global Mindset of the Leader and Internationalization of Sempertex

When I began work on this case I was certain that Emil Loewy, the patriarch of the family and a foreigner, was responsible for the success of Sempertex in the internationalization process.[9] However, as I discuss in this section, Oswald Loewy, the eldest son, was actually the architect of this outcome. Only 20 when he started to work for Sempertex, he was the CEO six years later. At that time Sempertex was a small company with 65 employees and only seven administrative staff. His first challenge was to consolidate Sempertex in the local context. According to Loewy,[10] his undergraduate studies in business administration were crucial for the national and international consolidation. This is in line with Kyvick et al. (2013) who state that formal education contributes positively to the forming of a global mindset. For these authors, higher education offers increased knowledge and competences and facilitates the understanding of foreign markets and cultures.

During the 1990s after achieving an impressive consolidation in the Colombian market, Loewy identified an opportunity in the G3 (a 1995 free trade agreement between Colombia, Mexico and Venezuela). Felício et al. (2012) posit that firms that choose to internationalize their activities generally have a significant level of experience in the domestic market. This is also in line with arguments that internationalization represents an intersection of entrepreneurship and internationalization theory. According to Casson (1982), entrepreneurs are always looking for and are able to identify the emergence of new opportunities. Some managers perceive free trade agreements as a threat, and this is more likely when firms have not started their internationalization processes. However, according to Kyvick et al. (2013), CEOs with a global orientation want to grow internationally and, like Loewy, see the world as one big marketplace.

When I asked Loewy about his international childhood experiences, he cited early trips to California, too short an exposure to be a major influence. However, he also asserts that "my biggest international personal experience was listening to stories of my father in Austria. The narrative in my house was quite international."[11] According to Arora et al. (2004), being part of an international family helps to develop an international mindset, and that assertion finds support in this case. Felício et al. highlight as an important factor in the development of a global mindset "the fact that the entrepreneurs, while growing up, had contact with other cultures, due to their parents residing in or traveling to different countries, and appreciation of international experience" (2012, pg. 480).

Regarding language skills, when Loewy started the internationalization process at Sempertex he did not know English but was fluent in German and Spanish. Self-taught, he is now also fluent in English, which allows him to close important business deals for Sempertex abroad. According to Felício et al. (2012), speaking multiple languages accelerates perception capabilities and supports the building of a cosmopolitan mentality.

When talking about his personal experience, Loewy asserts that he started as a common latex balloons exporter and, little by little, learned about the international market, the different segments in it and the relevance of quality. Today Sempertex is number one in the Chinese market, second globally, has more than 1000 employees, has presence on five continents and half of its sales comes from exports. According to Kyvik et al. (2013), the experiences and learning gained from firms' engagement on the international markets lead to a positive strengthening of the CEOs' global mindset.

Conclusions

This case reinforces issues that the literature has highlighted before. First, and most important, is the fact that the CEOs' global mindset has a strong relationship with firms' internationalization behavior. The mind of the leader shapes firms' growth horizon. Arora et al. (2004) and Tseng et al. (2004) demonstrate the relationship between a global mindset and the successful internationalization of firms. Felício et al. (2012) find that a global mindset is a positive influence on firms' internationalization, their international know-how and international networking activities.

Second, a global mindset could be best fostered during childhood. Encouraging the learning of different languages, creating early international experiences and offering an environment with a holistic view are elements that help to build a more complete view of the world.

But what if a manager has grown up without these opportunities? Then, third, it is necessary to help future leaders develop an international perspective and the sooner the better. The most effective channel to achieve this is formal education. Felício et al. (2012) find that education compensates for the lack of early international experiences and mitigates the relevance of childhood influence on the global mindset. Hence, to have business leaders with a global mindset, business schools have to foster the students' participation in international activities and have to offer an international curriculum.

Finally, according to Cseh et al. (2013) global leaders are continuous learners. Exposures to international experiences and engagement in international activities have their own knowledge spillovers. Hence, in regard to international experiences, the more the better. These conclusions are relevant for parents, formal education institutions and companies that understand the value of a global mindset to identify opportunities abroad, take advantage of them and succeed in this globalized world.

Notes

1. Interview with El Radar. Noticias Caracol. http://noticias.caracoltv.com/el-radar/este-barranquillero-conquisto-los-mercados-del-mundo-exportando-globos Accessed 24 April 2017.
2. D. Laueiro and H. Serna, "Sempertex, una empresa colombiana que vuela por el mundo", *Casos de Administración Universidad de los Andes*, ISSN 1900-8791, Diciembre 1, 2008.
3. See: http://www.semana.com/edicion/1513 Accessed 24 April 2017.
4. See: https://www.elheraldo.co/economia/el-barranquillero-oswald-loewy-elegido-emprendedor-del-ano-ey-2015-226652 Accessed 24 April 2017.
5. See: http://economia.elpais.com/economia/2017/02/03/actualidad/148611 9778_826587.html Accessed 25 April 2017.
6. D. Laueiro and H. Serna, "Sempertex, una empresa colombiana que vuela por el mundo", *Casos de Administración Universidad de los Andes*, ISSN 1900-8791, Diciembre 1, 2008.
7. See: http://economia.elpais.com/economia/2017/02/03/actualidad/148611 9778_826587.html Accessed 25 April 2017.
8. See: http://www.dinero.com/edicion-impresa/informe-especial/articulo/ plantas-industriales-alto-desempeno-colombia/198889 Accessed 25 April 2017.
9. The discussion on this section takes into account personal opinions of Oswald Loewy expressed during a personal interview that I carried out on April 20, 2017.
10. O. Loewy, personal interview, April 20, 2017.
11. O. Loewy, personal interview, April 20, 2017.

References

A. Arora, A. Jaju, A. G. Kefalas and T. Perenich, "An exploratory analysis of global managerial mindsets: a case of US textile and apparel industry", *Journal of International Management*, 10(3), 393-411, July 28, 2004.

H. Bradford, A. Guzmán and M.A. Trujillo, "Determinants of successful internationalisation processes in business schools", *Journal of Higher Education Policy and Management*, 39(4),435-452, May 18, 2017.

M. Casson, *The entrepreneur: An economic theory* (New Jersey, NJ: Barnes and Noble, 1982).

R. Clapp-Smith and L. W. Hughes, "Unearthing a global mindset: The process of international adjustment", *Journal of Business and Leadership-Research, Practice, and Teaching*, 3(99), 1-107, January 1, 2007.

S. L. Cohen, "Effective global leadership requires a global mindset", *Industrial and Commercial Training*, 42(1), 3-10, January 1, 2010.

M. Cseh, E. B. Davis and S. E. Khilji, "Developing a global mindset: Learning of global leaders", *European Journal of Training and Development*, 37(5), 489-499, March 25, 2013.

E. Davis, S. E. Khilji, A. J. Critchfield, M. Cseh, L. Yarr and W. Abou-Zaki, "Mirror, Mirror on the wall: Who has the Global Leadership Mindset (GLM) of them all? Proceedings: *International Leadership Association* Conference Global Leadership: Portraits of the Past, Visions for the Future, *10th ILA Annual Global Conference*", November 12–15, 2008.

J. A. Felício, V. R. Caldeirinha and R. Rodrigues, "Global mindset and the internationalization of small firms: The importance of the characteristics of entrepreneurs", *International Entrepreneurship and Management Journal*, 8(4), 467-485, August 30, 2012.

A. K. Gupta and V. Govindarajan, "Cultivating a global mindset", *The Academy of Management Executive*, 16(1), 116-126, February 1, 2002.

S. Hotho and K. Champion, "Small business in the new creative industries: innovation as a people management challenge", *Management Decision*, 49(1), 29–54, January 1, 2011.

G. Knight, "Entrepreneurship and marketing strategy: The SME under globalization", *Journal of international marketing*, 8(2), 12-32, Summer, 2000.

B. Kotey and G. G. Meredith, "Relationships among owner/manager personal values, business strategies, and enterprise performance", *Journal of Small Business Management*, 35(2), 37-61, Summer, 1997.

O. Kyvik, W. Saris, E. Bonet and J. A. Felício, "The internationalization of small firms: The relationship between the global mindset and firms' internationalization behavior", *Journal of International Entrepreneurship*, 11(2), 172-195, April 19, 2013.

M. Jones and N. Nummela, "International Entrepreneurship: Expanding the Domain and Extending our Research Questions", *European Management*, 26(6), 349–353, December 1, 2008.

O. Levy, S. Beechler, S. Taylor and N. A. Boyacigiller, "What we talk about when we talk about 'global mindset': Managerial cognition in multinational corporations", *Journal of International Business Studies*, 38(2), 231-258, March 21, 2007.

P. W. Liesch and G. A. Knight, "Information internalization and hurdle rates in small and medium enterprise internationalization", *Journal of International Business Studies*, 30(2), 383-394, June 1, 1999.

P. P. McDougall and B. M. Oviatt, "International entrepreneurship: the intersection of two research paths", *Academy of management Journal*, 43(5), 902-906, October 1, 2000.

D. Miller and J. M. Toulouse, "Chief executive personality and corporate strategy and structure in small firms", *Management science*, 32(11), 1389-1409, November 1, 1986.

J. Osland and A. Osland, "Expatriate paradoxes and cultural involvement", *International Studies of Management & Organization*, 35(4), 91-114, Winter, 2005.

C. H. Tseng, P. S. Tansuhaj and J. Rose, "Are strategic assets contributions or constraints for SMEs to go international? An empirical study of the US manufacturing sector", *Journal of American Academy of Business*, 5(1/2), 246-254, September, 2004.

7

Movile: Sustaining an Innovative Culture on a Global Scale

Luiz Artur Ledur Brito and Lilian Soares Pereira Carvalho

Abstract Movile is a global Brazilian company operating in the mobile market, developing and marketing apps in the O2O (online to offline) segment. From its humble beginnings, in 1998, as a startup from Campinas, it rose to world leadership in at least one segment, with the PlayKids app, providing content to children under nine years. After many mergers and acquisitions, it now operates in four main segments: content creation and distribution; food online ordering and delivery; movies, theaters and show tickets booking; and logistics intermediation. In the Brazilian market, it is the undisputable leader in the food online ordering and delivery segment: its iFood app has 80% of the market. Movile has offices in six countries in the Americas, including one in Silicon Valley in the United States, and has plans to expand to all continents. Fabricio Bloisi, the company's founder and CEO, is behind the company's business model and culture, combining the Brazilian passion with the result-oriented and high-tech mindset of the Silicon Valley. In this chapter, we outline the company's history, its innovative culture embedded in its business model and its future challenges.

L. A. L. Brito (✉) • L. S. P. Carvalho
Fundação Getulio Vargas EAESP, Madrid, UK
e-mail: Luiz.Brito@fgv.br

© The Author(s) 2018
S. Iñiguez de Onzoño, K. Ichijo (eds.), *Business Despite Borders*,
https://doi.org/10.1007/978-3-319-76306-4_7

Movile: A Global Player in the Mobile Market

In a big conference room, equipped with smart TVs exhibiting live feed from all branches of Movile worldwide, Fabricio Bloisi's eyes sparkle when talking about the company he founded, in 1998, under the name Compera. It has been almost 20 years, but now Bloisi's dream came true – he is the CEO of a multi-million-dollar company, with more than 1500 employees and 15 offices worldwide, being the undisputable leader in at least one segment globally, present in all continents, with the PlayKids platform and expanding into other segments. Figure 7.1 shows a map where Movile has offices.

Since its inception, in 1998, Bloisi's leadership has set the bar high: he accepts nothing less than fast returns and exponential growth, and is not afraid of reinventing his company repeatedly if necessary. Two years ago, in 2015, Movile's highest grossing product was PlayKids, an interactive content platform designed for kids. Nowadays, its star product is a food delivery app called iFood, present in Brazil and Latin America, responsible for 80% of the Brazilian market share.

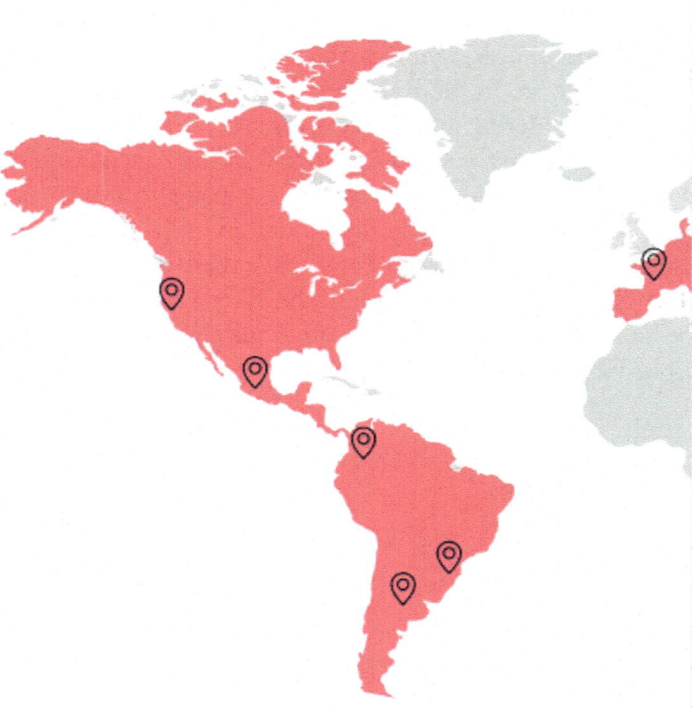

Fig. 7.1 Movile's Offices. (Source: Movile's website (movile.com))

Movile develops and operates platforms that link supply and demand in the mobile market. Movile operates in four main segments: content creation and distribution; food online ordering and delivery; movies, theaters, events and show tickets booking; and logistics intermediation.

The first segment is dominated by PlayKids, its best-known product worldwide. PlayKids is an educational platform for children under nine years, offering more than 3000 drawings and videos, 1000 e-books and 160 games and activities. Movile creates part of this content and distributes content from several partners such as Disney. The platform has been downloaded by 35 million families in over 100 countries. PlayKids is ranked #3 in the App Store[1] and #6 in the Google Play Store.[2] According to Bloisi, PlayKids is the #2 app in gross sales in the American market. In the content segment, Movile also has the app Superplayer, delivering music via streaming.

The second segment, food online ordering and delivery, features the iFood app. The app is a marketplace for restaurants in Brazil, Argentina, Colombia and Mexico delivering over four million orders monthly from 15,000 restaurants to final consumers. iFood became a synonym of food delivery in Brazil.

The third and fourth segments are still mainly focused on the Brazilian market. Movile operates in the events segment with Sympla, a platform for selling and promoting events. Lastly, Movile also has apps in the on-demand

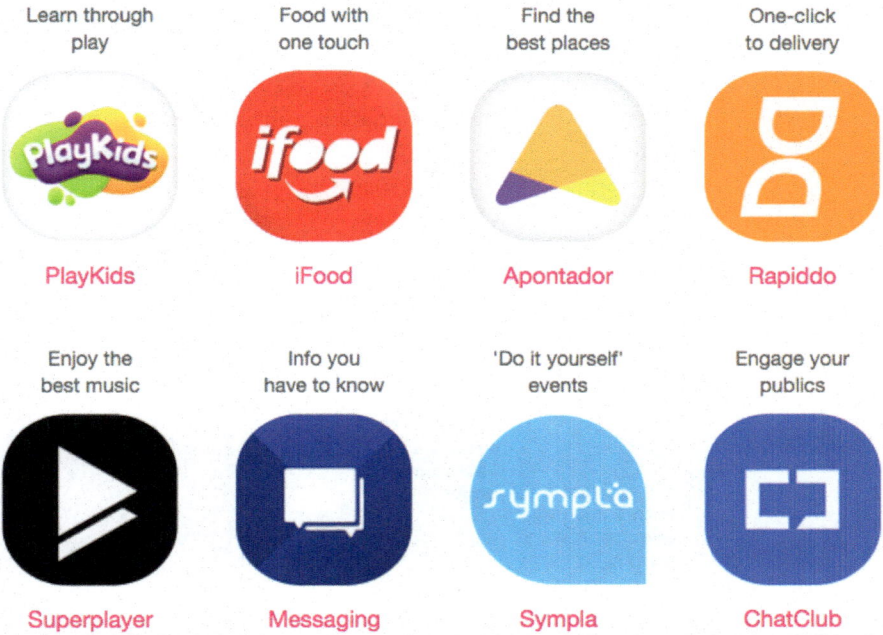

Fig. 7.2 Movile's main products. (Source: Movile's website (movile.com))

logistics segment, with the apps MapLink and Rappido helping logistics operators and manufacturers to connect and plan routes better. Other products explore new developing segments such as Messaging, Apontador and Chat Club. Figure 7.2 shows Movile's main products.

Company's History and Development

Bloisi founded Compera (later Movile) in 1998, just after graduating in computer science from Unicamp (University of Campinas, just 50 miles northeast of São Paulo, Brazil). It has always been his dream to found a company following the steps of Bill Gates (Microsoft) (Morgan et al. 2015).

Compera's products were games, stock quotes and news, usually delivered via text messages (SMS/MMS), since feature phones (before the creation of the first iPhone in 2007) did not support applications (apps). These phones lacked Wi-Fi or rapid internet access and were delivered to consumers via telecom carriers. Compera was a small entrepreneurial company, technology-oriented, exploring the nascent mobile market. The transformation of Compera into Movile can be better understood in the three phases shown in Fig. 7.3.

The first phase was quite typical of an entrepreneurial and ambitious firm facing successes and failures and working with limited resources. Relationships with the leading telecom companies were key to success, so efforts had to balance relationship building and technological innovation to create and deliver new products. The company had its first financing in 2001, with one million

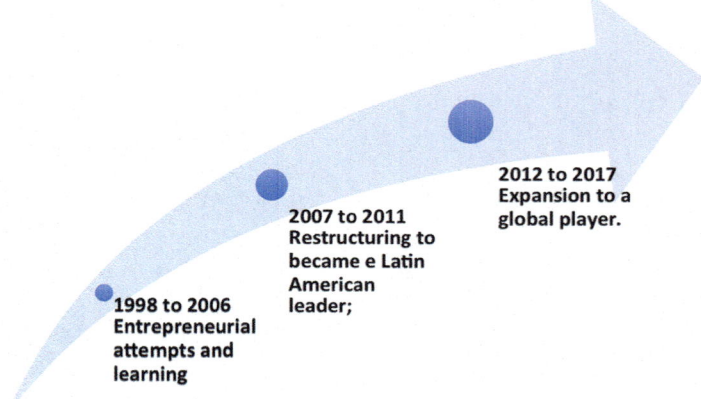

Fig. 7.3 Movile's timeline. (Source: Company's data)

dollars from Rio Bravo, a Brazilian investment fund. Compera achieved reasonable success and had 20 employees in 2004. From 2004 to 2006 it made its first attempts to internationalize. In 2004, it tried to expand to Peru, but had to retreat after a few months. Another attempt happened in 2006, in Spain, but limited resources made the company give up early. In early 2007, Compera opened an office in Mexico, but the business with Telcel, the local carrier, did not develop quick enough and Compera decided to focus on the Brazilian market. Bloisi says that these attempts were important to Movile's culture of experimentation: it taught them what not to try, and when Movile was ready to expand internationally again, it was much more successful. In 2007, Bloisi graduated with an MBA from Fundação Getulio Vargas in São Paulo, and his thesis was an analysis of high-growth technology startups. The thesis helped him to shape the future of the company.

The second phase was a dynamic series of mergers and acquisitions that turned the small startup into a Latin American leader in the mobile market. It all started with the merger with nTime, the fifteenth largest player in Brazil, in 2007. Although this first merger was difficult to handle, and they admittedly report having made "many mistakes", it gave Bloisi the experience he needed to make M&A a growth strategy that persists until today. The combined company became the seventh largest player with 90 employees. This more competitive size allowed Movile to get the support of Naspers, a South African investment fund, to finance Movile's further expansion. Naspers made the investment in 2008 and 2009, allowing Movile to acquire Yavox, a Brazilian mobile company with a complementary product portfolio (products sold directly to consumers instead of carriers). After the acquisition, Movile became the leader of the Brazilian market, with approximately 150 employees. Handling this acquisition in the middle of a world financial crisis was not simple to remain competitive. They had to reduce the workforce by a third. The final acquisition of this phase was Cyclelogic, in 2010. Cyclelogic had a large network dealing with 40 carriers in 23 Latin American countries. Movile had the products to exploit this large network. Integration was not easy given the cultural and geographical challenges, but it helped to forge the company's culture, or Movile's way that combines experimentation with efficiency and focus. By 2011, Movile was the leading mobile product provider in Latin America.

The third phase was the exploitation of this Latin American leader's strengths combined with creativity in new products to become a global player. A key decision was opening an office in Silicon Valley, in 2012. Bloisi states that opening the Silicon Valley branch gave Movile the recognition and access it needed to be considered a valuable partner by Google, Apple and Disney.

The launch of the iPhone in 2007 changed the mobile market with the rise of apps sold directly to consumers. Movile's success in this third phase is closely linked to this type of products. In 2011, the company started creating their own apps. Although most of them failed, an app that repurposed content for kids, called first Canal Desenho (Cartoon Channel in English), was the beginning of Movile's most successful product, PlayKids. This first attempt was the MVP (minimum viable product) and, according to its creators, had a terrible user interface. Nevertheless, it became the number one grossing app in Brazil in a few months, in 2013. In 2014, PlayKids became a top-ranked app in the United States, followed by an expansion to Canada, Europe and Australia. PlayKids was launched in China in late 2014 and became the market leader in early 2015.

PlayKids offers videos for streaming, but it also made them available for downloading, which catered to parents' needs when data services were unavailable or too expensive. The platform also includes e-books, lullabies and educational games, using an interface that is easy to navigate by children from three to nine years of age.

Movile launched several other apps during this phase with different success levels. The other remarkable success was iFood. Launched in 2014, it became the absolute leader in Brazil and is currently present in Argentina, Colombia and Mexico. Today, 80% of meals delivered via apps in Brazil are done via the iFood platform (Marzochi 2016). Figure 7.4 shows the growth in market share of the app in the Brazilian market since its launch and Fig. 7.5 the total growth in revenue since 2011.

The company currently has plans for new initiatives in several countries. Bloisi states that Movile does not want to only distribute its products on a global scale, as it does now. It wants to operate in all continents, have a truly

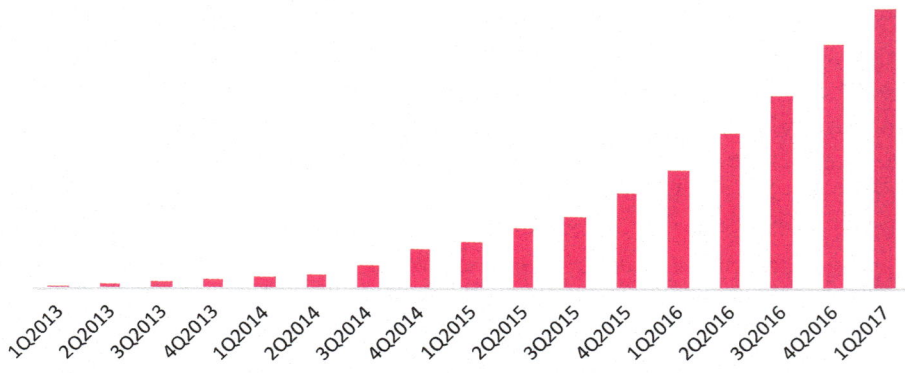

Fig. 7.4 iFood market share. (Source: Company's archives)

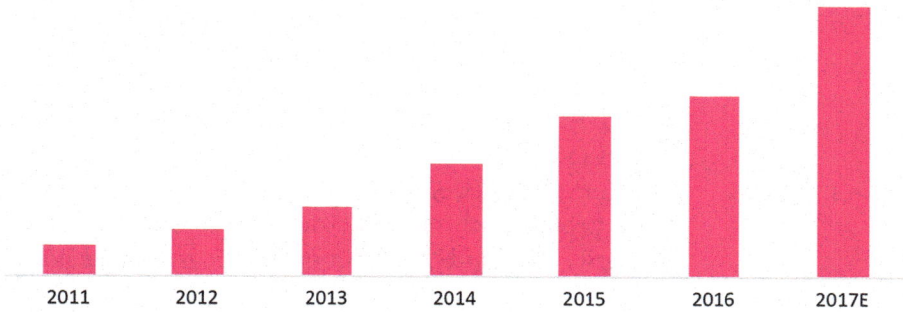

Fig. 7.5 Movile's revenues. (Source: Company's archives)

global presence and reap the benefits and the scale economies of a global presence.

The "Movile Way"

"We are not afraid of making mistakes." – Fabricio Bloisi

Bloisi's ambition is unmistakable: he talks about his company and its endeavors with passion and states "it's not culture, it's a religion." The company grew due to a combination of the working environment of Google with the passion for results of Ambev (Morgan et al. 2015), the Brazilian company that developed into the leading beer conglomerate AB Inbev after a merger with Anheuser-Busch. Ambev is a Brazilian multinational company that every majoring student of business and aspiring entrepreneur dreams of emulating. Created in 1999, in a merger between two major Brazilian breweries (Antartica and Brahma), Ambev's culture could be summarized as a relentless desire to grow and to succeed (Allen 2012). Bloisi shared with pride that one of Ambev's major shareholders is also one of Movile's investors.

The Values at Movile listed below summarize the strategy and the culture that drive the company's projects:

People: we attract and retain the best people, who are proactive, committed and passionate about what they do. We value teamwork and keep transparent relationships among ourselves.

Customer Focus: we want our customer to refer our products and services to their friends.

Innovation:	we have the creativity and agility necessary to innovate, making new products, services and processes a reality in order to positively surprise our clients. We encourage responsible risk taking and accept mistakes that lead to learning, fixing the source of errors.
Ethics:	we guide our actions by the highest standards of ethics and professionalism. We conduct our business with integrity. We guide our actions so that we would not be ashamed should they become public knowledge.
Results:	we are obsessed with aggressively achieving results, since it guarantees our investment breadth, compensating our shareholders and generating growth for the firm and employees alike.
Meritocracy:	we reward and offer opportunities so that people grow as fast as their results, with clear and complete performance assessment and clear goals, without any sort of privileges.

These values, in Portuguese, form an acronym "Gente FIRME", which means people you can rely on, who are responsible and committed to a cause or company, or loyal overall. Figure 7.6 shows the acronym from the company site.

Bloisi affirms that implementing these values at Movile was not difficult, but they demand continued efforts from the board and management. For instance, the stock options, one of the best rewarding programs in virtually all companies in the Silicon Valley, was not allowed under the old and anachronistic Brazilian labor law. To put it simply, in Brazil companies cannot establish their own contract with employees, and they have to follow the "Consolidação das Leis Trabalhistas – CLT" (Labor Law Act), created in 1943. One cannot express how these laws, created for an industrial world, hold back

Fig. 7.6 Movile's values. (Source: Movile's website (movile.com))

Brazilian companies today: it is difficult to establish temporary contracts, contracts by demand, and companies have to follow several unreasonable employees' benefits. Many Brazilians believe that the CLT holds companies' growth back and hinders them in competing in international markets. A full overhaul of the labor law is under review at the Congress now.

Nevertheless, the company persisted and promoted the stock options as bonus for results without breaking any of the local laws. The flat organizational structure was also an innovation in Brazilian companies. In Movile, Bloisi observes, there is no such thing as "this is not my problem". Every employee is responsible for creating a solution to a problem even by destroying a company's product and creating a new one. One of his challenges, Bloisi notes, is to "kill the bureaucracy".

Keeping the organizational structure simple is one of Bloisi's main concerns. Only 12 directors report directly to him. In addition, the company's headquarters has no cubicles or walls. During the interviews done for this chapter, if Bloisi had not pointed us to his table, we could not have differentiated the CEO's workstation from that of any other employee of the company.

This flat structure and the fast pace of growth support Movile's way of innovating: it flows from within and from outside the company. The structure that enables the company's innovative undertakings is settled under two tenets: many innovative threads running simultaneously and an aggressive marketing strategy.

Simultaneous Innovative Threads

Internally, innovative threads are usually divided into groups that work with small budgets and try to launch an MVP in the market. Mostly in the same way that the company did with the PlayKids platform. Bloisi maintains that the company runs under the principles of the lean startup manual (Blank 2012): try fast, launch fast, fail fast. When everything goes well, scale. They work also as an ambidextrous organization (O'Reilly and Tushman 2004), which means that Movile is not afraid of reinventing itself: "We change everything every 6/12 months", Bloisi says. And that is true: the fastest growing app three years ago was PlayKids, now it is iFood. iFood's growth is so remarkable that the share of international revenue (outside of Brazil) has diminished from 35% to 20%, due to its success locally.

But a company like Movile cannot rely on past successes and has to monitor new trends and technological developments. One of the next steps it could take is investing in Artificial Intelligence (AI). If the company decides to go through this route, Bloisi affirms that it would be done like this:

> *Instead of talking about it [AI] for six months, we would take a course at UNICAMP [Bloisi's alma mater], with 40 of our people, (...) and they would have to deliver something [a new product] in two, three months. They would test three or four products at a time, but probably all of them would fail. (...). Maybe one [product] has a better viability. I would find out what the leaders are doing well and say: build your team and deliver something better in three months.*

Decision-making is fast and decentralized maintaining the characteristic of an entrepreneurial small company. Bloisi says that in more established companies, the executives could take up to a year to decide if a product is viable and spend millions of dollars trying to make it work. Instead, using the lean startup approach, Movile invests a third of it as usual in the market, but tries to have several simultaneous innovative threads. The more competitive initiatives are launched and scaled if viable.

Innovating from outside the company comes through mergers and acquisitions (M&As), sustaining ambidexterity. When Movile acquires a new company, it quickly scans and identifies the product/solution that has potential synergy with the company's structure, and teams work to scale the product/solution further. Innovation also happens through what Bloisi calls a "consolidation merger". iFood, for instance, acquired by Movile in 2014, was a small app in the Brazilian market. After Movile's acquisition, its path to leadership was fueled by other M&As with local apps, such as Hello Food, Papa Rango and Central Delivery. M&As also contribute to innovation when entering new geographical markets. Again, with the iFood app they did this when entering the Mexican market, acquiring the app Hello Food. The scale-up in the new market benefits from the acquisition and is influenced by it.

Internal and external innovation compete with each other and interact in a synergistic way. Internally, it continues to continue to create solutions that, most often than not, compete with the acquired products and with other innovative threads. The most successful, or the most viable, product will survive and scale up to the consumer market.

Aggressive Marketing Strategy

The marketing strategy for innovative products works in the same way: aggressively and without fear of failure. With iFood, for instance, Movile invested a big chunk of its marketing budget in digital advertising, dividing its investments between Google AdWords and Social Networks (such as Facebook). Nevertheless, given its O2O (online to offline) positioning, it also invested in traditional advertising. The biggest star of iFood commercials[3] is Fabio Porchat, a Brazilian comedian best known for starting his own YouTube channel with the comedy group called "Porta dos Fundos" (backdoor, in English). These ads highlight the advantages of iFood against the traditional telephone ordering with a humorous approach. They established iFood as a synonym for food ordering.

Participative and Integrated Reporting and Control System

Inspired by Ambev's management system, Movile developed a participative system to monitor units, company's objectives and initiatives. The system blends quite well with the management style, culture and values.

Movile has a dashboard that tracks all of the company's goals and progress to their achievement: it gives everyone an overview of the company's goals and timeline to achieve them, broken down into departments, cells and individuals. Bloisi affirms that he follows it every day and that it is updated in real time. Bloisi attests that, even though the results are accompanied and tracked via dashboard, it could be easily done or accompanied offline. Plans and goals are kept simple and straight to the point. A plan for a new initiative with its goals should not take more than two pages: "it has to be simple so everyone can follow". Another striking feature of the Movile Way is decentralization: everybody monitors everybody.

Despite the fact that all company's plans are open, none of the numbers or core goals ever leaked outside. This is also related to its values and "Gente Firme": employees feel responsible for the company's results.

Movile has a monthly meeting in which all company's products and projects are reviewed, and results analyzed. The risk-taking approach is combined with a close monitoring and quick corrective action. The system also helps to promote accountability in a complex environment of many fast-moving initiatives. Bloisi makes sure that all branches and all departments follow the performance closely: they will be held accountable for their results in these meetings and they make sure that the company stays in the right track. Plans and goals are decided in a participative way. Goals are not set by top directors: each employee is responsible to negotiate and upload his or her own goals (up to five each year) and ensure that they are met.

This is what Movile calls its business model, or the Movile Way: infinite opportunities to innovate, results-oriented, decentralized structure, financial and merit recognition. But this is easier to achieve in the company's Brazilian headquarters. How is it possible to maintain this culture in its world subsidiaries? How to transfer the Movile Way in case of acquisitions?

Transferring the Movile Way to Acquisitions

"We maintain a cool and laid back relationship with the acquired companies". – Fabricio Bloisi

Movile has innovated and grown largely through M&As. Future plans are also based on continuous and numerous acquisitions. Many of these acquisitions are small companies as Compera in the past. A critical issue is how to maintain, evolve and take advantage of this unique culture and business model.

Movile never forces a CEO of a newly acquired company to follow its rules "top down". Instead, Bloisi brings the CEOs and top executives to visit Movile headquarters and asks them what he, as the CEO of Movile, could do to help the new company to grow and be profitable. Having been the owner of a small company in the past gives him a unique perspective on how CEOs and founders of companies think. *"It's their child"*, he says.

Bloisi gives the CEO of a newly acquired company freedom to decide and operate. No one should call the head office to ask permission to hire new employees or to make a new investment. The only thing that is non-negotiable is values: the newcomer has to adhere to their ethics code and core values. Movile does not hold back in sharing information with the acquired companies. They share knowledge, training opportunities and even employees. Also, Bloisi wants to make sure that the CEO knows that he or she will be responsible for results: and Movile wants them big and fast. The culture gradually, but quickly, permeates into the acquired company, naturally.

When a company enters into Movile Group, it makes what they call their "file intentions", which means stating the new company's mission, vision and goals. Then, for each goal they create strategic maps depicting how the goals will be achieved (via Balanced Scorecard methodology). Everything settled off the CEO goes to pursue his or her goals. Goal setting and negotiation is a key element to embed the new company into the Movile Way. Bloisi does not believe that ambitious goals are impossible. Movile has been achieving its goals systematically, impossible or not.

The first visit of the top executives of an acquired company to the Brazilian headquarters is usually a "culture shock". Learning about Movile's history, experiencing the office environment and openness and discussing plans and goals for the new company is a crucial test of fit into the Movile Way. It does not always work smoothly. Sometimes the old leadership of the company does not "buy" the new culture nor the new goals, deeming them "unachievable". The leadership of the new company needs to truly believe in the possibility of success. Bloisi puts it simply that there are two alternatives: either we convince and motivate the leadership or they will have to be replaced. That is a "no brainer" for Bloisi: Movile has a high turnover rate because of its fast pace. Nobody should stay too comfortable: "you are not the king of your castle not even of your own position". Movile's employees should embrace this fast pace with high spirits. In 2016, for instance, most of Movile's directors were relocated to other companies within the Movile group.

Regular operation flows easily with frequent communication and minimal red tape. Changing the company's structure is as easy as writing an e-mail. The management system keeps the acquired companies close, monitored and engaged.

Annual meetings are another way to foster integration. In 2016, they hosted an event named "Faster Together", bringing together top managers from all over the globe, connected to the Movile group. During this event, some of the newcomers were impressed to witness the passionate involvement of Movile's employees. One would easily see people screaming, cheering and chanting. Definably not an everyday business meeting. But Bloisi says it is not blind faith: it is this passion that helped him build Movile's success until today. The next successes are going to come from his apprentices.

Conclusion

Movile is an example of how a small entrepreneurial company can develop into a global player. At first, the small startup from Campinas did not have much future. According to the Brazilian Statistics Bureau (IBGE – Instituto Brasileiro de Geografia e Estatística) in 2014, 50% of the Brazilian companies closed their doors within five years from their foundation. Movile defied those odds courageously. It took calculated risks in controlled steps and took advantage of a window of opportunity created by the rise of smart phones that significantly changed the market for apps in the mobile industry.

Movile quickly realized that this new nascent market had important key success factors: scalability, global competition, innovation and agility. Its business model and growth history through M&A show that it became quite competent in exploiting these factors. This is an excellent example of what

Richard Rumelt (2011) calls "Good Strategy". A good strategy has a clear diagnosis, a guiding policy and a set of coherent actions. The diagnostic identified the new opportunity with the rise of smartphones and was precise in seeing the key success factors. Movile's business model with the Movile Way provided a proper guiding policy to exploit the nascent market at the right time. A coherent set of actions and continuous adjustment led the company to its current position.

Past success does not guarantee the future and Movile will have to continue to innovate and adapt. Competition is increasing and comes from unexpected players. Uber, for example, recently started a food delivery service in Brazil competing with iFood. Movile quickly reacted launching another app named SpoonRocket (Caldas 2016). Technology is constantly evolving and could change the game. As Steve Jobs said in Rumelt's book about Apple's strategy: "to wait for the next big thing". The "next big thing" is unknown and could be AI. Movile's flexibility and agility will be key to continuous adaptation, but challenges will be different.

Movile is a new type of Brazilian globalized company. Traditionally, Brazilian multinational enterprises operated in extractive or low value-added industries. According to a study done by Fundação Getulio Vargas and Columbia Center on Sustainable Development in 2016, the five largest Brazilian multinationals, in 2014, were Vale, Gerdau, Petrobras, JBS and BRF. Access to low-cost resources is a key element in their international competitiveness. Embraer and Weg, ranking 9th and 12th, are exceptions active in manufacturing higher technology products. Movile is totally different in terms of the market and the capabilities that underpin its success: a new global species.

Notes

1. Data provided by Movile for Jan – Jun 2017.
2. Data provided by Movile for 2016.
3. If you wish to see one of iFood commercials, check its YouTube Channel or follow this link: https://www.youtube.com/watch?v=z_e-WBiLzOI

References

J. Morgan, P. Ziebelman, G. Foster and K. Matsushita, "Movile: Going Global – Is Silicon Valley The Next Stop?" *Stanford Graduate School of Business*, Case: E-539A, Harvard Business Publishing, February 2015

R. Marzochi, "A fome do iFood", Isto é Dinheirom, 22 March 2016, http://www. istoedinheiro.com.br/noticias/mercado-digital/20160322/fome-ifood/354099

J. Allen. "The Beliefs that Built a Global Brewer", Harvard Business Review, 2012. Available at: https://hbr.org/2012/04/the-beliefs-that-built-a-globa

C.A. O'Reilly and M.L. Tushman, M. L. "The ambidextrous organization". *Harvard Business Review, 82*(4), 2004

R. Rumelt, *Good Strategy/Bad Strategy,* New York: Crown Business, 2011

S. Blank, *The startup owner's manual: The step-by-step guide for building a great company,* BookBaby, 2012

IBGE. Pesquisa de Demografia das Empresas (Brazilian Entrepreneurial Census), 2014

Edson Caldas, "Uber e Grupo iFood: a briga pelo mercado de delivery de comida no Brasil", Epoca Negocios, 18 November 2016, http://epocanegocios.globo.com/ Tecnologia/noticia/2016/11/uber-e-grupo-ifood-briga-pelo-mercado-de-delivery-de-comida-no-brasil.html

Center of International Financial Management Studies of the São Paulo School of Business Administration of Fundação Getulio Vargas and the Columbia Center on Sustainable Investment, "Leading Brazilian Multinational Enterprises: Trends in an Era of Significant Uncertainties and Challenges", January 20 2016, http:// ccsi.columbia.edu/files/2013/10/EMGP-Brazil-Report-2015-Jan-27-final.pdf

8

Delphi Automotive: An American Company … in Name Only

Salvador Carmona and Germán Pérez-Casanova

Abstract DELPHI Automotive PLC (DELPHI), a long time ago a General Motors' (GM) subsidiary, went public (DPH) and became totally independent from its holding company in 1999. Under the new ownership structure, DELPHI decreased its share as a GM supplier, and along with high labor costs, its poor financial situation saw the company filing for bankruptcy in the US in 2005, as non-US subsidiaries were not included and continued operations as usual. As part of its reorganization to emerge from bankruptcy, DELPHI designed a three-tier strategy: megatrends (See: Ernst & Young. *Megatrends 2016* (Madrid: E&Y, 2016)) (e.g., focus on core products), internationalization (e.g., footprint rotation, searching for best-cost countries instead of just low-labor-cost countries), and divestitures of non-core products and divisions. Accordingly, DELPHI enforced an aggressive strategy to penetrate in new, growing markets (e.g., China), as well as in getting close to key suppliers and major customers (e.g., Eastern Europe, North Africa). Our results show that internationalization and complexity are interlocked notions (e.g., personnel turnover, supply chain) and that geographical diversification should be implemented in conjunction with other strategic actions (e.g., focus on core products). Our findings also provide support for the notion that technological diversification benefits from internationalization and cultural

---

As shown below, this is taken from a quote by Steve Miller, Delphi's Chairman and CEO.

S. Carmona (✉) • G. Pérez-Casanova
IE University, Madrid, Spain
e-mail: salvador.carmona@ie.edu; gpcasanova@gmail.com

© The Author(s) 2018
S. Iñiguez de Onzoño, K. Ichijo (eds.), *Business Despite Borders*,
https://doi.org/10.1007/978-3-319-76306-4_8

105

diversity. Our results show that the internationalization strategy implemented along with the megatrends was successful (e.g., 70% of DELPHI's sales were international) and created the base for further focus on smart, high-tech products. Overall, our evidence shows that the three-tier strategy paid off and DELPHI emerged from bankruptcy in 2009 as a solid firm; it became a public firm once more, and its stock market value has quadrupled since 2011.

Filing for Bankruptcy

DELPHI, an automotive supplier, was a General Motors' (GM) subsidiary; it aimed at becoming a leading global supplier of mobile electronics, powertrain, safety, thermal, controls and security systems, electrical/electronic architecture (E/EA), in-car entertainment and communication technologies, and the aftermarket. In 1999, DELPHI became a totally independent company from GM and went public on the New York Stock Exchange (DPH). As a consequence of this change in its ownership structure, DELPHI designed a new marketing strategy to diminish its sales dependence on its former corporate parent; under the new ownership structure, it was expected that GM would enforce stiff competition between DELPHI and non-allied firms, and this would require significant changes in DELPHI's market strategy. In this new context, DELPHI would have to search for customers outside the GM group, as well as improve its competitive positioning to get access to contracts from GM assembly firms.

Labor costs became a central element of the new strategy; DELPHI was heavily unionized, and it paid its workers $65 an hour in wages and benefits. On the other hand, DELPHI's competitors paid their workforce as little as $25. Although the car component industry was technology intensive, such high labor costs made DELPHI a second-tier supplier. To enhance its competitive positioning in the car component market, DELPHI applied actions to diminish its labor costs, which resulted in a leaner organization, as well as in reducing its operations in the US market. As a consequence of these actions, DELPHI expanded its operations in Europe and Mexico and reduced its workforce in the US from 71,000 employees in 2001 to 33000 in 2005. However, high labor costs and the unionized labor force imposed major problems on DELPHI's operations and financial performance. As noted by Donald L. Runkle, Vice Chairman of DELPHI:

[E]verything was working well except [the loss] of GM business … there was no way you could get your productivity high enough [to compensate for high wages]

Under these circumstances, DELPHI's financial performance was steadily negative. Furthermore, and from the standpoint of external stakeholders, this situation worsened amid criticisms of earnings manipulation, which brought about the firing of DELPHI's CFO in 2005 for restating earnings between 1999 and 2004, including the misreporting of rebates, credits, and transactions with suppliers and customers. As DELPHI's financial situation did not register improvements, the firm had to enter a reorganization bankruptcy and filed for Chapter 11[1] in October 2005.

Emerging from Chapter 11

In 2005, the recently appointed chairman and CEO of DELPHI, Robert S. "Steve" Miller, expressed his vision of the car component sector, as follows:

> [T]he industry is structured to lose money, destroy capital and alienate customers, whose money fuels the machine.

To emerge in the best possible conditions from Chapter 11, DELPHI enforced a three-tier strategy, which comprised geographical diversification through internationalization, focus on core competencies (e.g., megatrends), and divestitures of non-core products and divisions (see Fig. 8.1).

Megatrends[2]

After working with consultancy firms and doing extensive homework within DELPHI, the firm identified three megatrends: safe, green, and connected. It was the intention of this plan to focus on stable, high-tech, and non-

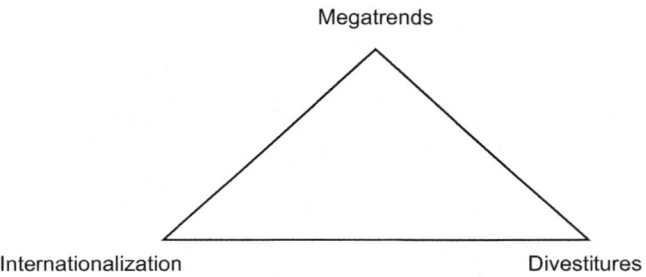

Fig. 8.1 DELPHI's strategic dimensions to emerge from bankruptcy

cyclical business that would guarantee the firm's growth in the long term. *Safe* is a must in the car industry. Fatalities per 100 miles have steadily decreased since 1965 due to improvements in the quality of roads and highways, as well as the implementation of seat belts, energy-absorbing bumpers, and active suspensions to name just some of the actions enforced to enhance safety. Along these lines, the car of the future has to be able to provide drivers with an extra 0.5 second of warning that would mitigate 60% of crashes, in a context that increasingly features traffic congestion in major metro areas around the world; more accidents; longer commutes; and higher stress levels. From the DELPHI standpoint, this situation resulted in a number of trends and, then, specific design and manufacturing actions: active safety systems (e.g., front, rear and side detection; radar and vision sensing; sensor fusion), driver state alerts (e.g., fatigue/drowsiness; distraction), and safety electronics (e.g., airbag control units; pressure, acceleration, combination, rollover, and pedestrian sensors). Additionally, DELPHI worked inter alia on a number of occupant classification systems, full and infant-only suppression, and seat-belt reminders.

Green constituted another megatrend; fast-growing economies require more fuel for mobile platforms. However, governments in different jurisdictions are enforcing regulation to make more stringent the emission of grams CO_2 per kilometer. To pursue this megatrend, DELPHI identified technology-related opportunities such as a cylinder deactivation system, alternative fuel systems/components, evaporative emissions canisters, diesel fuel injection systems, hybrid and electric vehicle technologies, electronics packaging, halogen-free cables, and power conversion products. Finally, *Connected* constituted the third megatrend. As early as 2005, DELPHI identified a growing, global demand for broadband access. Modern, connected vehicles will offer in-vehicle communications and entertainment (e.g., Wi-Fi); vehicle infrastructure interface and vehicle-to-vehicle interface; satellite audio, video, and data systems; digital receivers; advance reception systems; navigation systems; portable device interfaces; wireless connectivity security systems; and aftermarket telematics (see Fig. 8.2).

According to the Transformation Plan issued by Steve Miller on March 31, 2006, DELPHI would be organized around five divisions, which would produce the following product portfolio:

- *Electrical/Electronic Architecture*, which comprised electric and electronic distribution systems, primary wiring harness assembly, high-power wiring assemblies, and cable

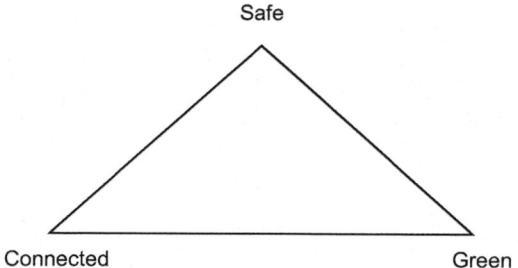

Fig. 8.2 DELPHI's Megatrends

- *Electronics and Safety*, which produced active safety systems, audio systems, driver information systems and controls, electronic control units, body computers, navigation systems, safety electronics, mechatronic products, reception systems, software, wireless connectivity, hybrid and electric vehicle electronics
- *Powertrain Systems*, which made fuel injection systems, ignition systems, air and fuel management, sensors and actuators, valve train systems, fuel handling systems, evaporative emissions systems, and transmission management systems
- *Thermal Systems*: condensers, radiators, fan modules, powertrain cooling systems, charge air coolers, evaporators, heater cores, air conditioner compressors, HVAC[3] modules, and microchannel heat exchangers
- *Product and Service Solutions:* vehicle electronics, engine management systems, fuel systems, heating and cooling, advanced diagnostics service products, training and component level technical assistance, original equipment service, and diesel systems

Divestitures

The Transformation Plan also established non-core product lines as those that "do not fit into the company's future strategic framework and ... [that] the company will seek to sell or wind-down..." Notwithstanding this strategic statement, the company expressed its intention to "continually evaluate its product portfolio and retain or exit certain businesses depending on market forces or changes in its cost structure". Non-core products included Brake & Chassis Systems, Catalysts, Cockpits and Instrument Panels, Door Modules and Latches, Ride Dynamics, Steering, and Wheel Bearings. Table 8.1 shows divestitures that took place under the Transformation Plan and that were executed during 2008–2010.

Table 8.1 Divestitures of DELPHI's divisions

Division	Divestiture
Total Fuel Systems (TFS) in Neumarkt	TFS operations located in Neumarkt, Germany, were sold on February 13, 2010 to Magna Steyr Fuel Systems GmbH. It was the company's only remaining production site for TFS (tank systems) worldwide
Passive Safety Assets in North America	Sold to Autoliv (announced on November 17, 2009). This operation includes North American airbag, seatbelt, and steering wheel assets. The acquired division will be consolidated into existing Autoliv facilities
Suspension and Brakes Business	Sold to BeijingWest Industries Co., Ltd. (November 2, 2009). Business comprised approximately 3000 employees, primarily located in France, UK, Poland, China, Mexico, and the US
Steering Business	Sold to GM. As a result of this operation, GM announced "Nexteer Automotive" as new brand name (October 6, 2009)
Airbag activities in Europe	Sold to iSi Automotive GmbH (August 2009), including site in Berlin, which comprised facilities for modern design, test, and engineering center
Global Exhaust Business	Sold to Mexican company *Bienes Turgon*—Business operating under the name Katcon Global (April 30, 2009). Included assets and shares in Blonie, Poland; Clayton, Australia; Port Elizabeth, South Africa; joint-venture interests in Monterrey, Mexico; technical centers in Auburn Hills, Michigan, USA; and Bascharage, Luxembourg
Power Products Business	Sold to Strattec Security, Witte-Velvert GmbH & Co. KG, Vehicle Access Systems Technology, LLC (November 30, 2008)
Kettering Facility (Ohio, USA)	Sold to Tenneco (May 30, 2008)
Wheel Bearings Business	Sold to Kyklos, Inc., a wholly owned subsidiary of Hephaestus Holdings, Inc. (May 1, 2008)
Global Interiors and Closures Business	Sold to the Renco Group (March 1, 2008)

Internationalization

DELPHI had a considerable number of international sites since it became a GM division. For example, in the case of Europe, there were sites in Austria, France, Germany, Italy, Portugal, Spain, and the UK. Despite this diversity, DELPHI was aware that organizational efficiencies could be obtained by taking the internationalization process further. In doing this, the firm developed the notion of *footprint rotation*. In the case of Europe, footprint rotation informed the move from high-cost manufacturing plants operating in Western Europe to new manufacturing sites in Eastern Europe, India, China, as well as North Africa (e.g., Morocco). Overall, footprint rotations were driven by the notion of low-labor-cost countries.

The experience gained with footprint rotation to sites located in Eastern Europe, Asia, and North Africa showed that labor cost was not necessarily the most significant portion of production costs. On the other hand, and for a considerable number of products (e.g., intensive in technology), labor costs were not as significant as transportation costs, especially if both supplies and deliveries were considered. Therefore, the concept of "low-labor-cost country" was replaced by the notion of "best-cost country", which comprised jurisdictions that could report the lowest production costs despite their high labor costs. According to the "best-cost-country" policy there might be sites in Western Europe, for example, that could outperform their Eastern Europe counterparts because of their overall efficiency and technological capabilities.

Investments in new manufacturing sites were selective. After careful consideration of each of the business plans, investments in China, Mexico, and Eastern Europe were made:

- China: Delphi Electrical/Electronic Architecture (E/EA), one of DELPHI's units, moved to China as a consequence of the best-cost-country policy. Delphi E/E produced connectors and cablings, an area in which DELPHI was the world leader. The development of production sites in China had to overcome two central problems: (a) personnel turnover, especially in the case of high-profile personnel; and (b) lack of manufacturing infrastructure (e.g., supplies), which made DELPHI approach its regular suppliers and persuade them to set up sites in China. Furthermore, major global technological centers were set up in Shanghai and Bangalore, which became operational in 2010.
- Powertrain: located in Europe, where major car assembly plants were established (e.g., France, Germany), as well as technologically advanced suppliers. Additionally, and to ensure penetration in the European market, investments were made in Romania, especially in areas that were not usually populated by the car industry, and that were useful to reduce personnel turnover and labor costs. In order to ensure hiring of high-profile personnel, DELPHI developed agreements with Romanian universities.
- Electronics: located in North America. This division enforced a strategy to diminish dependence on GM as a main customer. As a general policy, the largest customer of the Electronics division should not account for more than 30% of total sales.

DELPHI's manufacturing sites and locations were articulated around three major geographical areas: EMEA, China and India, and North America. DELPHI supplied most of its North American customers from Mexico, while Chinese plants were instrumental to serve Asian customers. Furthermore, manufactories in Eastern Europe (e.g., Czech Republic: Czeska Lipa; Poland: Gdansk, Ostrow; Romania: Iasi; Russia: Samara/JV; Slovakia: Senica) and North Africa (e.g., Morocco: Tangier I, Tangier II) supplied assembly plants in Europe (see Fig. 8.3):

From a financial standpoint, actions focusing on megatrends, divestitures, and internationalization paid off and DELPHI emerged from Chapter 11 Reorganization in the US; all but five plants in the US were sold, closed or returned to GM. Under these circumstances, the acquisition of DELPHI was now fully completed and the firm went private on October 6, 2009.

As a global company, the reorganization of the firm under Chapter 11 paid off; DELPHI was ranked 121 on the 2009 US Fortune list. Furthermore, the firm emerged as a major automotive supplier (see Fig. 8.4; the column reports sales in $billion):

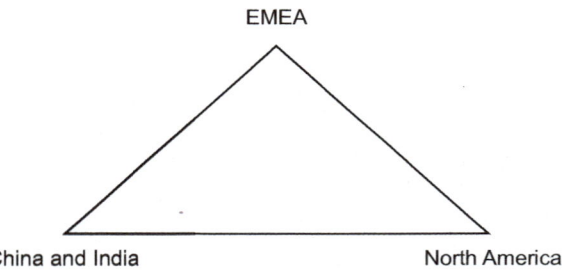

Fig. 8.3 Best-cost-country locations

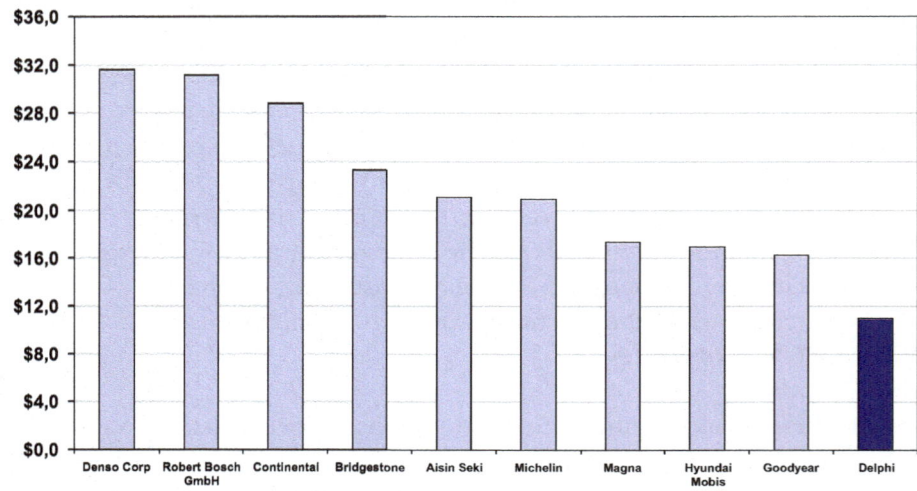

Fig. 8.4 Major automotive suppliers globally (2009)

In 2009, DELPHI was well established in Europe and sales in this region represented 42% of the firm's global sales. DELPHI was now well capitalized to invest in technology to assure a strong product portfolio and continue to provide the many industry-leading technologies and products demanded by their customers following the megatrends of safe, green, and connected. For 2010, two-thirds of sales would be outside North America and no single customer would represent more than 20% of its business. In 2010, gross engineering and R&D spending would be about 11% of sales.

Becoming a Global Player

After emerging from Chapter 11 and implementing its three-tier strategy along megatrends, internationalization, and divestitures, DELPHI enforced actions that would operationalize its strategy. Accordingly, DELPHI identified three dimensions that would enhance the company's competitive advantage and would make it a major player in the car components industry. Therefore, DELPHI:

1. Focused on delivering increased shareholder value

   - Enhance portfolio of market relevant products
   - Balance regional growth
   - Further diversify customer base and platform mix

2. Disciplined revenue growth

   - Ongoing footprint rotation to best-cost countries
   - Continuous improvement of Delphi Enterprise Operating System (EOS)
   - Increase leverage in operating model

3. Focused on cost structure optimization

   - Continue investment in organic and acquisition growth
   - Return cash to shareholders
   - Maintain investment grade ratings through the cycle

The operationalization of the strategy, following the specific metrics, focused on aspects related to internationalization and geographical diversification, to ensure "balanced regional growth" and "footprint rotation to best-cost countries". The footprint expansion involved actions to grow beyond the traditional European Union footprint, as well as to improve local support (e.g., engineering and manufacturing) for all customers. Therefore, DELPHI set up the new Powertrain Yantai (Diesel) and Beijing Wanyuan Manufacturing (GDi) and the Tech Center, in 2012, which was instrumental in boosting DELPHI's competitive advantage. In 2012, the distribution of bookings by regions was as follows:

- Asia: 34%
- Europe: 32%
- North America: 29%
- South America: 5%

The strategy of internationalization was successful, and DELPHI made a fruitful Initial Public Offering (DLPH) in November 2011 at $21.37 per share.

Smart Products

We began the conversion to smart products over a decade ago … We wanted to sell sophisticated black boxes –'thinking' products. We have done a great job adding intelligence to our products. –Rodney O'Neal, President and CEO, 2015

In pursuance of the megatrends and considering technological developments in the industry, DELPHI made a step forward on the way to become a premier company in the industry. In 2015, DELPHI sold its Thermal Division to Mahle GmbH for $727 million as part of the firm's plans to focus on core products and technology. The Thermal Division had generated sales about $1.6 billion in 2013 from 13 manufactories located around the world, with a workforce of 6700 operators. Furthermore, the After-Market Division (Product & Service Solutions) merged into Powertrain Systems. Therefore, DELPHI was no longer organized around the five divisions that were used to handle its Chapter 11 reorganization, but around the following three divisions: Electrical/Electronic Architecture, Electronics and Safety, and Powertrain Systems. In May 2017, DELPHI announced its plans to spin off its $4.5 billion Powertrain Systems Division into a separate publicly traded company. Currently, Powertrain has 20,000 employees and 5000 engineers, and the spin-off is planned to be completed by March 2018.

With these organizational changes, the once-bankrupt DELPHI is now work-ing to reinvent itself, transforming from a low-margin, commodity parts supplier (e.g., steering) to a purveyor of high-margin technology in the safe, clean, and connected areas. In the high-tech sector, DELPHI is currently working on areas such as autonomous driving, mobility services, data, and connectivity.

The company has strategic partnerships to accelerate product innovation. In August 2016, the company announced a partnership with Mobileye (acquired by Intel in March 2017), to accelerate the time to market for an SAE Level 4/5 Automated Driving Solution for 2019. In August 2016, Delphi also announced that it had been selected by Singapore Land Transport Authority for the Autonomous Vehicle Mobility-on-Demand Program. Delphi will provide a fleet of fully autonomous vehicles and will develop a cloud-based mobility-on-demand software (AMoD) suite, opening up new potential autonomous markets for its customers. The three-year pilot program is slated to transition to operational service by 2022. The Singapore project will be used to test suburban vehicle sharing, autonomous bus or taxi services, logistics, and long-distance truck platooning. Delphi also plans pilot projects in other jurisdictions (e.g., Europe, North America).

Overall, geographical diversification and focus on core, high-tech products have put DELPHI in a premier position in the competitive automotive sup-ply industry. For example, Fig. 8.5 reports the steady growth in reported and adjusted bookings during the period 2011–2016:

Fig. 8.5 DELPHI's reported and adjusted bookings (2011–2016)

As far as financial results are concerned, 2016 was an excellent year; sales turnover was $16.7 billion, which represented a growth of 8%. Operating income was $2.2 billion, 13% higher than in 2015; and earnings per share $6.28, meaning a 20% increase with respect to 2015. Finally, DELPHI has quadrupled the company's stock since 2011 when it went public at $21.37 per share. The price was $87.01 on May 3, 2017.

In 2017, less than a third of DELPHI's sales turnover is reported from the US. Furthermore, the company is legally based in the UK. The whole process that led DELPHI to emerge from bankruptcy may be summarized in Michigan Radio's quote from Steve Miller, "the turnaround kid", when he said that the company was "an American firm in name only."

International Strategy and Performance

As noted by Sapienza et al. (2006), the most profound business phenomenon of the twentieth century has perhaps been the internationalization of large, small, established, and new venture firms (see also Hitt et al. 2016). However, we still have much to learn about the determinants of performance improvements and the extent to which geographical diversification and internationalization can enhance organizational efficiency (Hitt et al. 2017). In this respect, the case of DELPHI can provide some perceptive insights into the ongoing, empirically supported discussion on the underpinnings of internationalization.

As shown in the case of DELPHI, a firm's international strategy cannot be driven by the sole effects of geographical diversity. At the time of filing for bankruptcy under Chapter 11 reorganization, DELPHI was already highly international, with a substantial number of manufactories based in Western Europe (e.g., France, Germany, Spain, UK). Despite this high international profile, DELPHI's decision to go for footprint rotation was part of a wider strategic design comprising megatrends and divestitures. In this sense, the timing of the move to footprint rotation suggests that such a decision was made at the right moment (e.g., five years after becoming a totally independent company) and considering the speed of the process. According to extant empirical evidence, premature internationalization may result in inefficient organizations. On the other hand, late decisions may jeopardize the internationalization process because of issues with organizational inertia. Furthermore, and although DELPHI was formally a young company, it had operated as a GM subsidiary for several decades, and the fact that footprint rotation was enforced amid a severe financial crisis was helpful to overcome situations of organizational resistance (e.g., divestitures).

During the implementation of the footprint rotation strategy, DELPHI had to face complex problems. For example, DELPHI's subsidiaries in China (e.g., Delphi E/EA) had to deal with high personnel turnover as a consequence of growing markets for high-profile personnel (e.g., engineers). Furthermore, and to decrease transportation costs with suppliers, DELPHI had to persuade them to set up subsidiaries in China, which brought about long-term agreements with core suppliers. In a similar vein, issues surrounding hiring high-profile personnel in the manufactory located in Iasi (Romania) required cooperation agreements with local universities to ensure access to technologists and engineers.

The degree of internationalization is measured through the ratio of international sales/total Sales. In this ratio, DELPHI rates highly, with 70% of its sales being done internationally. As noted by Marano et al. (2016), high levels of internationalization bring about product diversification, and this was also the case of DELPHI, which diversified its product portfolio along five divisions that covered a wide range of technologically advanced products. Furthermore, Marano et al. (2016) also suggest that technological diversity is positively affected by internationalization and cultural diversity. In the case of DELPHI, with manufactories located in four continents and with technological centers based in Shanghai and Bangalore, its high degree of internationalization and cultural diversity certainly boosted technological diversity. Overall, DELPHI's international strategy was part of a wider move to focus on megatrends and core products. It rendered high financial performance, as shown by the value of the company's stock—which has quadrupled since the firm went public in November 2011—as well as improvements in bookings, sales turnover, operating income, and earnings per share.

Conclusions

- A financial crisis (e.g., filing for bankruptcy) provides firms with good opportunities for reorganization (e.g., divestitures) and redesign of their organizational strategy.
- The timing and the speed of the internationalization process are critical for its success.
- Internationalization strategies should be accomplished through other strategic actions such as megatrends (e.g., focus on core products), and divestitures on non-core products and divisions.

- Internationalization strategies (e.g., footprint rotation) should be informed by the notion of best-cost country instead of the traditional, low-labor-cost country.
- Best-cost countries should be selected after careful examination of cost drivers, as well as the wider institutional (e.g., personnel turnover, supply chain) and cultural (e.g., technology savvy) conditions of the host country.
- A firm's technological diversification is linked to its internationalization and cultural diversification.

Notes

1. Delphi non-US subsidiaries were not included in Chapter 11.
2. The notion and the operationalization of megatrends are still valid in the car industry (see, EY 2016).
3. HVAC: heating, ventilation, and air conditioning.

References

Ernst & Young. *Megatrends 2016* (Madrid: E&Y, 2016).

M.A. Hitt, S.E. Jackson, S. Carmona, L. Bierman, C.E. Shalley and M. Wright, "The Future of Strategy Implementation", in *Handbook of Strategy Implementation: The Management of Strategic Resources* (Oxford: Oxford University Press, 2017).

M.A. Hitt, D. Li and K. Xu, "International Strategy: From Local to Global and Beyond", *Journal of World Business*, 51(1), 2016.

V. Marano, J.L. Arregle, M.A. Hitt, E. Spadafora, and M. van Essen, "Home Country Institutions and the Internationalization-Performance Relationship: A Meta-Analytic Review", *Journal of Management*, 42(5), 2016.

H.J. Sapienza, E. Autio, G. George and S.A. Zahra, "A Capabilities Perspective On the Effects of Early Internationalization on Firm Survival and Growth", *Academy of Management Review*, 31(4), 2006.

9

Cineplanet: Developing South American Markets

Fernando A. D'Alessio

Abstract Surviving and growing in today's cinema industry is complex: it faces competition from illegal downloads and streaming: in response, movie theatres have introduced redesign processes and layout to attract customers. Despite many cultural and linguistic commonalities, the nations of South America have never been able to cooperate, and few regional agreements have progressed. Different consumption patterns and behaviours also need to be considered.

Cineplanet, a Peruvian company that dominates the domestic market, has begun expanding regionally, building on its success in Chile. The board of directors is divided over the expansion policy, with one experienced director opposing it and a dynamic successful CEO trying to expand markets. The CEO needs to present a sound strategy of global expansion to receive the agreement of the board of directors.

Current Situation

In August 2016, Raffael Dawson, the Chief Executive Officer of Cineplanet (Appendix), could not sleep. He was concerned about a meeting he had with the board of directors a couple of weeks ago. After a long conversation with the six members of the board, five directors agreed that the cinema industry

F. A. D'Alessio (✉)
CENTRUM Católica Graduate Business School, Lima, Perú
e-mail: fdaless@pucp.pe

© The Author(s) 2018
S. Iñiguez de Onzoño, K. Ichijo (eds.), *Business Despite Borders*,
https://doi.org/10.1007/978-3-319-76306-4_9

119

would increase and mature in Peru the following year and that it was time to look for new opportunities in other countries; however, one director, Tomas Bauver, disagreed (Appendix). He believed that this was not the time to develop new markets and thought that Cineplanet should work on penetrating the Peruvian and Chilean markets. Dawson was undecided because of the vision of the company: "To be one of the top three largest cinema chains in South America making a difference with an excellent customer service" encouraged him to keep expanding; however, he had to take into account the expertise of senior board member Tomas Bauver.

From his office in Lima, Peru, Dawson reflected on the rapid growth of the global cinema industry and the contribution of Cineplanet to the national market. With a commercial and finance background, Dawson started his career in his early 30s at Cineplanet as head of an inexperienced commercial team. Three years later, he was promoted to Operations Manager as a result of his leadership skills and his excellent results in increasing sales. He finally became CEO in 2011 after the former CEO took an important role in one of the companies of the Intercorp group, which is one of the most important economic groups in Peru, and to which Cineplanet belongs.

Even though the company has developed the Chilean market over the last 12 years, Dawson needed to pursue an aggressive strategy to fulfil the board's requirements. He had the company information he had requested from marketing, along with the marketing studies of different countries in South America, including a summary of the Doing Business Ranking (Table 9.1). He had to consider all the characteristics of the market and choose wisely. The cost of investment was very high, and directors wanted a quick result. Would Cineplanet's current position in Peru and its market in Chile be enough to achieve the aggressive goal that shareholders wanted? On the other hand, would it be necessary to expand it into a third or fourth country?

Table 9.1 Ease of doing business ranking

Doing business rank	Economy	Starting business rank	Getting credit rank	Dealing with construction permits rank
48	Chile	62	79	24
50	Peru	97	15	48
54	Colombia	84	2	38
116	Brazil	174	97	169
117	Ecuador	166	97	74
121	Argentina	157	79	173
157	Bolivia	178	126	150
186	Venezuela	186	109	125

Source: The World Bank (2016). Doing Business 2016: Measuring Regulatory Quality and Efficiency

The Peruvian Cinema Industry

Since the early years of the twentieth century, the cinema industry has been the most popular form of entertainment in Chile. It is backed by a huge production industry that, despite being a risky business, keeps producing millions of dollars every year.

The most recent player in this industry is Movie Theatre, which negotiates with different distributors; however, powerful distributors pit cinemas against each other for maximum film rights. Distributors try to get a high percentage of the ticket cost (The Gateway 2010). Cineplanet belongs to exhibitors who buy films from distributors and show them in movie theatres. It is important to mention that film production is increasing every year. Nevertheless, some of these films will never be shown in theatres because of Hollywood's domination. The majority of blockbusters come from Hollywood and cinemas are willing to give up a high percentage of the ticket cost to get them because they know they will make money.

In 2016, the Peruvian cinema industry was at an incredible moment in its history (Fig. 9.1). This was a consequence of the growing economy of the country. Peru had registered continuous GDP growth for 85 months, according to the National Institute of Statistic and Informatics (INEI). This improvement in the Peruvian economy reduced poverty and allowed people to spend money on entertainment. Another important factor is the growing population. According to INEI, the population in Peru in 2015 was over 31 million and, for 2050, will increase up to 40 million. This increase will see increased

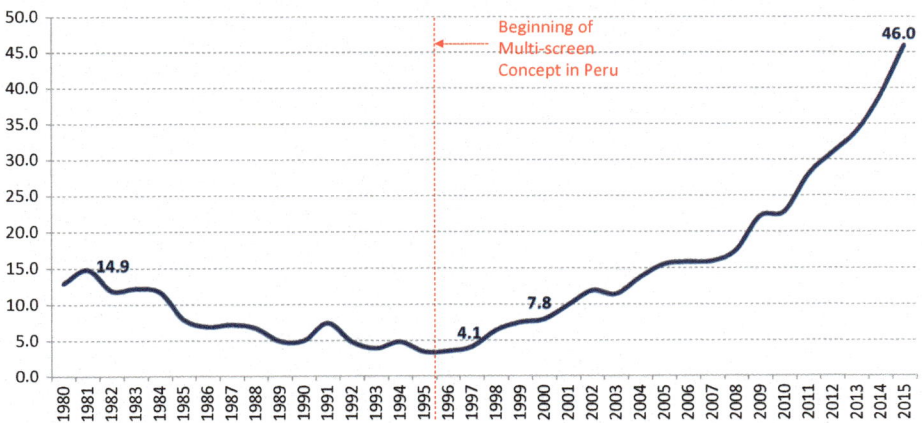

Fig. 9.1 Evolution of moviegoers in the Peruvian market (1980–2015) in millions of people. (Source: Cineplanet. Memoria Anual 2015)

demand in the entertainment industry. Another peculiarity of the Peruvian cinema industry is the location of movie theatres. Ten years ago, they were all in coastal regions, and mainly in the capital; however, the cinema industry is expanding to other cities inland. This rapid expansion makes it difficult for cinemas to find attractive cities that can justify the investment to build a movie theatre in them.

The cinema industry in Peru was an oligopoly. There were three big companies: Cineplanet, Cinemark and UVK Multicines. Cineplanet had the highest market share in Peru with 46.3% of the total market. It had more than 230 screens in 31 movie theatres in Peru: 16 of them in Lima and 15 in the major cities. This made it a leader not only in terms of market share, but also in installed capacity. Cineplanet also saw an increase in revenue. In 2014, it made almost 250 million soles.[1] From 2013 to 2014, the company saw an increase in turnover of 25.7% (Table 9.2).

The second largest movie theatre company in Peru was Cinemark, which started operating in 1997. Cinemark was an American movie theatre chain owned by Cinemark Holding Inc. operating in North, Central and South America. It was headquartered in Texas and it was the second largest theatre chain in the world. In Peru, Cinemark had 13 movie theatres. The third cinema chain was UVK Multicines. It was a Peruvian chain, founded in 1998, which grew rapidly in Lima, with eight movie theatres. It is important to know that the Peruvian cinema industry has many entry barriers as well as a large investment costs. These three companies are well positioned. This cinema industry is explained by Porter's Five Forces model: for more details see Fig. 9.2. The customer is king and movie theatres need to attract them not only with a comfortable seat, but with interesting side offers.

The global cinema industry is being challenged by Netflix and Amazon, as well as by other streaming companies. Despite the advance in the global market by these two giants, the idea of leaving home for distraction is still quite

Table 9.2 Distributions of income and growth category for Cineplanet

Income (millions of s/.)	December 2014	December 2013	Growth
Takings	138,108	112,631	22.60%
% Income	56.50%	57.90%	
Snack Bar	92,544	71,899	28.70%
% Income	37.80%	37.00%	
Other	13,876	9944	39.50%
% Income	5.70%	5.10%	
Total Income	244,528	194,474	25.70%

Source: Cineplanet. Memoria Anual 2015

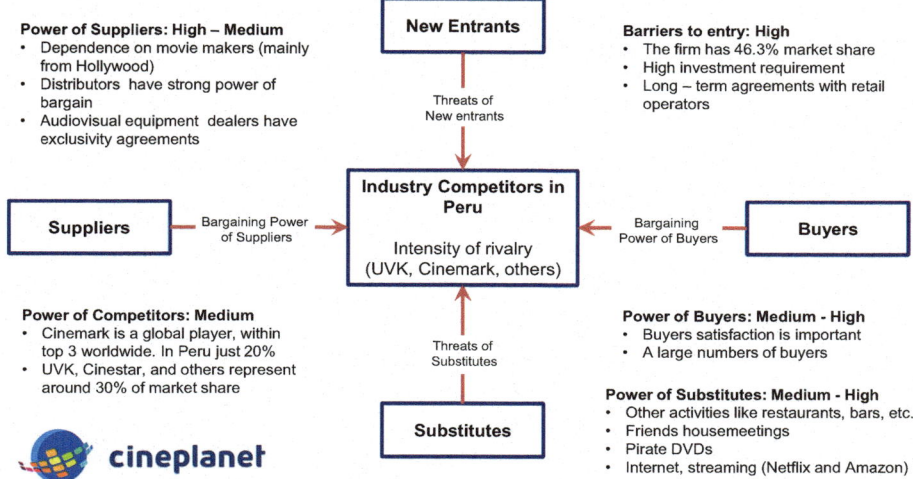

Power of Suppliers: High – Medium
- Dependence on movie makers (mainly from Hollywood)
- Distributors have strong power of bargain
- Audiovisual equipment dealers have exclusivity agreements

Barriers to entry: High
- The firm has 46.3% market share
- High investment requirement
- Long – term agreements with retail operators

Power of Competitors: Medium
- Cinemark is a global player, within top 3 worldwide. In Peru just 20%
- UVK, Cinestar, and others represent around 30% of market share

Power of Buyers: Medium - High
- Buyers satisfaction is important
- A large numbers of buyers

Power of Substitutes: Medium - High
- Other activities like restaurants, bars, etc.
- Friends housemeetings
- Pirate DVDs
- Internet, streaming (Netflix and Amazon)

Fig. 9.2 Porter's Five Forces Analysis for Cineplanet

important for families. This industry attractiveness is relatively low because investors are not willing to spend capital on movie theatres.

Cineplanet

Cineplanet was born as Cineplex Inc. because of the multiple divisions approved by the board of The Nomad Group Inc. and Inmobiliaria Sytasa Inc. The firm started operations on July 1, 1999, managing four movie theatres located in Lima: Cineplex (today Cineplanet San Miguel), Adan y Eva (today Cineplanet Centro), Metro (closed) and Alcazar (today, Cineplanet Alcazar). In February 2000, Nexus Films Corp—a company that had CDC Capital Partners (a British government unit oriented to invest in the private sector of emerging countries) and Nexus Capital Partners as shareholders—acquired the firm. The change of the company's board was consolidated in the same year and it brought original ideas about developing a cinema chain with an important level of penetration nationwide, as well as pursuing a strategy of differentiated experience and high-quality customer service. Both ideas were conceived for the new brand called Cineplanet (Memoria Anual 2015).

The early 2000s was a period of exploration and expansion. In 2001, the company launched its Planet Premium customer loyalty programme, the goal of which was to attract and retain customers and to identify habits and trends.

This information was used in subsequent marketing strategies. In the same year, positive financial results were achieved for the first time and have been maintained until now. In 2002, the firm followed an expansion strategy in Peru by going into underserved markets or places where the competition was not consolidated.

In 2013, the company developed a different concept of theatres: Cineplanet Prime, the new high-end brand of the company. This idea responded to an under-attended demand segment: more sophisticated adult customers that value comfort and personal attention when choosing entertainment options outside home, including the cinema. The cinemas were well designed and equipped with giant screens with reduced seating capacity: 60, providing comfort to moviegoers. Cineplanet Prime movie theatres have ergonomic and reclining couches with footrests, tables and lamps, which require large spaces. This new kind of infrastructure allows on-site personalized attention for food and beverage without compromising customers' comfort (RPP Noticias 2013). Since then, Cineplanet Prime has positioned five complexes, four in Peru and one in Chile.

In 2014, Cineplanet pursued an aggressive expansion plan. In the same year, eight new complexes were opened in Peru and in 2015, two more in Chile. In order to fund this new investment, the company issued bonds for PEN 119,947,000 (Class and Asociados 2016). The company went from 236 to 301 screens in two years and, by the end of 2015, the firm had captured 46.3% of the Peruvian Market share (Fig. 9.3) and almost 20% in Chile. As a result, Cineplanet is well distributed throughout Peru, mainly along the coast where there is a higher density of people (around a third of the Peruvian population lives in Lima). Around half of these theatres are in Lima (Fig. 9.4).

The market research team at Cineplanet carried out a complete analysis of all the countries in South America. Based on pros and cons, costs and benefits, the team decided to choose four potential options and write down the main factors that made them interesting targets. Bolivia's market represented 2.5 million moviegoers in 2009, which was 11.5% of the Peruvian market and 17.3% of the Chilean market (Banegas 2011). Since it was the smallest market in the region, it was not attractive for the company; moreover, reliable and recent information was not available.

In 2004, Cineplanet went regional. After the company reached agreements with different retail operators in Chile, Cineplanet was able to open five new cinema complexes through the constitution of its subsidiary Cines e Inversiones Limitada. Four of these five complexes opened in 2005 and Cineplanet Costanera, which is located in the most important mall in Chile, started operations in 2012. In order to achieve the internationalization plan,

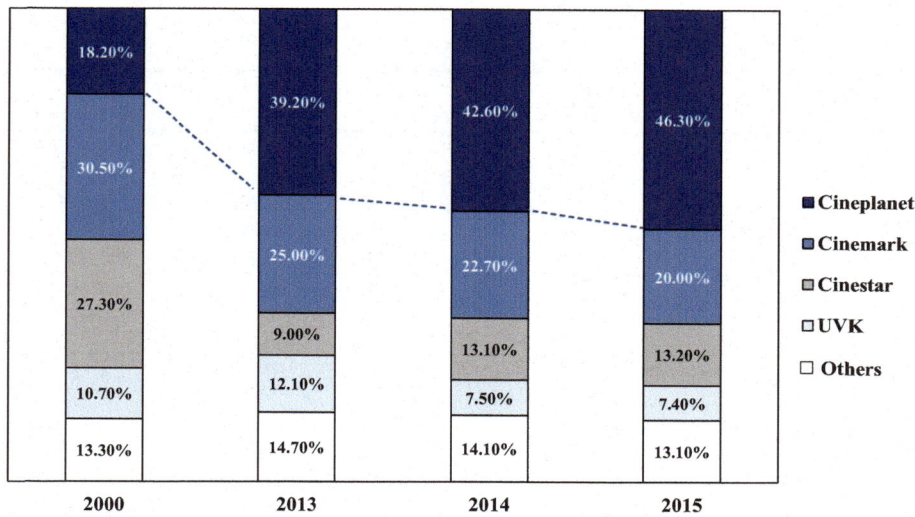

Fig. 9.3 Evolution of market share in the Peruvian market (2000–2015). (Source: Cineplanet. Memoria Anual 2015)

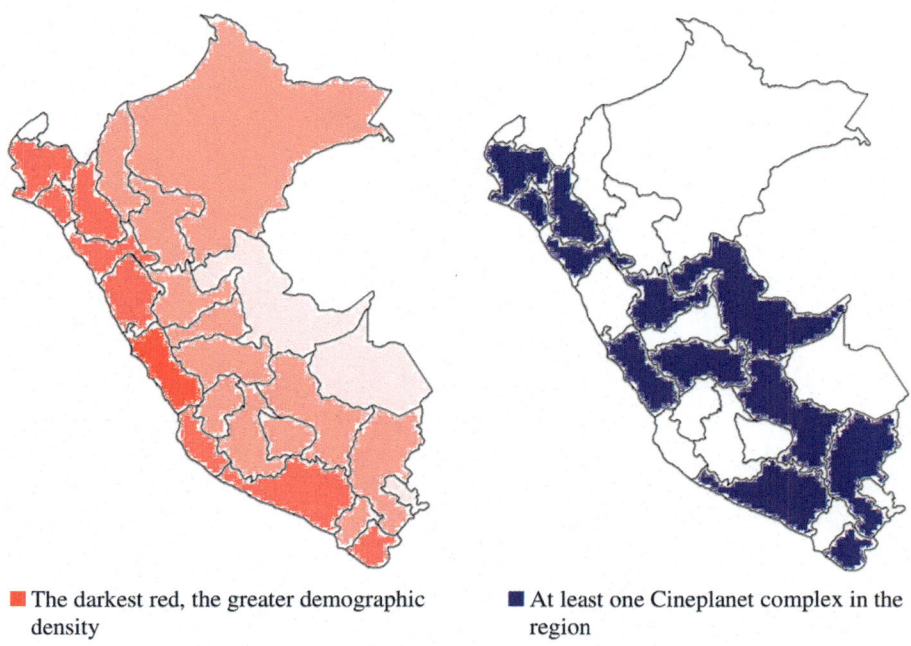

■ The darkest red, the greater demographic density

■ At least one Cineplanet complex in the region

Fig. 9.4 Demographics and distribution of Cineplanet movie theatres in Peru. (Source: Cineplanet. Memoria Anual 2015 & INEI (2015))

Table 9.3 Exhibitors ranking 2014 in Chile, including the number of screens and percentage of tickets sold

Brand	Number of centres	Number of screens	Attendance %	Attendance
Hoyts	21	143	45.60	10,029,425
Cinemark	16	113	34.60	7,615,079
Cineplanet	7	59	15.20	3,338,912
Independent	5	19	2.90	637,601
Pavilion Entertainment	2	8	1.20	261,628
Cinema Star	3	5	0.60	133,238
	54	347	100.00	22,015,883

Source: Cámara de Exhibidores Multisalas en Chile A.G. (CAEM) (2015)

the firm was funded through the issuance of US$8 million bonds in 2005. However, not everything was good news. Even though Cineplanet successfully executed its plan, it was not able to use this brand in the Chilean market for the first eight years; the company went into a legal process, emerging with a favourable ruling in 2012. Since then, Cineplanet has unified its identity in Peru and Chile. By the end of 2012, the company operated 26 complexes: 21 in Peru and 5 in Chile, and in 2014 the company market share in the southern country was 15.2% (Table 9.3).

A New Wave of Expansion

The following countries were analysed:

Brazil: A Great Opportunity

The largest country in Latin America, both in geographical size and population, is Brazil. Brazil also has its own movie industry (Fig. 9.5), which has received less recognition in North America and other parts of the world than it has deserved. Per capita GDP in Brazil is US$8670 (Table 9.4). Steve Solot, President of the Rio Film Commission, confirms that despite the country's general economic slowdown, the film and, especially, TV, industries are emerging, boosting demand for content in all audio-visual segments. The Global Competitiveness Report ranks Brazil 75th, and the report indicates that the most problematic factors to be competitive are taxes, restrictive labour regulation and corruption (World Economic Forum 2015), which are also very important factors in Peru. Hence, companies have to learn how to deal with them.

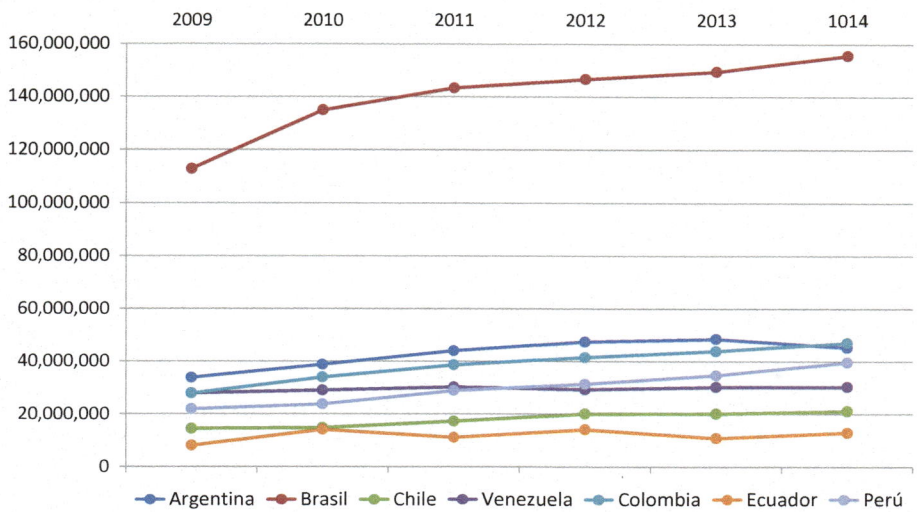

Fig. 9.5 Comparison of moviegoers in Peru, Chile, Colombia, Ecuador, Brazil and Venezuela. (Source: Conferencia de autoridades cinematográficas [Conference of cinematographic authorities] (2015). Statistical indicators)

Table 9.4 The global competitiveness index 2015–2016 rankings, world economic forum

World rank	Economy	Score	Prev.	GDP Per capita USD
35	Chile	4.58	33	14,477
61	Colombia	4.28	66	8076
69	Peru	4.21	65	6458
73	Uruguay	4.09	80	16,199
75	Brazil	4.08	57	11,604
76	Ecuador	4.07	n/a	6286
89	Trinidad and Tobago	3.94	89	21,311
106	Argentina	3.79	104	12,873
117	Bolivia	3.60	105	3061
118	Paraguay	3.60	120	4305
121	Guyana	3.56	117	3748
132	Venezuela	3.30	n/a	6757

Source: World Economic Forum (2015). The Global Competitiveness Report: 2015–2016

Brazil is the only Portuguese-speaking country in the continent. It is challenging to translate English content into Portuguese, although many movies are translated. The culture is different mainly because of its origins. Peru was conquered by Spain, while Brazil was colonized by Portugal. Both countries are predominantly Catholic. Another important factor is that Brazil is not part of the Andean Community and it does not have a free trade agreement with Peru. In geographic terms Rio and Sao Paulo are 3800 km from Lima, around five hours by airplane from Sao Paulo. Furthermore, Brazil has a different time zone to Peru (it is two hours ahead). Brazil showed no GDP growth in 2015 and had a high unemployment rate (7.5%). Brazil is the main commercial partner of Peru in South America. In 2015, trade represented more than $3 billion dollars. At a global level, Brazil is Peru's fourth-largest trading partner (Ministerio de Comercio Exterior y Turismo 2016).

The film industry in Brazil is supported by the government; however, it is not equally distributed and is largely concentrated in Sao Paulo (66.9%) and Rio de Janeiro (26.06%). Together, these two states account for almost 90% of the total. In 2016 Q1–Q3, Brazil's box office was $711 million, with an audience of 146.1 million, representing a growth of 10.5% in audience and 15.1% in box office over the same period in 2015. Domestic films' share of box office was 12.1% in 2016. Brazil is now home to 3098 cinema screens. Additionally, 99.19% of those screens are digital. The key to this growth is the strong connections between the US and Brazilian film industries. From 2010 to 2014, the two countries worked together to generate over 100 co-produced films. These co-productions are a creative venue for cultural exchange and mutual economic growth.

Colombia: The Only Risk Is to Stay

The Colombian government has enacted legislation to promote its film industry, funded by a tax that distributors, exhibitors and cinema producers must pay towards the "*Fondo Mixto de Promoción Cinematográfica PROIMAGENES en Movimiento* [PROIMAGENES Joint fund for film promotion]". In 2015, Colombian box office revenue reached US$179.2 million. At the end of the year, the country had 935 screens; the cities with most screens were Bogota, Cali and Medellin with 262, 81 and 74, respectively (63,200 people per screen) (Anuario Estadístico de Cine Colombiano 2015).

Colombia currently maintains a relationship with Peru through three main trading blocs: the Pacific Alliance, the Andean Community and the Union of South American Nations. In addition, both countries maintain bilateral relationships through embassies to settle cooperation between them, fight against drug traffic and to boost trade with Europe (Embajada de Colombia en Perú n.d.).

As in most Latin American countries, local companies have to import most technology. However, the country ranks 54th in the "Ease for doing business" index, and third in Latin America and Caribbean (Table 9.1). The capital of the country is Bogota and the distance from Lima is around 2908 kilometres;

the flight time is nearly three hours. GDP per capita in Colombia is about $8074, according to the Global competitiveness report (Table 9.4), higher than in Peru (around $6400).

Venezuela: Trouble=Opportunity?

The distance between Peru and Venezuela's capital, Caracas, is about 4330 kilometres. The flight time from Lima to Caracas is nearly four hours. This country has a $7744 GDP per capita (Table 9.4) and a population of around 31 million people.

Venezuela and Peru have both experienced political crisis: Peru during the 1980s and 1990s, and Venezuela at present. In the past, Venezuela took in more than 90,000 Peruvians (RPP Noticias 2016) and gave them all the facilities to start a new life. Nowadays, Peruvians are very grateful for what Venezuela did, and now that Venezuela is in political and economic crisis, it is concerned about receiving Venezuela immigrants. Pedro Pablo Kuczynski, the president of Peru, is looking at extending the visa for Venezuelans for an unlimited period.

Given Venezuela's ongoing problems, (Table 9.1); there is little encouragement to invest.

Despite the current crisis, the country has continued to make films, and, in terms of tickets sold, the film industry has grown over the last decade (El Universal 2015) (ticket sales increased from nearly 3.32 to 17.6 million). Political problems make it difficult to import equipment from the United States. In short, doing business at this moment in Venezuela is clearly not recommended.

Ecuador: From Adversaries to Allies

Peru and Ecuador nowadays are active members of the Andean Community. Doing business between Peru and Ecuador is relatively easy and a more attractive investment for the private sector.

Ecuador and Peru share similar cultures. The country has many traditional celebrations around the cities, which keep alive the essence of their culture. In addition, with a distribution of 65% people of mixed race, 25% natives, 10% Caucasians and 7% afro descendants (Ecuador Explorer 2013), Ecuador is considered a multi-ethnic culture. It has a population of 16 million people (Datos Macro 2015) and a GDP per capita of almost $6500 (Datos Macro

2015), close to Peru's $6200 (World Bank 2016) (Table 9.4). Ecuador's middle classes are growing, as in Peru. Both countries enjoy trade, and employment is being driven by Small and Medium – sized enterprises (SMES), while consumption is increasing as well (Revista Lideres n.d.), and the government encourages local employment. These factors are the main reasons for the growth of the GDP per capita. Almost 60% of Ecuadorans watch domestically produced TV programmes. Furthermore, traditional arts and music is well appreciated by young people, who are proud of their culture. Ecuador is ranked 105th in the world corruption chart. The culture, tastes and tendencies are similar between both countries.

In recent years, Ecuador has improved its people's living standards. A stable democracy, it is open to global investment. The country is seen by external investors as stable and has attracted inward capital. The government has also focused on the development of the media, especially through the Internet. Ecuador is looking for sustainable growth and technological development. The government believes that the Internet is the most powerful tool used to improve education. In 2012, 60% of the population had Internet access and the country is expecting to eradicate the digital analphabetism (Ministerio de Comunicaciones n.d.). Ecuador is concerned about its natural resources and increased energy usage, which in the last decade had almost doubled (El Comercio 2015). Figure 9.6 shows a comparative chart about the related topics among Ecuador and some other countries. It is an interesting opportunity for Cineplanet, but it must show that it is well constituted in Peru and that it can meet all the requirements. Finally, Cineplanet must have at least one rep-

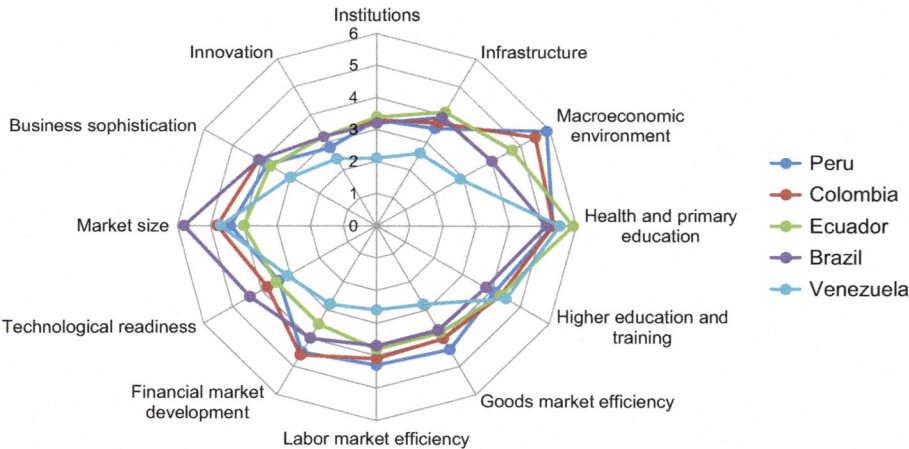

Fig. 9.6 Competitiveness comparison among Peru, Colombia, Ecuador, Brazil and Venezuela. (Source: World Economic Forum (2015). The Global Competitiveness Report: 2015–2016)

resentative who can manage the operating functions all the time in Ecuador (Derecho Ecuador 2014).

Caught Between Four Stools

While Dawson decided which new markets to develop, he also had to show Bauver that developing new markets is the best option, taking in as many factors as possible. His team provided him with valuable and useful information. However, he was concerned there was valuable data he still needed, so he decided to formulate some questions to his team that would help him win over the board of directors.

Why should Cineplanet continue developing new markets?

How attractive is South America for investment?

What are the risks of developing a new market?

How important are the cultural and geographical factors between Peru and its neighbours in making a decision?

Are there other factors to consider in the analysis?

Which country will be easier to enter and which will be the most difficult?

Which country should we enter, and why?

Dawson had to demonstrate and convince his fellow directors that developing new markets was the right path, and explain the reasons for choosing certain countries. Dawson was motivated because it could spell success for him both professionally and financially.

Takeaways

Developing new markets is a challenging strategy and needs to be developed very carefully. Despite most global expansion starting regionally, consumer behaviour is different, even in countries that share language, traditions and religion, as is the case in Latin America.

Each potential country's movie industry needs to be very carefully studied, taking in the main players, consumers, suppliers, competitors, substitutes and entrants. Cineplanet's advantage is having studied the "field" previously and knowing the critical success factors for that industry.

This is a vital decision and one that involves many risks. The board of directors plays a decisive role and needs full agreement on the decision and the strategies to be pursued. It is difficult when an experienced member of the board opposes a proposal, and in this case the CEO needs to present convincing strategies and a well-supported external and internal analysis of the company, as well as a sound competition and substitute's analysis.

The expansion of Netflix and Amazon, along with other streaming companies, presents an important threat to companies like Cineplanet, as did DVDs and piracy before them. This is not a particularly attractive industry for many investors, who are not willing to put money in movie theatres.

Leadership is needed to transform a company and an industry. Dawson has been successful with Cineplanet in Peru and Chile and now has the challenge of expanding that success to other neighbouring countries, as seen in Table 9.1: Ease of Doing Business Ranking in South America.

Appendix: Character Profiles

Raffael Dawson

Raffael Dawson (40) is the Chief Executive Officer of Cineplanet since 2011 to the present. Raffael Dawson started in the company as a chief of an inexperienced commercial team in 2003. After great results in sales, he became the Operations Manager. He engineered fast growth in Cineplanet due to his leadership skill, which led him to become CEO in 2011. With a degree from Lehigh University, he has a strong background in marketing and global corporative finance. These two management fields and his leadership skills gave him a different vision of the organization. Before Cineplanet, Raffael worked in Pennsylvania at Israeli pharmaceutical company TEVA. He started as a trainee, and after one year he began as a junior analyst in the marketing area. His career at TEVA was very promising; but he had to return to Peru after he was unable to renew his work permit. Dawson's approach is theoretical rather than pragmatic; he conducts a lot of research before making a decision. This way of working led him to make very few mistakes in his decisions and earn an excellent reputation for his capacity. Dawson is sociable and says he wants to meet his personal goals before starting a family. He is very disciplined and has earned the respect of the entire organization.

Tomas Bauver

Tomas Bauver (58) is the oldest and most respected member of the board and is a veteran of the cinematography industry. He studied Business Administration in Films at the University of California Berkeley. He graduated with honours and he was recruited by Cinemark USA. He started from a low position as assistant and was soon promoted due to his business skills until he became Operations Manager for North America. He then decided to return to Peru to start a cinema company. Along with other members of the board, he founded Cineplanet. He knows every aspect of the company and how the industry behaves. He is very authoritarian and usually always gets what he wants. He is a very difficult person to persuade, and the only way to convince him is demonstrating with facts that he is wrong.

Notes

1. 1 US Dollar is approximately 3 Soles (PEN).

References

Anuario Estadístico de Cine Colombiano (2015) Dirección de Cinematografía Ministerio de cultura, http://www.mincultura.gov.co/areas/cinematografia/estadisticas-del-sector/Documents/Anuario%20Estad%C3%ADstico%20Cinematograf%C3%ADa%202015.pdf

Banegas, C. (2011) Industria cinematográfica latinoamericana: políticas públicas y su impacto en un mercado digital. El caso boliviano, https://www.academia.edu/3517155/Bolivia_Ley_del_cine_y_su_impacto_el_mercado_cinematogr%C3%A1fico

Camara de exhibidores multisalas de Chile A.G. (2015) El cine en Chile en el 2014, http://www.caem.cl/index.php/informes-anuales/item/19-informe-caem-2014

Cineplanet, (2016) "Memoria Anual 2015", *Empresas en la BVL*, March 30.

Class & Asociados, "Fundamentos de Clasificación de Riesgos CINEPLEX SA", May 30, 2016.

Conferencia de autoridades cinematográficas (2015) Observatorio Iberoamericano Audiovisual Indicadores estadísticos, http://www.oia-caci.org/es/estadisticas/espectadores/?filter=1&ano[]=2009&ano[]=2010&ano[]=2011&ano[]=2012&ano[]=2013&ano[]=2014&paises[]=29&paises[]=42&paises[]=45&paises[]=60&paises[]=148&paises[]=193&graph=bars&graph=lines

Datos Macro (2015) Expansion, http://www.datosmacro.com/demografia/poblacion/ecuador

Datos Macro (2015) Expansion, http://www.datosmacro.com/demografia/poblacion/peru

Derecho Ecuador (2014) Las compañías extranjeras, http://www.derechoecuador. com/articulos/detalle/archive/doctrinas/derechosocietario/2014/07/08/ las-companias-extranjeras

Ecuador Explorer (2013) Ecuador su cultura y su gente, http://www.ecuadorexplorer. com/es/html/cultura-ecuatoriana.html

El Comercio (2015) 2015 El año del reciclaje en Ecuador, http://www.elcomercio. com/tendencias/reciclaje-ecuador-contaminacion-basura-playas.html

El Universal (2015) En medio de la crisis florece el cine venezolano, http://www.eluniversal.com/noticias/entretenimiento/medio-crisis-florece-cine-venezolano_26794

Embajada de Colombia en Perú (n.d.) Mecanismos bilaterales entre Colombia y Perú, http://peru.embajada.gov.co/colombia/mecanismos_bilaterales

INEI (2015) https://es.scribd.com/document/350006033/Cineplanet-Memoria-Resumen-2015

Ministerio de Comercio Exterior y Turismo (2016) Acuerdo de profundización económico comercial entre la República del Perú y la República Federativa de Brasil, http://www.acuerdoscomerciales.gob.pe/index.php?option=com_content &view=category&id=194:inicio-brasil&layout=blog&Itemid=213

Ministerio de Comunicaciones (n.d.). Ecuador continua creciendo en tecnología, http://www.telecomunicaciones.gob.ec/ecuador-continua-creciendo-en-tecnologia/

Revista Lideres (n.d.) El sector mypes está en pleno crecimiento, http://www.revistalideres.ec/lideres/sector-mipymes-pleno-crecimiento.html

RPP Noticias (2013) Cineplanet anunció apertura de las primeras salas Prime en el Perú, http://rpp.pe/economia/negocios/cineplanet-anuncio-apertura-de-las-primeras-salas-prime-en-el-peru-noticia-564385

RPP Noticias (2016) Centenares de venezolanos llegan a Perú cada semana huyendo de la crisis, http://rpp.pe/peru/actualidad/opositores-venezolanos-piden-a-peru-regularice-a-centenares-de-compatriotas-noticia-966453

The Gateway (2010) How it works: the film industry, http://thegatewayonline.com/ commercial-awareness/business-analysis/how-does-the-film-industry-work

The World Bank, *Doing Business 2016: Measuring Regulatory Quality and Efficiency*, 13th ed. (Washington, DC: World Bank, 2016).

World Bank (2016) GDP per capita (current USD), http://data.worldbank.org/indicator/NY.GDP.PCAP.CD?end=2015&locations=PE&start=2004

World Economic Forum, *The Global Competitiveness Report: 2015–2016*, 36th ed. (Geneva, Switzerland: World Economic Forum, 2015).

10

Innovation Beyond Technology: Unilab

Jikyeong Kang, Maria Antonia OG Arroyo, John C Orlina, and Ariel T Lopez

Abstract Making a mark in the global business community is a daunting task for any organization, especially when multinational companies (MNCs) have the resources to set market standards and define trends in industry innovation. This leaves local players in expansion limbo; once they implement innovation initiatives to "catch up" with MNC leaders, the market would have been flooded by similar offerings, leading to small-scale competition among laggards, while market leaders have already identified and are pursuing new trends.

Companies of all sizes should have innovation in mind, but it should not be pursued for its own sake. All innovation initiatives should result in making the firm measurably more competitive. Novel strategies and business models that have little to do with high-technology equipment or systems the big players use can prove to be just as successful (and more cost effective) in terms of scaling and expanding one's business.

How does a business grow through innovation when it operates in a sector that has high barriers to entry, particularly in an innovation ecosystem that favors importing mature "turn-key" solutions that have been proven to work in the developed world? The pharmaceutical sector is one such area, heavily controlled by a few multinational players who have the resources to take big bets on multiple R&D projects and constantly churn out new products.

J. Kang (✉) • M. A. O. Arroyo • J. C. Orlina • A. T. Lopez
Asian Institute of Management, Makati, Philippines
e-mail: JKang@AIM.EDU

© The Author(s) 2018
S. Iñiguez de Onzoño, K. Ichijo (eds.), *Business Despite Borders*,
https://doi.org/10.1007/978-3-319-76306-4_10

The sector is affected by both local and global forces because stringent government regulations vary from country to country while global advances in biomedical technology by large players make costs prohibitive. This forces smaller, local companies to pursue incremental innovation.

To succeed in this globalized economy, pharmaceutical companies must take advantage of other avenues for development, looking for different means of tapping the various areas and relationships within their value chain. One such example is United Laboratories Inc., a Philippine pharmaceutical company that has managed to grow itself from a small, local pharmaceutical supplier into a regional giant in South East Asia, in an industry that the country is not known for.

Unilab (Philippines), Incorporated

United Laboratories is a privately owned and controlled Filipino pharmaceutical company, now more commonly known as Unilab (Philippines) Inc. It has come a long way from its simple beginnings as a corner drug store in 1945. With the culmination of the Pacific theater of World War II, the Philippines lacked medicines and medical supplies. Founders Jose Y. Campos and Mariano K. Tan, seeing the need to provide these products at a highly affordable rate to the average citizen given the circumstances, established United Drug Co. The firm's bias toward a market-driven culture thus began as a necessity.

By 1959, 14 years from its creation, the company would see itself become the largest Filipino pharmaceutical company, possessing the lion's share of the country's pharmaceutical market. Now in its 72nd year of operation, the conglomerate has grown to possess a substantial share of the Philippine market, holding more than 20% consistently over three decades. Its portfolio consists of some of the biggest and highly popular prescription, consumer healthcare, and personal care brands of the country.[1] Brands like Bioflu, Biogesic, Decolgen, Alaxan, Kremil-S, and Neozep for pharmaceutical products; and Tiki-Tiki, Revicon, the Enervon line of products, Swish, and Conzace for consumer healthcare have long become household names for all Filipinos.

The company also possesses significant shares of the Asia-Pacific market, rivaling top multinational firms. As of June 2015, figures from QuintilesIMS, formerly IMS Health (Table 10.1) showed that the Unilab Group was ranked the highest of the Top 20 ASEAN Pharma companies, overtaking multinational players like Pfizer, Novartis, GlaxoSmithKline, and Sanofi.

Table 10.1 Unilab Group ranking in 2015

Top 20 ASEAN corporations		USD millions	% growth
1	Unilab Group	946	5
2	Pfizer	864	0
3	Novartis	714	10
4	GlaxoSmithKline	657	6
5	Sanofi	622	5
6	Kalbe Pharma	515	−5
7	Merck & Co.	508	4
8	Roche	442	10
9	AstraZeneca	383	5
10	Bayer	350	3
11	Boehringer Ingel	317	8
12	Abbott	296	7
13	Johnson & Johnson	287	−2
14	Sanbe	249	−3
15	Dexa Medica	227	−1
16	Merck KGAA	210	8
17	Allergan	193	1
18	Takeda	191	1
19	Otsuka	157	8
20	Servier	156	1

The pharmaceutical conglomerate operates across the South East Asian region, with manufacturing plants and offices in select countries such as Indonesia, Thailand, and Vietnam. Their subsidiary companies operate with relative autonomy from the mother company to further increase their respective growth and penetration in their areas of operation.

Building a Culture That Fosters Innovation

As a privately owned and controlled family corporation, Unilab can make decisions quickly and is under no pressure from outside shareholders to sacrifice long-term strategy for the sake of hitting short-term, year-end targets. Coupled with the conscious effort to maintain competitive advantage by pioneering affordable products for countries in Southeast Asia, the firm balances its steady expansion with rapid blitzes of market-driven product development.

Central to this balance is building a critical mass of senior managers who can craft, lead, or implement strategic innovations.

These are the same people who are expected to deliver revenue. Including innovation in their key results areas when these projects are filled with uncertainty is not enough. They will factor in the risk of cannibalization, opportunity cost, and their personal accountability if the project fails. We had to create a culture that emphasized learning from these projects so that the right people can thrive. Managers who are willing to fail on the way to success, who are passionate enough to see things through but not so attached to the project that they can't pull the plug. We value people who are able to say: 'We tried it. It didn't work out. But these are the things we learned.'[2]

Unilab has made it a consistent policy to hire early and promote internally, allowing company culture to be nurtured and leadership to remain stable. Since a manager's short-term decisions will directly affect them in the future, accountability and ownership have become a company norm across all positions leading to complete buy-in and execution of new directions that the company takes.

This behavior differs from most regional headquarters of pharmaceutical MNCs as they have a volatile leadership structure where upper management changes every 3–6 years, usually assigned by corporate headquarters. While initiatives can continue, transitioning to a new country and learning the lay of the land are time consuming and may even be repetitive—allowing for those with quicker decision-making capability to get new products to market faster and influence market trends.

Aside from being able to quickly react to market opportunities, Unilab views innovation as a core capability and not as an event relegated to the recesses of R&D departments and conference rooms of well-intentioned brainstormers. Instead of following the normal view of pharmaceutical innovations: drug discovery, improved efficacy/reduction of side effects, or efficient/convenient drug delivery, Unilab takes a more general approach and defines it as *"the creation of new businesses or new ways of doing business that*

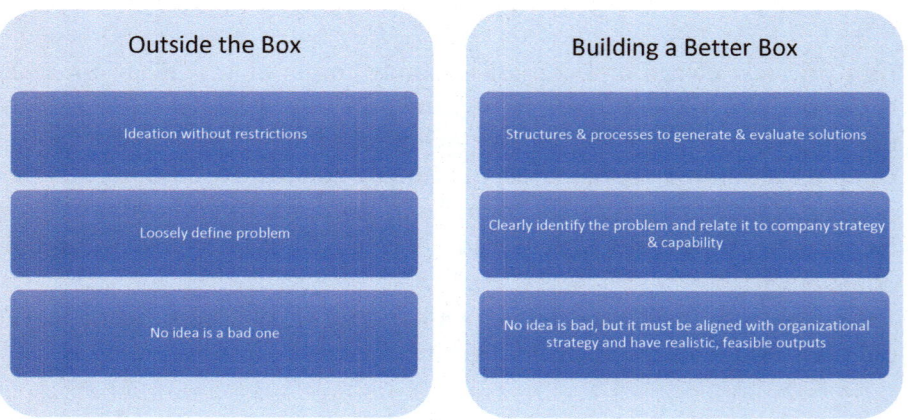

Fig. 10.1 Unilab's innovation strategy: "building the better box"

generate value for the customers and the company.[3] This holistic view allows them to ideate quickly, adapt to market needs, and implement projects efficiently. Innovation strategy at Unilab is not about "thinking outside the box" but in "building a better box" that is tailored to customer needs in each country and to the firm's overall strategy (see Fig. 10.1).

Early on, Unilab established a system of "tailored boxes" in their business units, allowing each unit to focus on competing with a particular foreign company's brand and formulate their own respective strategies. To keep initiatives relevant to company objectives and feasible to company operations, structure was built in to the autonomy to prevent the customer from solely defining Unilab's innovations and thereby defining the company itself. By creating innovation charters, which spell out goals, objectives, guidelines, and specific parameters, the business units can conduct small market tests that are geared to increase insight and not revenue.

The effectiveness of this strategy is apparent from Unilab's development of individual product brands in their early years instead of focusing on a single corporate brand. Immediately after World War II, foreign brands were viewed as better quality and more reliable. Efforts on building the brand first, instead of competing with product features and performance kept innovation initiatives focused on the major hurdle to overcome—establishment of a reputable, credible pharmaceutical company rather than a company with the latest, greatest discovery. Initiatives included highlighting product brands as ones that doctors trust as they were a main influencer in drug recommendation. By keeping brands separate, Unilab could remain flexible to market changes while remaining synchronized with the vision of value creation for both customers and shareholders.

Small Experiments Within a Better Box

Unilab's culture of experimentation aided in turning their "tailored boxes" into successful products. As with any experiment, everything that is desired to be known is not tested all at once. Rather than treating new product launches as quick-to-market, short-term revenue generators, Unilab took an entrepreneurial mindset and placed small bets early on with the intention of gaining deep customer insight versus profit generation. In the first 3 years of a product launch, losses were not seen as failures; the only failure would be if no product or market insights were identified and acted on in subsequent years, with breakeven achieved by year 4. In their use of the scientific method to test

	Our hypothesis was validated by the experiment	Fund a larger market test
Testing Market Hypothesis	Our original hypothesis was wrong but we found a different path that looks promising	Learn
		Create a new hypothesis
	Our original hypothesis was wrong and we should kill the idea	Learn
	Our experiment did not give us enough data to validate the hypothesis	Failure

Fig. 10.2 A methodical approach to testing market hypothesis

market hypotheses (see Fig. 10.2), Unilab could roll out new products, quickly pivot at a minimal loss if necessary, and scale new product launches.

Further market penetration for the firm involved multiple initiatives that were made possible by this culture of experimentation. Taking advantage of Philippine legislation that called for more affordable medicine to be made available to the average Filipino, Unilab established generic over-the-counter (OTC) medicines, produced through one of its subsidiary companies, Amherst Laboratories. This allowed Filipinos from lower economic classes to gain access to the generic versions of known Filipino brands like Biogesic (Paracetamol) and Alaxan (Ibuprofen). The branded versions were normally seen as relatively out of reach to the lower-class working Filipino. Middle-class Filipinos tended to purchase the generics since they had the scientific literacy to understand that the medicine was biologically equivalent to the originator's product and felt no shame in cutting their healthcare costs. Whereas the poor felt "safer" purchasing "the real thing."

Unilab worked with the hypothesis that Filipinos are generally brand conscious, seeing branded items as higher in quality over the generics. Given Unilab's strength in brand image, they experimented with branding their generics under a single name—RiteMed. This was a risky strategy as it cannibalized the sales of branded generics for a uni-branded generic drug. A large marketing campaign was launched so that customers who needed Paracetamol would not buy Biogesic (the Unilab-branded generic) and would instead request for "RiteMed Paracetamol." The RiteMed brand was associated with Unilab's image of quality OTC medications. After the introduction of RiteMed, sales of individual branded generics decreased but overall revenues skyrocketed since Unilab was able to tap the socio-economic class that makes up 54% of the Philippine population.

While RiteMed is still a successful brand, it does not mean that failures were not encountered when testing new markets. One example was Unilab's failed approach to reach the Philippine Business Process Outsourcing (BPO) market for RiteMed. At a size of almost 1 million people with medium-to-high spending power, the BPO market seemed to be a potentially lucrative market. The assumptions to test were that BPO professionals had the disposable income and desire to help their aging parents, many of whom were taking maintenance medicines.

Targeting a small sample size to test these assumptions, Unilab was able to see that this was not the case. The BPO professionals did not have the money, and a number of them were actually in debt since they chose to purchase cars, gadgets, or travel. Purchasing maintenance medicines for their parents may have been stated as a priority but their actual spending behavior was quite different.

Bespoke Innovation Process

Not all innovation is created equal, and a "one size fits all" approach doesn't always work, especially in a highly regulated, capital intensive industry, such as pharmaceuticals. As Unilab's brands grew, they found that focusing only on new product development would be unsustainable. New opportunities would be passed up to focus on their core business, and while being the Philippine market leader was a great accomplishment, the threat of foreign players would not be staved off by brand image alone.

The firm's internal innovation process evolved to differentiate core and ancillary business opportunities, moving beyond product innovation and including business model innovations targeted at untapped or under-served markets. By splitting innovation into two groups (mainstream innovation and market insight innovation), they were able to ensure that resources were allocated properly and find solutions that would still be relevant to the needs of the organization (see Fig. 10.3).

In their new process, mainstream innovation would fall under Unilab's core competency of prescription and OTC drug development. The problem with product innovation in the pharmaceutical industry is that it is highly regulated and even changing the delivery of a drug (i.e., from a patch to oral) will require a completely new set of clinical trials though the drug is essentially the

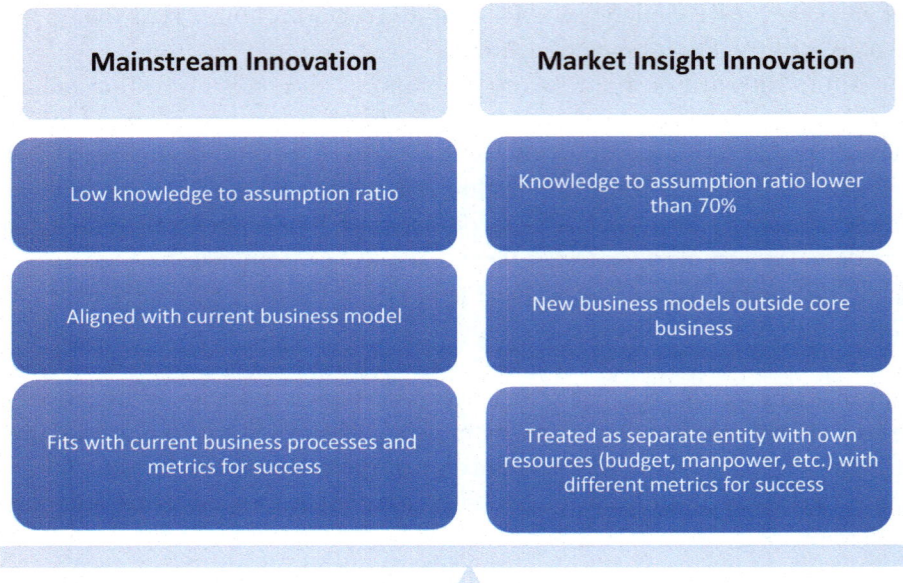

Fig. 10.3 Unilab's innovation split: mainstream and market insight innovations

same. Even with generic medicines, one must still show they are the bio-equivalent to the original patented drug.

Thus, mainstream innovations for Unilab are incremental changes rather than breakthroughs, and investments in technology and R&D are limited to platforms that will improve current products and operating systems. Investments are calculated and pursued only if they are aligned with the current business model and easily integrated in current manufacturing and distribution systems. For instance, in 2010 the firm had the only SAP direct-to-automated material handling system and retail performance standard tracking system in Southeast Asia. In the same year their R&D platforms veered away from breakthrough drug discovery and instead focused on improving the taste, dosage efficacy, and stability of products that Unilab currently distributes.

You can't really do a lot of disruptive innovations from a product standpoint because it usually requires a whole new set of clinical trials. It's not like consumer goods where you can easily vary the taste, the color – you can vary anything and call it an innovation. That's why the innovations will have to come from non-product avenues, such as the business model innovations that we came up with here like RiteMed. Especially when it comes to expanding into Southeast Asia – it's all about finding new routes-to-market, new ways to reach more consumers, new ways of capitalizing on the relationships with the customers.[4]

While these initiatives are safe bets, the returns they provide are small and will serve more to limit competition from stealing market share rather than increasing it. Too many small safe bets, in the long run, are unsafe to the business. Unilab thus made a concerted effort to have a diverse but balanced innovation portfolio driven by their market insight innovation group. This group was treated as a separate entity from Unilab with a structured and more entrepreneurial process that allowed market experiments to be created outside of Unilab's core business. As shown in Fig. 10.4, the market insight innovation group had to first pitch the idea internally and gain a set of champions within the conglomerate to support the project. Rather than implementing immediately and learning on the way, planning and market research was then performed to see if the potential innovation could satisfy certain criteria such as:

- Key solve-rate metrics (% of problem solved/customer pain eliminated)
- Implementation metrics (% of solution implemented, time to market, costs)

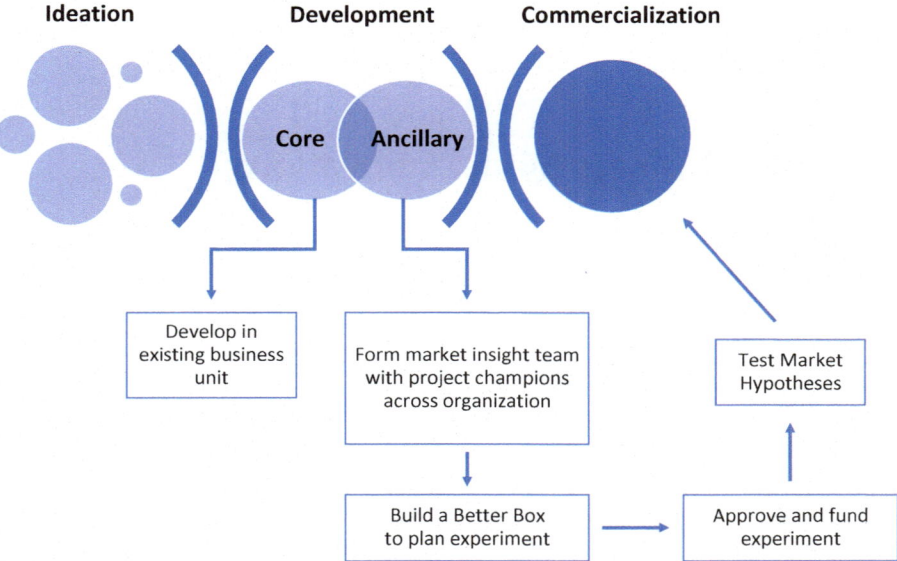

Fig. 10.4 The market insight innovation group's process

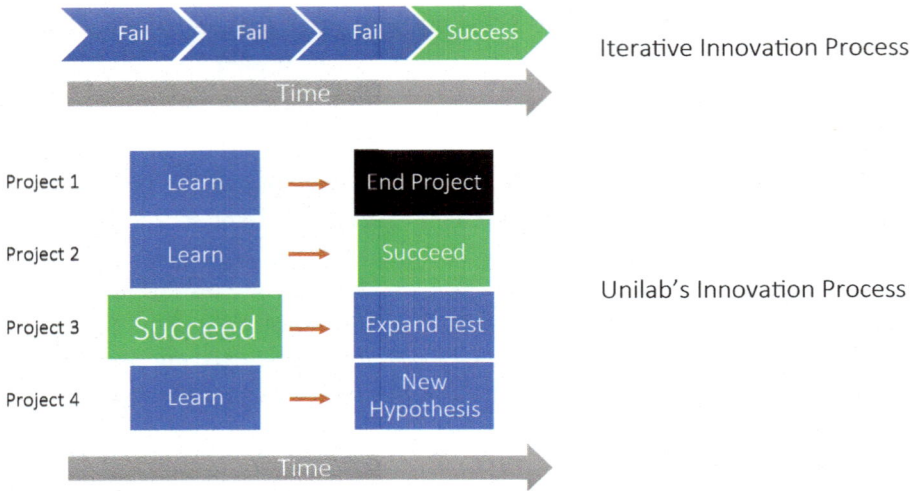

Fig. 10.5 Evolving the iterative process into multiple small-scale projects

- Value capture metrics (increased revenue/cost reduction, ROI, breakeven point)

Only when a solid set of hypotheses could be tested with minimal losses and a maximum amount of learning would Unilab's internal strategic investment group fund the project. To speed up the process even more, multiple small-scale investments were made to allow failures and successes to happen at the same time versus an iterative process (see Fig. 10.5).

Localized Business Model Innovations

An example of the market insight innovation group at work can be seen in Unilab's SafeBirth initiative. Unfortunately, 72% of the Filipino population pays for their healthcare out of pocket with only a small percentage covered by either personal or corporate-sponsored health insurance. Government health insurance does offset some of the costs for basic healthcare, including prenatal and maternal health services. However, most Filipinos cannot easily access standard hospital facilities for safe delivery of their children. Most of the lower working-class Filipinos go to third-party lying-in facilities or call for the services of midwives to help deliver their babies. These third-party facilities tend to be overcrowded, with as many as three women per bed, and consequently unsanitary.

SafeBirth was created to capitalize on this opportunity and venture beyond their core business. These lying-in clinics had facilities that operated with the efficiency and aseptic environment of a hospital, offered at a price range affordable to the poor. Pregnant women are cared for by an accredited, highly trained staff of midwives and a doctor, fulfilling the standards for a safe delivery. The facility's system of operations also enables quick referrals to the nearest capable hospital facility if it is necessary for the patient to be transferred for further observation and care. SafeBirth remains within the financial reach and capacity of Filipinos who cannot afford the usual hospital rates. It also offers another channel aside from drugstores for RiteMed prenatal vitamins.

Business model innovations such as RiteMed and SafeBirth would not have been approved or even perceived to be successful if not for the high level of empowerment given to managers who innovate.

> Nobody gets fired here for making a wrong decision because we know that over the course of time, you will make decisions that may not necessarily be wrong, but a decision whose time has yet to come. And what we encourage [everyone] to do is: evaluate it, analyze it, distill the lessons, document it, store it, then maybe a few years from now when the time is right, we pull it out and see if we can try again.[5]

Removing the fear of being vilified for the wrong decision has greatly pushed Unilab professionals to be able to explore that pioneer mentality; to commit those mistakes as early, as quickly, and as cheaply as possible.

Regional Expansion

The company's focus was always to expand within Southeast Asia, and the founders always expressed that they would go into areas in which they could understand the culture with relative ease. Southeast Asia, despite its varying cultural groups, was such an area in which the adaptability rate for understanding was high for the company.

> We put up manufacturing plants in Thailand, Vietnam, and Indonesia because their laws stated that you had to build a factory before you could sell your products in their country. In fact, in Vietnam, we were the first 100% foreign-owned pharmaceutical company that established a manufacturing facility there. In China later on, we had a joint venture with the University of Shanghai. And the technology used for the first products in China, such as an oral cholera vaccine (from the People's Liberation Army), were all licensed.[6]

In parallel to their local growth, Unilab was also able to utilize their culture of innovation and experimentation, to port their innovation process outside of the Philippines, and to apply the same structured autonomy seen in domestic business units to their foreign affiliates. Initially there would be a team there that would conduct a study of the market. Then small retail experiments were funded in the target country, selling a few brands from the Philippines and registering them with the local authorities. Manufacturing plants would then be built when a significant amount of traction in the market had been achieved.

Structured autonomy empowered foreign business units and gave them the flexibility to make decisions on product rollouts, packaging, and branding that catered to local needs and expectations, yet remained aligned with overall company strategy. Rather than set up regional headquarters in their expansion countries, Unilab took various routes to establish their position based on what worked and what was needed in that country.

In places where they had to set up a factory before selling their product, such as Thailand and Vietnam, subsidiaries were not created under the Unilab name (and at times brand names were changed as well) to better blend in with the countries' respective pharma industry and competitors' product offerings. Unilab further differentiated themselves in international markets by varying their product formulations to suit locals as most multinational pharma companies only make minute packaging changes while keeping the formulation standard across all countries where they distribute. Rather than coast on the strength of their brand, Unilab actively engaged local doctors and customers to gain deep customer insight on what locals really wanted (in terms of taste, delivery mechanism, stability, etc.) to produce a product that met these needs and made their generics the brand of choice.

Indonesia's years of being solely a manufacturing partner to produce Unilab products, soon aided the affiliate in gaining the necessary expertise to provide toll manufacturing services for other companies who wanted to scale their drug production. Unilab executives also had enough foresight to take advantage of new marketing channels that greatly increased sales.

In Indonesia, we were probably the first to do OTC marketing. Until around the late '80s, all TV channels in the country were state-owned, with very limited audience. We took advantage of the establishment of private TV channels by heavily funding direct-to-consumer advertising. All our local competitors in Indonesia were reluctant to spend so much up-front without any assurance of yielding positive results. We knew how to reach out to millions of people with lower incomes and build a rapport with customers for quality healthcare. This allowed us to gain an advantage in Indonesia, Vietnam, and Myanmar.[7]

Unilab's presence in the Southeast Asian Region captures nine of the ten ASEAN countries, as well as Hong Kong and the People's Republic of China. The penetration of Unilab's products and services is mixed throughout the entire region. In Indonesia, they currently rank at 12. In Myanmar, the company is positioned as the biggest in the market. Thailand is a heavily dispersed market, so ranking is not as clearly defined in that territory. In terms of absolute value, the conglomerate sees the markets of the Philippines, Indonesia, and Myanmar as its biggest targets. While China is a large market, competition is fierce among local players and instead of targeting their people, Unilab utilized China's R&D and expanded their innovation portfolio to include drug discovery, the traditional means of pharma innovation, jointly developing two specific niche products with small but high-value markets.

An automatic assumption for the territorial involvement in China would be that its original founders were of Chinese descent, and that family connections to the mainland played a part in their entry, like that of the many Filipino Chinese Taipans who have successfully established businesses in the country and in the region. This was not the case for Unilab.

> The Chinese link is not very strong from a family perspective. It was purely about the market opportunity and our potential partners. We were so used to going to markets that multinationals wouldn't touch, and that initiative was a loss leader for the first decade.[8]

Now that the conglomerate can take a chance on investing in high-risk/high-reward projects, China may be the linchpin for a venture into biotechnology-based products and drug discovery.

For most international expansion initiatives, the company made strategic decisions to enter into countries that most multinationals stayed away from due to the many conflicts, political instability, and uncertainties present.

> 'Early-to-market' definitely gave us a huge advantage over everyone else. We are ahead of many of the local companies in [our expansion] countries today, as well as many multinationals. They came in when things were already clear, while we came in when things were not. We also have stayed through the years in those countries, both in good times and in bad. There are highs and lows in the political life of any country, affecting the economy of a country. We don't get discouraged by that. We take the long view.[9]

Rather than fearing the unknown, Unilab saw expansion into these countries as an opportunity to get "first-mover" advantage not only in product launches, but also in clearly defining and understanding the countries' respective nuances in their innovation ecosystems with a long-term strategy of having significant influence on how the countries' pharmaceutical rules and regulations would evolve through the years.

Unilab also ensured that their company culture extended to their international units. They operate with relatively high levels of autonomy and are free to make decisions on what products would best fit their respective markets, unlike multinationals where there tends to be centralized deployment of major products to be marketed and sold.

> Going out there, among the things that we've learned is that you have to adjust; you have to adapt to what you find there. Government regulations will be different from country to country. Healthcare concerns will also be different as well as the reactionary responses of the market. That's why we've adopted a sort of country-specific approach for our international operations.[10]

Unilab executives also knew that if they were to enter these territories on their own, they would have to be able to establish economies of scale to even come close to replicating the level of presence in the Philippines—an endeavor that they knew was prohibitively expensive.

Country-specific strategies enabled the conglomerate to decide where and when to colonize a market like China where they focus on profitable niches, and when to consolidate a market like Myanmar by being a judicious fast mover. In all Southeast Asian countries, the firm leveraged their existing relationships and partnerships with third-party distributors, logistics groups, and marketing firms.

Expanding from the Core Throughout the Region

Unilab plans to take advantage of the massive projected growth rates for Southeast Asian economies and the region's young population whose per capita income will rise by transitioning from a pharmaceutical company to a healthcare company. The policy moves throughout the region to provide greater access or even universal access to healthcare also create opportunities for Unilab. These policies will enable national health insurance services to provide greater coverage to a larger number of people. These changes in the region dovetail with Unilab's plans to expand from their core business. The conglomerate is well placed to leverage its culture, processes, and insights learned from market experiments to move beyond pharmaceuticals and into consumer care, specialized clinics, natural products, and biotechnology.

Evolution of any kind is always a challenge but blindly latching on to what other companies are doing, adopting technologies, or performing R&D outside of one's core business will only lead to extinction. Unilab's culture of experimentation and learning has allowed them to innovate beyond technology, setting their own market standards and making sure that they were always the ones who defined themselves. The practice of building "better boxes" tailored to consumer needs as well as acting on market insights quickly and cost effectively has allowed them to evolve in synch with their markets, while remaining true to the company vision. As the company scaled and revenues grew, Unilab could have easily followed the industry standard of pursuing higher risk-reward opportunities in drug discovery, remaining content with the value they had provided to their core customers and the market share they had gained in the Philippines.

Yet if one listens to market needs and learns from industry trends, they can craft creative, cost-effective solutions that have little to do with technology, as seen in Unilab's RiteMed. Innovation with the company's vision always in mind will make the most of new avenues for opportunity, not only creating new markets, but benefiting markets already addressed, as seen in Unilab's SafeBirth clinics.

Unilab's innovation process is one that puts customer opportunities first and only looks to technology if it is absolutely required or will optimize processes. With any learning process, there will be failures, but Unilab has shown that by failing early and failing fast but absorbing all data to improve, one can quickly pivot and continue to remain competitive, and grow to effectively deliver value to their customers.

Notes

1. Read more about Unilab here: http://www.unilab.com.ph/about/
2. Ochave, Atty. Jose Maria. 20 Apr. 2017. Senior Vice President for Growth Leadership – Unit 2; Chairman of the Board – Pharex Pharmaceuticals.
3. Ochave 4.
4. Ochave 9.
5. Engwa, Manuel P. 21 Jun. 2017. Corporate Senior Vice President, Office of the Chairman of the Board, Unilab (Philippines) Inc.
6. Ochave 12.
7. Engwa 13.
8. Ochave 13.
9. Engwa 14.
10. Engwa 14.

11

LATAM Airlines Group: From the End of the Earth to No. 10 in the World

Cristián Larroulet and Jorge Ardiles

Abstract This chapter describes the consolidation of LATAM into the leading airline company in Latin America, along its internationalization process through growth in different foreign markets, which has required new structure designs, respect of diversity, and cross-cultural management.

LATAM is the continuation of LAN, a Chilean state-owned air transport company created in 1929 and privatized, after 60 years of existence, in 1989. Only 20 years later, it became the 11th company in the world in terms of the number of passengers carried. Its recent business history illustrates both the importance of a global economy and the contribution of a company to the progress of Latin America as a result of this new scenario.

In May 2017, Enrique Cueto and Ignacio Cueto, the company's senior managers and controlling shareholders, explained that companies in a globalized world must differentiate themselves through their ability to adapt to a changing environment.

"We have faced four major change processes and we have given a name to each one of them. The first period was called 'Transformation Phase' and ran from 1994, when we purchased the company, to 2000. We merged two Chilean passenger air transport companies, LAN and LADECO, and one freight air transport company, FASTAIR".

C. Larroulet (✉) • J. Ardiles
Universidad del Desarrollo, Santiago, Chile
e-mail: clarroulet@udd.cl; jardiles@udd.cl

S. Iñiguez de Onzoño, K. Ichijo (eds.), *Business Despite Borders*,
https://doi.org/10.1007/978-3-319-76306-4_11

"In 2001, we decided to export our project, which gave rise to the second phase that we called 'Regional Expansion'. We created LAN Peru, LAN Argentina, LAN Ecuador, and LAN Colombia."

"In 2005, our company was poorly valued on the New York Stock Exchange, despite the growth attained. Therefore, we launched the third phase, called 'Efficiency', as a result of which we moved from a Stock Exchange value of US\$2.2 billion ("Billion" refers to one thousand million) to a position as the most highly valued company trading on the NYSE in the world, at US\$14 billion."

"In 2011, we launched our fourth phase, called 'Consolidation', during which we merged with the Brazilian company TAM and formed LATAM."

From 1994 to date, the company's DNA has been based on three pillars: safety, efficiency, and service. These pillars have always been delivered with a flexible vision in order to take advantage of existing opportunities in an ever-changing world.

Company Milestones During Its State-Owned Phase

The airline was founded in Chile by Army Air Services Commander Mr. Arturo Merino Benítez (whose name was given to the main airport in Santiago) and started operating on March 5, 1929, under the name of Línea Aeropostal Santiago-Arica (Fig. 11.1).

At the beginning, the airline used small Havilland Gipsy Moth twin-engine airplanes essentially devoted to the transport of mail and some bold passengers. To travel to Arica (located at a distance of 2041 kilometers from Santiago), the pilots of these airplanes had to fly a perilous route with transit stops in the cities of Ovalle, Copiapó, Antofagasta, and Iquique, both from and to Santiago. This trip was very dangerous because there was no support from meteorological or communication services at that time.

The new company was quickly accepted by the Chilean public. During its first year of operations, Línea Aeropostal carried 762 passengers.

As a result of the success attained, flights to the south of the country were launched in 1930. During its second year of existence, the company managed to carry more than 5000 passengers.

In February 1931, the company received a sign of confidence when it was required to carry the Prince of Wales (the future King Edward VIII) and his brother, the Duke of Kent, between the cities of Antofagasta and Santiago, during their visit to the country as guests of the Chilean government.

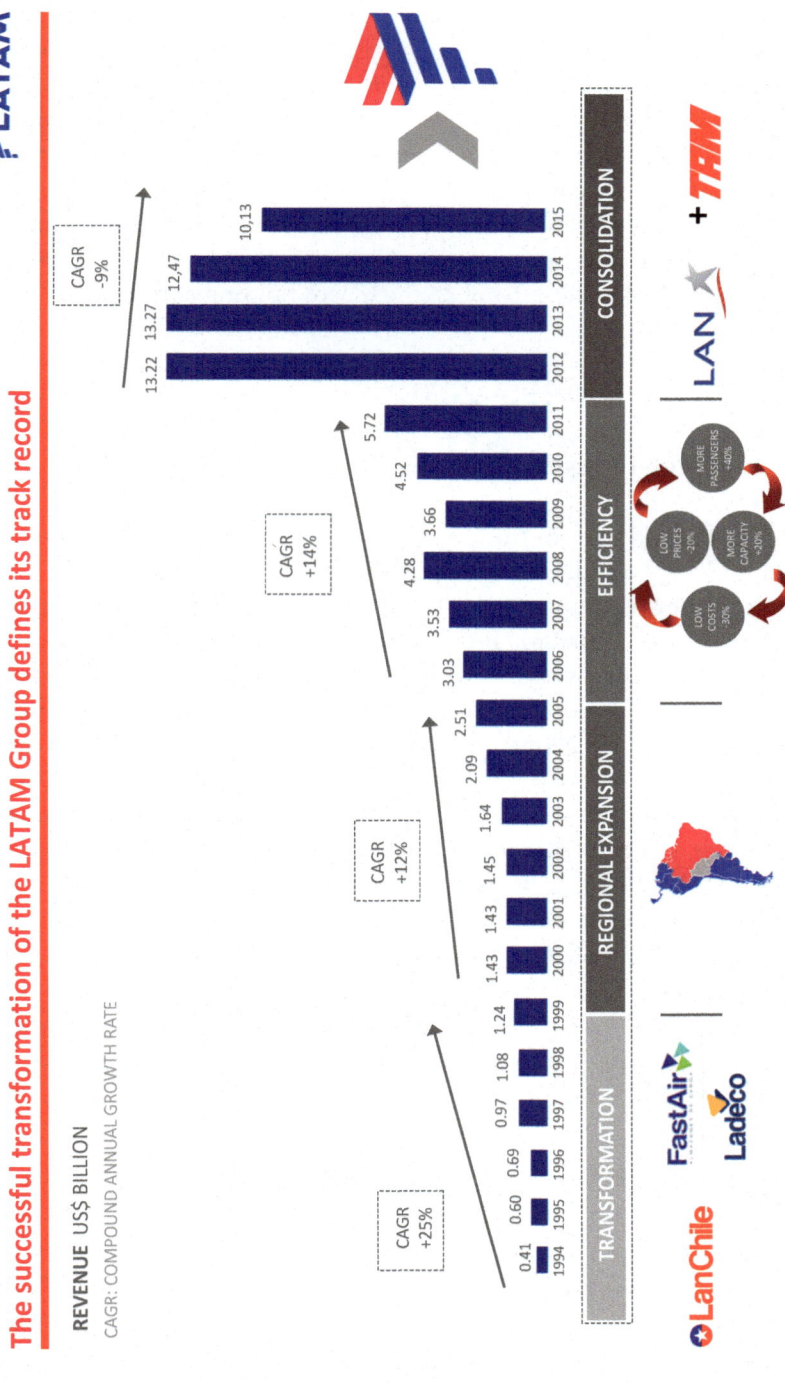

Fig. 11.1 The successful transformation of the LATAM Group defines its track record

In 1932, the company was renamed LAN Chile and became a state-owned company, starting international operations by flying to Buenos Aires, Argentina, in 1946. In addition, the first flight to the United States took place in 1958 and the first flight to Europe in 1970. In 1974, LAN Chile made its first nonstop flight across the South Pacific, connecting South America and Australia. This was a highly significant event for the company.

In 1989, the Chilean government privatized the airline, selling the majority interest to Icarosan and Scandinavian Airlines System (SAS). In 1994, LAN Chile was sold to its current owners, the Cueto holding company.

Recent History: 1995–2016

Transformation Phase: 1995–2000

One of the first activities in this phase was the merger of the companies LAN and LADECO—both devoted to passenger air transport—and FASTAIR—a freight air transport company. All three of them were Chilean companies. The smallest of these companies, FASTAIR, finally bought the other two. The reason for this merger was that LAN and LADECO shared traffic rights to São Paulo. Thus, LAN flew to this city on Tuesdays, Thursdays, and Saturdays, and LADECO flew on Mondays, Wednesdays, and Sundays. However, their Brazilian competitor, VARIG, flew on a daily basis. Chile had an open-market economy, and its air transport legislation strongly promoted competition. The merger enabled the integration of the few international rights owned by Chile—also including freight as another crucial element—thereby being able to compete under better conditions in the Latin American context.

In this regard, Enrique Cueto stated, "During this phase, in 1997 we listed the company on the New York Stock Exchange. At that time, we had two objectives in mind: margin improvement and growth. LAN and LADECO had good margins, but our business had to be internationalized. This gave rise to the second phase."

Regional Expansion Phase: 2000–2005

Chile is a small country, and the company had the maximum market share that could have been expected at that time. As Ignacio Cueto said: "We came to the conclusion that the only way to grow was to export this project to other countries." LAN Peru was therefore created, first participating in domestic flights in that country and subsequently adopting a similar strategy in Argentina, Ecuador, and Colombia.

In 2005, the company's senior managers observed that the Brazilian airline GOL and the Panamanian airline COPA had also been listed on the New York Stock Exchange. By then, "GOL was worth US$7 billion, TAM (another Brazilian company) US$5 billion, and LAN US$2.2 billion, while COPA was valued at US$1.6 billion" (Fig. 11.2).

Efficiency Phase: 2006–2011

The company became aware of the existence of a serious problem: while it was present in multiple countries—carrying both passengers and freight—it was scarcely valued on the market. Consequently, the Cueto brothers set a new goal: to enter the Brazilian market, despite the great difficulty of "buying another company, if one's own worth is between half and one third of the worth of the company you want to buy." Therefore, they decided to increase efficiency levels by increasing passenger numbers and reducing stops, since nonstop flights result in substantial cost reductions.

During this period, the company removed in-flight hot meals from its service. Enrique Cueto recalls,

> The consultant of a prestigious institution asked me, 'How much does the omelet that you offer at breakfast cost? I answered that it cost US$1 per passenger. 'No, Sir, you are wrong,' he said. 'Apart from saving one dollar per passenger, if you had no ovens on short-haul flights, you could include an additional row of seats; since your plane has 120 seats, the incorporation of 6 seats would generate an additional 5% more passengers.' And he added, 'Furthermore, free newspapers should no longer be available on your plane. Cleaning the airplane during transit stops takes 5 more minutes, because as newspapers are free of cost, the majority of the passengers leave them on their seats. If you can save 5 minutes from the time devoted to cleaning the plane, you could have one more flight every 12 short-haul flights.

The company put these suggestions into practice, and thanks to the ensuing cost reductions, it was able to lower the price of the ticket for the Santiago-Punta Arenas segment by 10%. The response was surprising: there was a 20% increase in the number of passengers. Many analysts indicated that this result was obtained just by chance. Ignacio Cueto recalls, "To verify this fact, we lowered the price by another 20%, and the number of passengers increased by 40%. As a result of this, we doubled our traffic in one month."

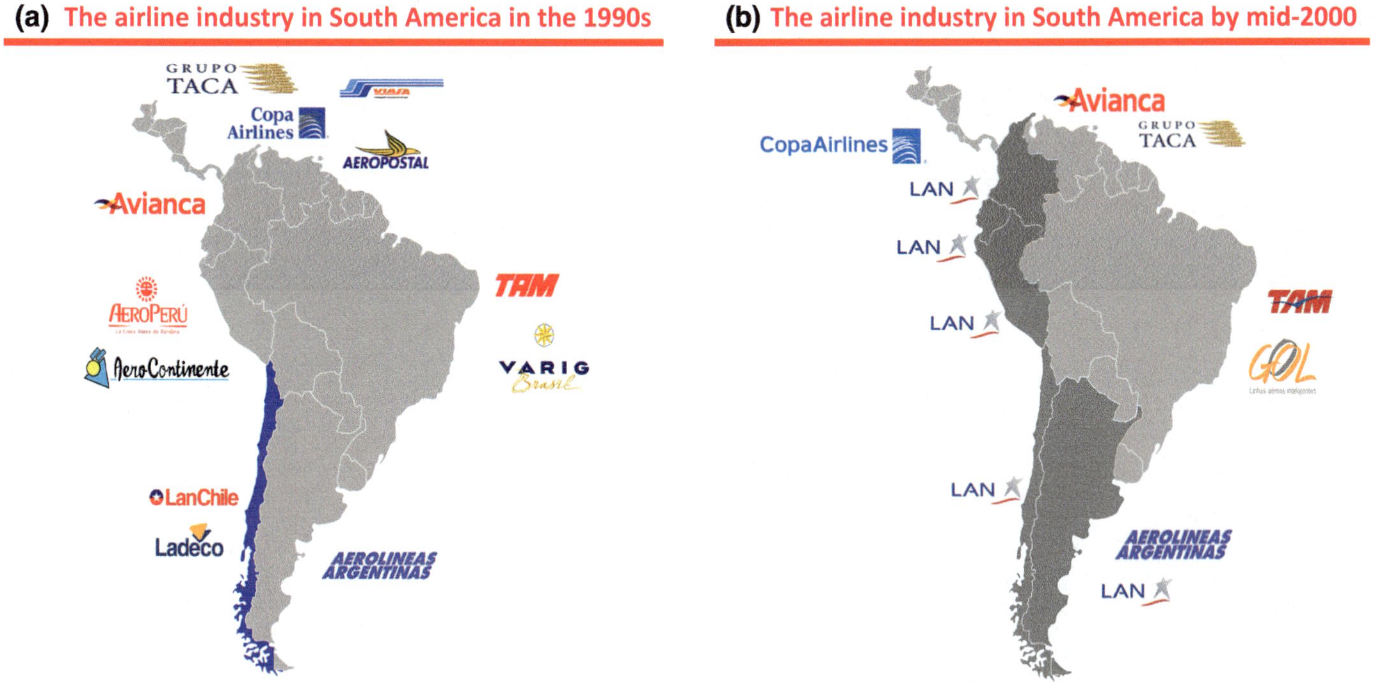

(a) The airline industry in South America in the 1990s

(b) The airline industry in South America by mid-2000

Fig. 11.2 (a) The airline industry in South America in the 1990s. (b) The airline industry in South America by mid-2000

During this period, the company managed both an efficiency and a profitability increase; the number of passengers rose by an annual 15% in all short-haul markets, which implied going from a domestic traffic of 3 million passengers to 10 million passengers in Chile. "We realized that a large part of the increase was accounted for by new passengers," said Ignacio Cueto.

Finally, the Cueto brothers fulfilled their objective. Their company was worth US$14 billion, while the Brazilian airlines GOL and TAM were worth US$700 million and US$1.5 billion, respectively. As a result, LAN could implement its consolidation model.

Consolidation Phase: 2011–2016

However, competition continued. LAN's presence in the South Pacific was continuously and increasingly challenged by other companies, especially in secondary cities, and the company was forced to withdraw and defend its positions.

Negotiations were held with VARIG and TAM to evaluate entry into Brazil or some other new market, for which an alliance with the Panamanian airline COPA was explored.

At the beginning of this phase, major economies in the region were facing serious economic problems, a situation that, according to Enrique Cueto, "did not knock us down because we had diversified into many markets" (Fig. 11.3).

This phase ends with the merger with TAM and can be summarized as follows: "One brand name, one continent, one network." There is no other airline in the world named after a continent (LATAM), and this makes it easier for passengers to fly across the region. LATAM is very attractive as a partner in Joint Business Agreements (JBAs), and this is why British Airways, American Airlines, or Qatar Airways, for example, are willing to form global alliances with LATAM. As illustrated by Ignacio Cueto, "Commercial aviation must be understood in the same way as the mobile phone industry: if our customers go to China, they will want to use a telephone, but since we cannot install antennas in that country, we must have a partner" (Fig. 11.4).

However, the implications of being a global airline as LATAM have continued, a fact attested to by the issue of 10% new shares that were fully acquired by Qatar Airways, as a result of which the company received US$600 million at the end of 2016. During this period, the industry in the region had poor results due to the crisis in Brazil, which affected all airlines operating in that country.

Under this scenario, such a substantial capital injection was highly attractive for LATAM and very beneficial for the Qatari company. Qatar Airways

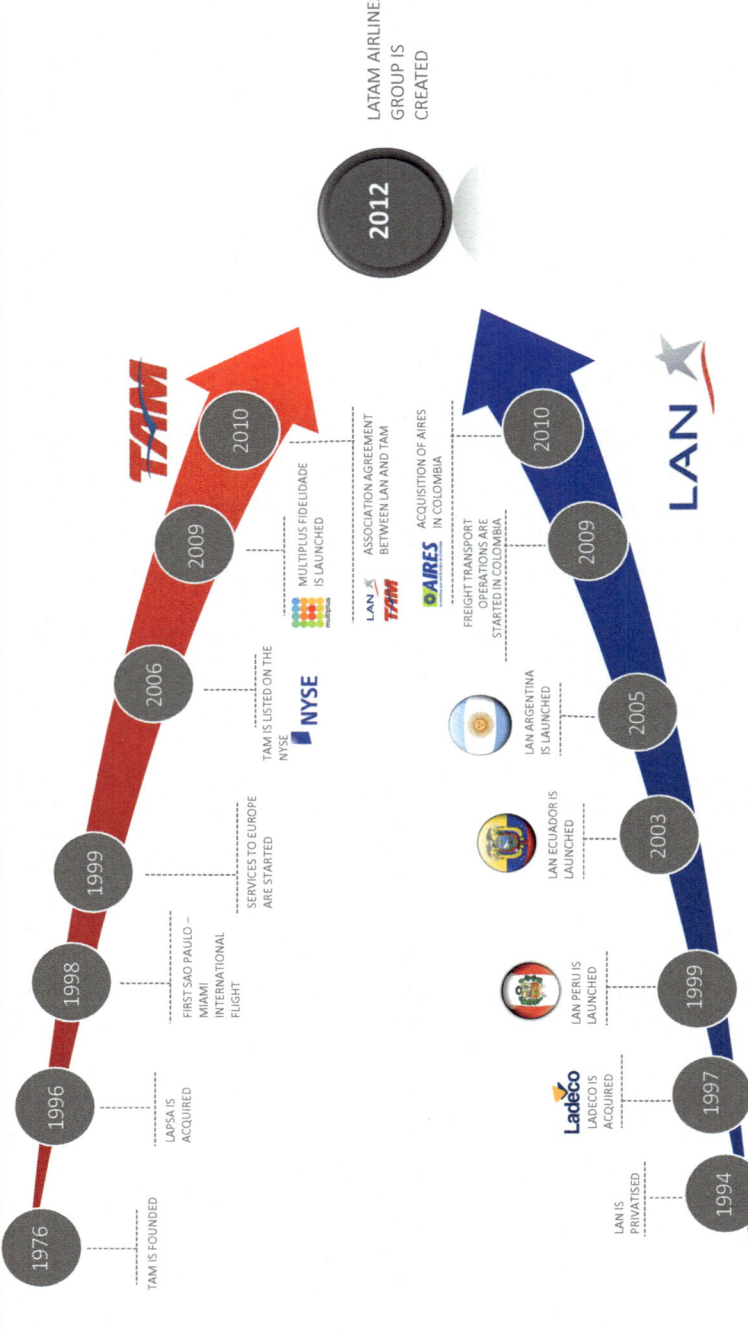

Fig. 11.3   Two South American carriers join forces to become the leading airline group in the region

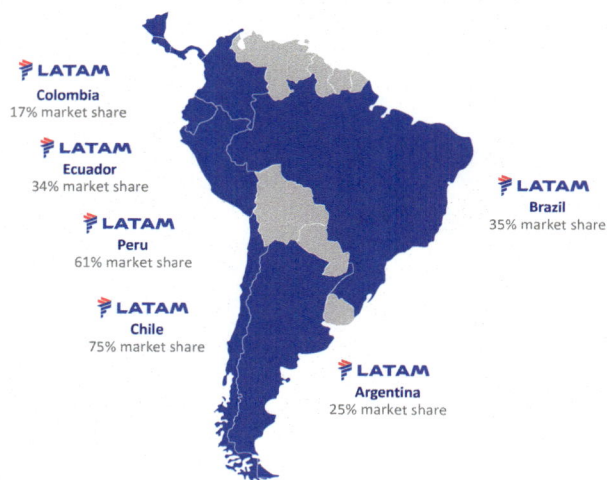

Fig. 11.4   LATAM GROUP/one brand name, one continent, one network

has a long-term vision under which South America is a region with tremendous growth potential, with LATAM being very well positioned. As explained by Gisela Escobar, LATAM's Corporate Affairs Manager, "This was a recognition by an investor with a long-term perspective of what we have constructed throughout the years. Qatar is a partner that gives us great confidence regarding the future, and this was also perceived in a very positive way by the market."

LATAM: Lessons Learned and the Future

At present, the company is entering into a phase focused on changing the domestic business model, transforming short-haul operations, concentrating on business class passengers, and getting passengers used to paying in accordance with the type of flight they prefer, for instance, with or without luggage, being among the first or last to board the plane, or what they want to eat and drink. This will undoubtedly also contribute to cost reductions, and hence lower fares.

"On the international market, we are working on Joint Business Agreements (JBAs) in order to get together and create a yet-larger network with American Airlines for flights to the United States from anywhere in South America, and

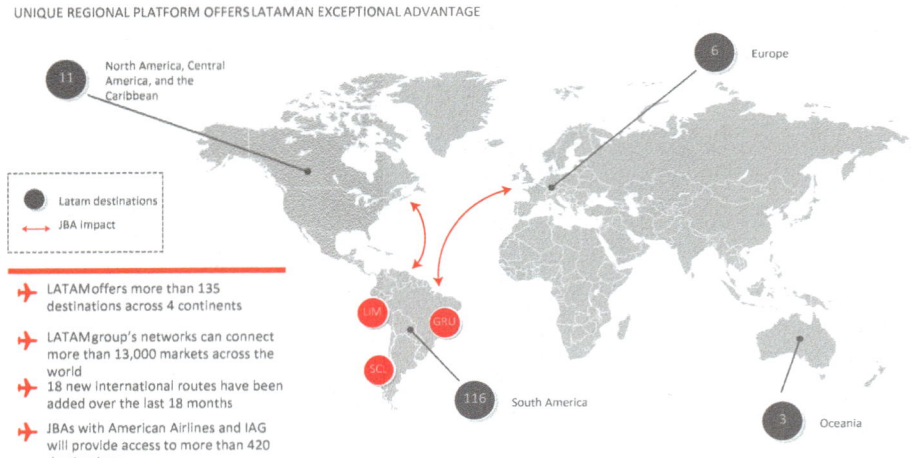

Fig. 11.5 The LATAM group continues to strengthen its networks through new routes and strategic alliances

with Iberia and British Airways for flights from anywhere in South America to Europe," said Enrique Cueto. Through JBAs, LATAM will gain access to more than 420 destinations (Fig. 11.5).

The airline industry in the world is currently much more than it was before; today, it is a public service on a massive scale.

Lessons Learned by LATAM

A relevant area in the development of creative thinking has been a shift from a subtractive to an additive approach.

From this perspective, LATAM has created different nodes, to subsequently put these nodes together, thereby creating a network connecting different cities in different countries and continents. Based on this network, it has created connections with other networks, attaining wider service coverage.

Needless to say, internationalization processes bring about cultural exchange and a clash between local and corporate executives, as a result of which strategic decisions are different in each country. In this regard, Enrique Cueto stated, "The most dramatic case was that of Brazil. It took us a long time to make strategic decisions, so in order to solve this problem we hired a company that told us which executives had to be replaced, which executives had to be hired, and how corporate ranks had to be distributed. In addition, it helped us with compensation issues. However, nothing turned out as we expected. Joining two cultures within one company is difficult."

Another drawback, and consequently another lesson learned, concerned the company's partners in each country. As these are foreign companies and current legislation usually prevents them from owning 100% of a company, they are compelled to choose local partners. This results in a big valuation problem due to the amount of cross-benefits and cross-costs associated with a holding company. Local partners are the owners of only a portion of the company in the country, not the entire holding company; consequently, the cost-benefit proportion can hardly be valued with respect to one country alone.

LATAM's partners made this mistake in relation to their first company in Peru. As a result, after two years, they closed the company, and no flights were carried out for some time. Finally, they reached an agreement with their original partner and resumed activities. Ignacio Cueto illustrates this as follows, "We learned the lesson; from now on, cross-costs and cross-benefits will be clearly explained to new partners." Caution must be exercised in deciding how to select and who to select as partners, bearing in mind a partner profile that represents the company and generates public confidence.

Public policies in each country are also considered crucial by the company, since the industry is one of the most regulated on the planet. The existence of simple, homogeneous regulations would be highly welcome in a globalized world, but in fact each country has a different regulatory framework, and this results in higher costs and increasingly stronger competition.

One of the most relevant policies is that concerning boarding taxes, which make tickets more expensive. Boarding taxes in Chile are among the highest in Latin America, representing as much as 50% of the ticket value. This means that no matter how much the company strives to reduce costs in order to lower fares and increase demand, this is offset by the high boarding taxes applied.

On the other hand, regulations raise barriers that hinder the required modernization and expeditiousness, generating a loss of new business options.

It should be noted that the airline industry offers quality employment to people in all the countries and cities where airports exist, generating true clusters stemming from the air transport business. The positive externalities associated with the growth of the airline business must be analyzed. The sole arrival of an airplane in a city brings well-being and economic development, not only through job creation, but also because this contributes to the development of the tourism industry in the region.

Projections

According to Gisela Escobar, LATAM's Corporate Affairs Manager, "Joint Business Agreements (JBAs) are long-term agreements and are here to stay."

The focus is on implementing agreements with airlines in other regions. This way, passengers can be assured that they will have global coverage, even if it is not the company itself that provides all the required transport. This enables a streamlined route offer and a more rational economic operation.

Air traffic growth rates in the United States and Europe range from 1% to 2% on an annual basis. In contrast, China and Latin America are estimated to grow at a 7% annual rate over the next 20 years. American and European airlines are aware of this, and it is unlikely that Qatar or European and American airlines will fly throughout Latin America. Instead, they will need distribution, and this is precisely what LATAM can offer.

On the other hand, the industry operates under a rationale based on "hubs," which implies the need to reach these points with airplanes having a large passenger capacity—ensuring lower costs—to subsequently distribute passengers from there to other destinations.

Another projection involves a strategic change with respect to the freight transport business. Before LATAM was created, LAN covered the freight transport business using either cargo planes or the free spaces available on passenger planes. For its part, TAM did not operate cargo planes but considered freight as an additional revenue, carrying cargo on its own passenger planes, where possible, and outsourcing the transport of the cargo they could not carry. The combination of both companies' business operations generated an immediate synergy because TAM's entire freight business was absorbed by LAN, enabling widespread cost reduction and providing a significantly improved freight-carrying capacity within the network. The operation of cargo planes could also be reduced because now TAM's aircraft hangars were available.

The trend toward low-cost airlines has started to reach the region. However, today there are no low-cost airlines plying the traditional model in South America, with the exception of the Colombian airline VIVA COLOMBIA. The rest of the airlines using the concept, such as GOL, SKY, and others, are not comparable with Ryanair. Gisela Escobar adds, "South America is a market that is becoming attractive for these ultra-low-cost airlines. We have observed groups of investors starting to develop business models such as VIVA COLOMBIA, while the entry of VIVA PERU has recently been announced.

In Chile, the entry of an airline called JETSMART, owned by VOLARIS, an ultra-low-cost Mexican air transport company, has been announced."

Projections indicate that corporate passengers grow one and a half times the rate of GDP, while non-corporate passengers grow seven times more. Consequently, LATAM is working on constructing a model enabling it to maintain corporate passengers—who pay five times more on average than non-corporate passengers but are not growing in numbers—and at the same time to take advantage of growth in terms of non-corporate passengers—who pay one fifth of what corporate passengers pay but grow seven times more.

It is important to underline that long-haul flights have no low-cost precedents. There was only one such flight between London and New York during the 1970s.

Conclusions

Over a period of 20 years, the company was able to progress from being a small company in a small country located at the end of the earth to becoming the 10th company in the world in terms of passengers carried, mainly due to the decisions made by its controlling shareholders, allowing the company to adapt to the major changes occurring in the world and to take advantage of the market opportunities detected.

Throughout the growth period, the company showed an ability to learn from its own mistakes to avoid repeating them. It also understood that each country is characterized by different cultural aspects, and that instead of hiring foreign executives and allocating them to the company's country of origin, hiring local professionals is preferable.

A company that opts for internationalization and requires business partners in countries where it is going to start operations must be very careful in defining the required profiles and developing the selection process.

Compliance with current legislation is also very important, as well as relationships with government authorities in each country where operations are carried out (Fig. 11.6).

Latin America currently represents 6% of the world's air traffic and has strong growth potential. Air traffic growth rates in the United States and Europe range from 1% to 2% on an annual basis; in contrast, China and Latin America are estimated to grow at a 7% annual rate over the next 20 years. This represents a big opportunity for a company such as LATAM, Latin America's leader.

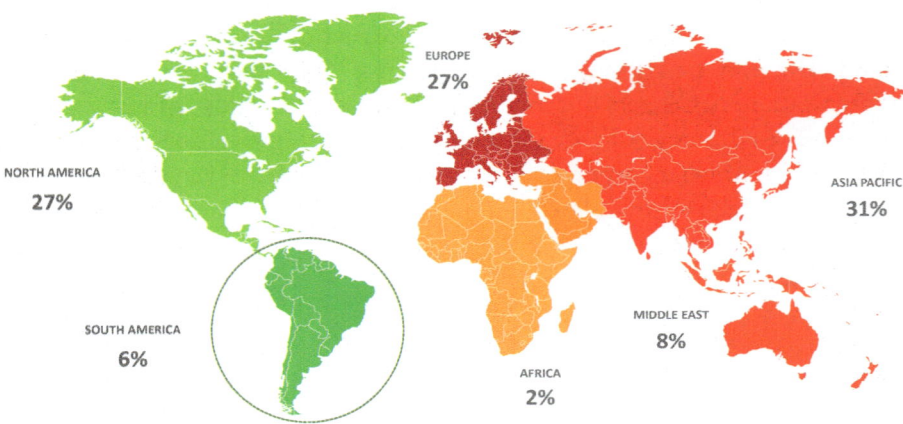

Fig. 11.6   South America is a small region

Further Bibliography

C. Larroulet y F. Mochón, Economía (Santiago, Chile: McGraw-Hill/Interamericana,2003).

J. Ardiles, De Empresa y Estrategia, Ideas y Casos (Santiago, Chile: Gráfica Metropolitana, 2012).

www.latamairlinesgroup.net

www.latam.com./es_cl

12

General Motors: Globalization, Disruption, and Sustainability

Daniel R. LeClair

Abstract Built originally for scale and efficiency, General Motors (GM) found itself ill-equipped to react quickly to companies exporting better, more fuel-efficient cars to the US. That, along with a global recession and credit crisis, nearly killed the company. Now it is confronted with the threat of disruption from not one source but from many—autonomous vehicles, electrification, and ride sharing.

This chapter considers the ongoing story of the iconic industrial corporation. It was selected for this volume not as the epitome of a modern global enterprise, but rather because of the range of issues that it now faces. A profoundly different global species is emerging. GM is now a smaller, more market-driven, and agile company that leverages its international network to innovate. It is more likely to be inspired by global sustainability challenges than by the blind pursuit of profits.

Scale and Efficiency: Bigger Is Better

By end of the 1970s General Motors' (GM) dominance in its home market was being seriously challenged by German and Japanese automakers exporting cars to the US in large numbers. Spiraling fuel prices encouraged consumer interest in the better, more fuel-efficient vehicles they offered. GM was

D. R. LeClair (✉)
AACSB International, Tampa, FL, USA
e-mail: dan.leclair@aacsb.edu

© The Author(s) 2018
S. Iñiguez de Onzoño, K. Ichijo (eds.), *Business Despite Borders*,
https://doi.org/10.1007/978-3-319-76306-4_12

making bigger, less economical cars and was slow to respond to the competitive threat. It had become too large and bureaucratic. In the US alone, GM employed more than 600,000 people; worldwide it employed more than 850,000 (AP 2009). In 1978 American automakers sold 12.87 million units and produced 82.3% of the cars purchased in the US. By 1982 they made only 6.95 million units, and their share had dropped to 72.1% (Foner and Garraty 1991). Between 1984 and 1986 GM's share of the US market shrank from 44% to 34% (Scaruffi 2013).

What happened next is well known. GM and the whole American automobile industry eventually went through a series of massive restructurings, with cutbacks in plant capacity and personnel. They increased focus on quality management processes and eventually invested in plant modernization and retooling. Companies began taking redesign more seriously and built cars that were smaller, more fuel efficient, and safer. GM made inroads globally, especially in emerging markets. But it was too late.

In 2008, a major recession hit the US and sparked a global credit crisis. Car sales cratered, and GM was in trouble, unable to attract private funding. The US Treasury offered a bridge loan, mandating that the company accelerate the restructuring of its US operations.

So how did GM come to find itself in such a difficult situation? To continue setting the scene, it is useful to start from the beginning.

GM was founded in 1908, just as Henry Ford introduced the Model T and moving assembly line process. Ford took an early lead in the industry based on its manufacturing advantage, which included significant economies of scale and its commitment to pay "$5 per day," more than double the market wage at the time. But thanks to pioneering managerial innovations by CEO Alfred P. Sloan, GM soon caught up and took over as the global market leader. Sloan wanted to produce a car "for every purse and purpose," and to achieve that he pioneered the multidivisional form, dividing the company into autonomous divisions by brands. He installed central organization functions deemed essential to the development and control of the corporation's activities. On these and other innovations, Sloan transformed GM into a company built for mass production, where scale and efficiency mattered most. The structure and culture he built would lay the foundations of GM's financial success and, according to many scholars, its eventual decline in the face of global competition.

Systematic strategic planning also played a crucial role in GM's development. In Sloan's process, each GM model was updated or redesigned annually. It worked well for GM initially, but over time the number of models and options proliferated. Its cars became bigger and heavier, as they were fitted with extra gadgets. Surface-level aesthetics took the place of functional design, as well as safety and economy objectives. Defects become routine. Not surprisingly, the 1960s brought new regulations covering a range of safety and emissions standards in the US. Industry leaders complained that these regulations stifled their ability to compete with Japanese and German firms.

Now the story has come back to the 1970s and the disastrous results that would follow. This version of how GM got there is admittedly a stylized one, ignoring numerous details in order to set the stage for the rest of this chapter. Nonetheless, it serves two purposes. First, it establishes an important connection between the strategy and objectives of GM, and the structure and culture developed to achieve them. Second, it introduces the first of three important characters in our story—Alfred P. Sloan, a larger-than-life CEO who famously said the primary object of the corporation was to make money, rather than motorcars.

Regionalization: The Reality of "Distance"

The second of the three main characters in our story is Theodore Levitt. He wrote in a now classic *Harvard Business Review* article published in 1983 that the globalization of markets is "at hand" and it will bring about the end of the multinational company. In its place will rise truly global companies that "sell the same things the same way everywhere." He argued that markets were drifting toward a homogenization of preferences and business methods, and that "success in world competition turns on efficiency in production, distribution, marketing, and management, and inevitably becomes focused on price" (Levitt 1983).

At the time it would have been easy to see Levitt's world emerging in the Japanese and German penetration of the US market. In fact, international integration in the industry did accelerate in the 1980s. However, it would not be the flat world Levitt described; instead, it is best characterized as regionalization, a strategy that combines countries to minimize within-group differences relative to differences between groups. Through regionalization strategies, companies are able to achieve some, though not all, of the efficiency gains from scale, while also exploiting differences through product adaptation. In other words, it was neither completely local nor completely global.

This approach was not inconsistent with GM's strategy. Early on under Sloan, the company added two brands to its domestic portfolio, Vauxhall Motors of Great Britain in 1925, and Adam Opel AG of Germany in 1929 (Associated Press 2009). By 1930, the company already had more than a dozen plants outside of the US (General Motors 2017). That was followed by a steady march toward scale economies and local adaptations. However, it wasn't until the 1980s that GM accelerated its globalization efforts, along with the industry as whole. In 1982, for example, GM made its largest expansion outside of North America when it opened a new complex in Zaragoza, Spain, to build the Opel Corsa (General Motors 2017). It added joint ventures in China and India, and took Saab and HUMMER into the GM family. The company expanded both the reach and variety of vehicles it sold worldwide (General Motors 2017).

The GM pattern illustrates that top automakers have long invested in manufacturing close to their customers. Just-in-time manufacturing also meant that suppliers followed. Local content requirements were also important, so much so that the patterns of regionalization in the auto industry have mostly been shaped by the integration of regional trade blocs to take advantage of the free-trade agreements. To be tariff-free under the North American Free Trade Agreement (NAFTA), for example, 62.5% of the content of a car must have been produced in the NAFTA region (*The Economist* 2017). Other political sensitivities, such as the importance of vehicle production in times of war, also favored local production, at least in the final assembly stages.

Distance can also be measured by differences across countries. Of course, there are cultural differences at work in the auto industry. There is the question of whether to design for driving on the left or the right. Then there is the infamous story about a company that, in order to cut costs, enabled the power windows to be operated only from the front seat. The car was designed for India where most car buyers had to be relatively wealthy—and tended to hire chauffeurs! Geography matters too, in determining, for example, whether air conditioning or an engine heater is needed. Differences in regulations have been particularly powerful in shaping adaptation in the automobile industry, determining minimum fuel economy standards and maximum emissions standards, for example.

In the regionalization of automobile strategies, emerging markets have been especially important in recent years. Established markets (like the US and Europe) are now responsible for less than half of all vehicle sales, and that is expected to drop to 40% by 2020. That means small vehicles, such as microcars and subcompact vehicles, will increase in popularity. More than 60% of these types of vehicles are sold in emerging markets, and more specifically in urban areas (Schwartz 2013).

Distances and differences will continue to matter in the global automotive landscape. But disruptive trends will likely change what matters most and bring about modifications in the regional aggregation strategies of automakers such as GM. The trouble is that there is no universally accepted view about what the disrupted future of mobility will look like.

Disruption: The Future Is Definitely Not What It Used to Be

The GM story has thus far been a fairly simple one. GM was built for scale and efficiency, and gravitated toward regionalization in its global strategy. Technology is changing that—the future of the auto industry is, as they say, not what it used to be.

There are multiple disruptive trends in the automobile industry, and it is not clear how and when they will converge. According to McKinsey and Company (2016), digitization, automation, and business model innovations that have revolutionized other industries will give rise to four disruptive technology-driven trends in the automotive sector: diverse mobility, autonomous driving, electrification, and connectivity. It would be impossible to outline each of these trends in detail. Instead, some brief explanations and simple examples are presented to explore the global evolution of GM.

First, attitudes toward automobiles have been changing. Car ownership is becoming less of a dream than a burden, especially among young people in densely populated urban locations, and that is increasing demand for car-share (e.g., Zipcar) and ride-share (e.g., Uber) services. For automakers, this means customers are moving from owning a vehicle to use for multiple purposes to wanting on-demand access to vehicles or rides depending on the purpose. Experts estimate that by 2030 one out of every ten cars sold could potentially be a shared vehicle (Gao et al. 2016). This will create new automobile segments based on purpose. For example, vehicles for ride-sharing services might be designed for higher utilization and additional passenger comfort. The car- and ride-share markets are still small. That is, they have huge potential. Of the three trillion vehicle-miles driven in America last year, only 0.15% were undertaken in ride-sharing services such as Uber and Lyft (*The Economist* 2017). That is expected to rise on continuing urbanization of the population, especially in developing economies.

Second, rapid advances in connectivity and other autonomous vehicle technologies will have a broad impact across the automotive sector. In the self-driving future, the car becomes a platform for drivers and passengers to use their time in transit to do other things, such as consume media and play games. Cars will be upgradable like computers and consumers will pay more attention to technological advances, creating new opportunities for aftermarket sales. Forecasts indicate that by 2020 more than 250 million connected cars will be on the road (Amelie 2017). And this is a wide open space, with experts estimating as many as 1700 highly disruptive startups in areas ranging from cybersecurity to sensors and parking (Singh 2017). However, the pace of autonomous vehicle market development will depend heavily on consumer understanding, as well as safety concerns and regulatory systems, all of which can be more local than global.

Third, there have been huge advances in the space of electrified vehicles. The market already has an array of such vehicles, and the technology has been improving. Ultimately, the long-term disruptive potential of electrified vehicles will depend not only on how much and in what direction the technology advances, but also on the development of local infrastructure (e.g., charging stations). And that will hinge on environmental policy and regulation. Regardless, electrification will have a major impact on sustainability, and will be discussed in more depth in the next section.

There are wildly different views about the disruptive potential of each of these trends for companies like GM that make cars. And these cover only a few of the most directly disruptive technologies. Further complicating the matter are new technologies cutting across the automotive value chain, impacting suppliers and distribution networks. These include everything from robots (disrupting production) to block chain (disrupting finance) and the Internet of Things (disrupting secondary markets); all are potentially relevant to the changing landscape of mobility.

For this case it is most useful to explore the interaction of disruption and globalization strategies. To start, most industry observers believe these trends will slow but not reverse the steady growth in global demand for automobiles. However, they all point to shifts in strategies for global segmentation and aggregation. The basis for segmentation will become more granular. For example, the city or sub-city level will become more important than countries or country groups. Local-level population density, traffic patterns, regulation (e.g., congestion fees), and the availability of parking will increase in importance for segmenting mobility markets.

Unfortunately, even the experts at McKinsey (2016) say "there is still no integrated perspective on how the industry will look in 10 to 15 years as result of these trends." For companies like GM, that leaves many strategic questions unanswered. What business or businesses will they ultimately be in? GM already considers itself a mobility company, rather than an automotive one. Who are they competing with? Toyota, Ford, and Tesla, or Google and Apple? Or is it Uber? Or any one of 1700 startups across the automotive and mobility space? Are they still a hardware company, or are they becoming a software firm—or both? Regardless, from this point forward the GM competitive landscape is irreversibly complicated by twin forces: the continuing push and pull of globalization along with the exponential growth and urgency of disruption.

Innovation: From Scale to Agility

GM was built largely on the benefits of scale and efficiency. With a presence in every major global market, it was among four global manufacturers (including Volkswagen, Toyota, and Renault-Nissan) that each produce about 10 million cars per year (*The Economist* 2017). Now, as discussed in the previous section, the industry is about to undergo a major transformation, although the ultimate destination is not clear. This section explores GM's response and the next phase of its evolution as a global species.

Most visibly, GM is getting smaller as a global enterprise. It is already out of Russia and Indonesia and has slowed operations in Thailand. In 2017 it announced a pullout of Europe, selling Opel to France's PSA Group. In May 2017 it decided to stop selling cars in India and to leave South Africa. Overall GM aims to pull back production to 8.5 million (*The Economist* 2017). Executives say the company can no longer be "all things to all people in all places." In addition to North America, GM is staying in China and, for the time being, Latin America. GM was huge, at one time bulging with more than 850,000 employees worldwide. Today it employs 225,000 people (General Motors 2017), less than half the size it once was.

Analysts usually welcome such market focus, the willingness to make tough choices about where to compete and not to compete. And the practice itself could be valuable to GM; gaining experience in quickly exiting markets could be profitable. But this case study does not benefit from digging more deeply into the financial management of GM. Instead, the intent is merely to draw attention to a larger story—one that will cause us to recall the corporation that Alfred Sloan built and the one that Levitt envisioned. It turns out that neither is useful when it comes to reinventing the GM of the future.

Buried among the articles about contraction are headlines like "GM says it's ready to produce self-driving cars" (Snavely 2017). The company had just finished making 130 self-driving Chevrolet Bolt test vehicles. GM's CEO and Chairman, Mary Barra, said: "The level of integration in these vehicles is on a par with any of our production vehicles, and that is a great advantage. In fact, no other company today has the unique and necessary combination of technology, engineering and manufacturing ability to build autonomous vehicles at scale" (Snavely 2017). The third and last character in our GM story has now been introduced.

And there have been other headlines, like "GM Buying Self-Driving Tech Startup for More Than $1 Billion" (Primack and K. Korosec 2016), which emphasized the company's commitment to autonomous vehicles. In January

2017, GM announced Book by Cadillac, a $1500 per month on-demand concierge subscription service for Cadillac cars and SUVs in New York. In 2016, GM launched Maven, its own car-sharing service to which it will "supply cars that customers can rent by the hour or for days" (Woodall 2017). By 2017 Maven was operating a fleet of about 10,000 GM vehicles in 17 US cities allowing customers to use a mobile app to locate and reserve a vehicle. Customers have already logged more than 130 million miles in Maven-branded GM vehicles. In 2016, GM invested $500 million in ride-hailing service Lyft (Reuters 2017). Again, GM supplies vehicles for Lyft drivers to rent on a short-term basis. The two companies are also working together on autonomous vehicle technology.

What's most interesting about Book and Maven? It is that GM is using hybrid strategies, combining physical with digital, while many other companies have responded to digital disruption by "straddling," creating a digital product or service, but keeping it distinct and separate from their core market.

Another media theme highlights investments in research and development (R&D). The company announced in 2012 that it would spend $1 billion on construction and renovations to its Warren Technical Center. The plans called for creating 2600 jobs in engineering, IT, and design (*Crain's* 2015). GM also opened its global research center in Shanghai in 2012. The focus of the GM China Advanced Technical Center is not only on China's auto market, but also on advanced electric car battery technology, taking advantage of the fact that "new energy" research has clustered in Northeast Asia (Shirouzu 2012).

The point is that for decades GM considered Warren to be the center of its commitment to R&D. But now it is just one part, albeit the most important one, of a global network of laboratories, science clusters, and collaborative relationships involving suppliers, governments, universities, and other partners. Considering the broad opportunities for disruption, the foci of this network have expanded beyond basic research and vehicle design and now include manufacturing and business model innovation.

Imagine the network as creating a marketplace of ideas and it is easy to grasp how GM Ventures creates value. Formed in 2010, it is "a business unit that makes investments in technology startup companies" (General Motors 2017). And a significant amount of the fund goes to internal startups, including "off-roadmap projects, game-changers, breakthrough innovations, high-risk projects, not things on the technology roadmap." Globalization has become more about the flow of ideas and less about scale and efficiency. As noted earlier, the startups disrupting the automotive industry are geographically scattered. Israel, for example, "has over 300 startups with a core focus on cybersecurity, smart mobility, artificial intelligence, smart city, and more." Over 50 ride-hailing startups have grown in the last year in Africa (Singh 2017).

GM's R&D experience illustrates the tensions between centralization and decentralization. While more centralized R&D can increase the likelihood of breakthrough advances, it can also cause a disconnect between R&D and company needs. It can be slow and cumbersome, and fall into the "valley of death" trap with technology deployment. On the other hand, decentralized structures can suffer inefficiencies from duplicated efforts, but this approach encourages alignment and has shorter time to market. The current GM objective favors decentralization, as it is focused on developing technologies that can be put into use in years, rather than decades. These examples also reinforce the importance of cross-border differences. For example, in R&D, relationships between industry, government, and academia can vary considerably across geographies. So globalization in the auto industry is no longer just about aggregating to manufacture cars in the right countries; it also means creating a global network supporting research and technology development and innovation.

Similar tensions arise in the overall corporate setting. Structurally, will GM be better positioned to compete in a disrupted industry by leveraging its century-long history with administrative hierarchies? Here the headlines are also helpful to surmise GM's direction. For example, the headline "Mary Barra shapes a new GM: Fast, focused, and decisive" appeared in the *Detroit Free Press* on June 25, 2017 (Phelan 2017). Then there was "Mary Barra is Remaking GM's Culture—and the Company Itself" in *Fast Company* on October 17, 2016, which outlined her plans to "replace a culture of blame and bureaucracy with one driven by accountability, speed, and collaboration" (Tetzeli 2017). The article also describes GM 2020, which builds cross-functional "co-labs" to address problems across the organization.

Sustainability: What Business Are You Really In?

This chapter has traced the global development of GM, an iconic industrial company, from its disciplined inception to today, a time of great uncertainty about its disrupted future. There is reason to believe that a new, more innovative type of global organization is emerging, one that is transforming itself from a company that seeks international markets to achieve scale economies to one that leverages global networks to be more innovative and agile. But something is missing.

Sloan's GM was built to make money. And we have seen in GM the power-ful and lasting impact that strategy can have on the structure and culture of a company. The company that Sloan built ultimately made it difficult for GM to compete when globalization accelerated in the 1980s. It took a bankruptcy and safety crisis to create an opportunity for change. But the opportunity for change is usually not enough. Perhaps the threat of disruption, combined with bold leadership, will be sufficient to set it on a new course. But will it be enough for the company to thrive? To what end will the company strive?

It is hard to believe profits can continue to serve as a meaningful purpose. Disruption has made it entirely unclear how best to make more of it. Some people suggest committing to an intense focus on customers. In fact, GM's current stated purpose is to "earn customers for life" (General Motors 2017). That is close, but there are signs that a larger purpose is emerging. According to Mary Barra in 2016, the disruption gives GM "an unprecedented opportu-nity to develop new mobility solutions that lead to a world with zero emis-sions, zero congestion and zero crashes."

There is a lot of power packed into that statement, which appeared in GM's 2016 Sustainability Report, aptly titled "Moving Forward." She focuses atten-tion on impact and crystalizes the transformation that GM is undertaking. A typical car company is concerned about meeting pollution standards (regulation), the customer driving experience (congestion), and customer safety (crashes). But a mobility company is inspired by the potential to elimi-nate pollution, congestion, and crashes. In GM's case, it can achieve these bold objectives by innovating in electric cars (e.g., Chevy Volt), building car-sharing and ride-sharing models (e.g., Maven) that put fewer cars on the roads, and advancing autonomous driving technologies (e.g., Cruise Automation). Car companies find it very hard to move away from defining success by the number of cars sold. As a mobility company, success could mean selling fewer cars, or none at all.

There are many ways to pursue sustainability. At the very least, auto com-panies can view compliance with emission requirements as an opportunity. Complying with the most stringent standards means a company can deploy a single norm and benefit from economies of scale. Staying at the cutting edge of regulation can put companies in a better position to work with regulators and spot business opportunities first. Ideally, sustainability-oriented compa-nies go further by driving sustainability product designs into supply chains. Ultimately, purpose-driven companies create new business models and plat-forms for sustainability.

It is useful at this stage to bring back Theodore Levitt, this time for a differ-ent article called "Marketing Myopia" (1960), in which he poses a simple question: What business are you really in? The question puts the business leader in the position of the customer, who, as Levitt was known to say, "doesn't want a quarter inch drill." Rather, "he wants a quarter inch hole" (Levitt 1960). We know Sloan's answer to Levitt's question; GM was in the business of making money rather than motorcars. For the new GM under Barra's leadership, the answer is mobility. And that is one giant step closer to sustainability than making cars to chase profits.

Conclusions and Takeaways

What came out of the Sloan years at GM has been institutionalized into our understanding of industrial companies. The ideas have been baked into the curricula of business schools around the world, and that by itself will influence the future of business. This case challenges these ideas and offers new insights into the complex interplay between global strategy, structure, and purpose. It encourages the reader to consider the underlying dynamics that could undermine an organization's capacity to change. Regardless of what eventually happens at GM, this case shows not only that it is possible to reinvent an iconic company, but also that doing so requires a larger vision. It requires redefining and elevating the purpose of the corporation.

This case offers three general takeaways for any manager:

- Build more agile, network-driven organizations when faced with disruptive technologies.
- Go beyond country-level groupings and identify meaningful segments based on more granular data.
- Define the business your company is really in and elevate it to create a meaningful purpose.

There are also some things to be learned from the small cast of characters involved. Certainly, the CEOs have shown that the job of leaders is not at all limited. As a whole, they have demonstrated the power of ideas, framing and reframing them while shaping the future of a company, an industry, and society.

References

T. Levitt, "The Globalization of Markets", *Harvard Business Review*, May/June 1983.

E. Foner and J. A. Garraty (eds), *The Reader's Companion to American History*, 1991. Accessed at: "Automobiles", History, http://www.history.com/topics/automobiles

P. Scaruffi, "A Timeline of the Automobile Industry", 2013. http://www.scaruffi.com/politics/cars.html

Associated Press, "GM: History of An Automaker", cnbc.com, June 1, 2009. http://www.cnbc.com/id/30962998

General Motors, "Acceleration: 1910–1929". http://www.gmchina.com/gm/en/aboutGM/GMGlobal/historyandheritage/acceleration. Accessed June 24, 2017.

General Motors, "Globalization: 1980–1999". http://www.gmchina.com/gm/en/aboutGM/GMGlobal/historyandheritage/globalization. Accessed June 24, 2017.

"The pitfalls of renegotiating NAFTA", *The Economist*, February 11 2017. https://www.economist.com/news/americas/21716660-revision-north-american-trade-deal-will-not-give-donald-trump-what-he-wants

A. Schwartz, "3 Ways the Automotive Industry Will Change By 2020", *FastCompany*, September 5, 2013. https://www.fastcompany.com/3016741/3-ways-the-automotive-industry-will-change-by-2020

P. Gao, H-W Kaas, D. Mohr and D. Wee, "Disruptive trends that will transform the auto industry", *McKinsey&Company*, January 2016. http://www.mckinsey.com/industries/automotive-and-assembly/our-insights/disruptive-trends-that-will-transform-the-auto-industry

"General Motors is getting smaller but more profitable", *The Economist*, June 24, 2017. https://www.economist.com/news/business/21723869-yet-uncertainty-about-how-it-will-fare-future-still-weighs-its-share-price-general-motors

M. Amelie, "These 3 megatrends are disrupting the automotive industry", *Planet Entrepreneur*, February 15, 2017. http://planet.telenor.com/2017/02/15/these-3-megatrends-are-disrupting-the-automotive-industry/

S. Singh, "Over 1,700 start-ups are disruption the automotive industry", *Forbes*, May 17, 2017. https://www.forbes.com/sites/sarwantsingh/2017/05/17/over-1700-start-ups-are-disrupting-the-automotive-industry/#27f9cb525145

General Motors, "Our Company". http://www.gm.com/company/about-gm.html. Accessed June 24, 2017.

B. Snavely, "GM says it's ready to mass produce self-driving cars", *Detroit Free Press*, June 13, 2017. https://www.usatoday.com/story/money/cars/2017/06/13/general-motors-we-can-mass-produce-self-driving-cars-now/102805626/

D. Primack and K. Korosec, "GM Buying Self-Driving Tech Startup for More Than $1 Billion", *Fortune*, Mar 11, 2016. http://fortune.com/2016/03/11/gm-buying-self-driving-tech-startup-for-more-than-1-billion/

B. Woodall, "GM's Cadillac to start car subscription service in NYC", *Technology News*, January 5, 2017. http://www.reuters.com/article/us-gm-cadillac-idUSKBN14P2BD

Reuters, "GM has pieces in place to develop ride sharing, self-driving cars", *Fortune*, June 1, 2017. http://fortune.com/2016/06/01/gm-ride-sharing-self-driving-cars/

"GM to invest $1 billion, create 2,600 jobs at Warren tech center", *Crains Detroit Business*, May 14, 2015. http://www.crainsdetroit.com/article/20150514/NEWS/150519917/gm-to-invest-1-billion-create-2600-jobs-at-warren-tech-center

N. Shirouzu, "GM opens China research center to focus on 'new energy'", *Reuters*, November 29, 2012. http://www.reuters.com/article/us-autos-china-gm-idUS-BRE8AS09920121129

General Motors, "About Us"GM Ventures. http://www.gmventures.com/. Accessed June 24, 2017.

M. Phelan, "Mary Barra shapes a new GM: fast, focused, and decisive", *Detroit Free Press*, June 25, 2017. http://www.freep.com/story/money/cars/mark-phelan/2017/06/04/mary-barra-general-motors/352853001/

General Motors, *Moving forward: General Motors* 2016 *Sustainability Report*, 2016. http://www.gmsustainability.com/_pdf/downloads/GM_2016_SR.pdf

R. Tetzeli, "Mary Barra is remaking GM's culture—and the company itself", *Fast Company*, May 23, 2017. https://www.fastcompany.com/3064064/mary-barra-is-remaking-gms-culture-and-the-company-itself

T. Levitt, "Marketing myopia" *Harvard Business Review*, 38, July/August 1960.

13

Unconventional Internationalization of Huawei: The Role of Core Values

Ziliang Deng, Yufeng Zou, and Ji-Ye Mao

Abstract This chapter discusses how corporate core values enable an emerging market enterprise to enter sophisticated international markets and achieve technology and brand upgrade. The chapter starts with a brief introduction of Huawei. The main body of the chapter first examines the manifestation of its core values, namely "staying customer-centric" and "inspiring dedication". We then discuss how core values support the strategy implementation of Huawei in terms of local immersion, dynamic location choices, and heavy investment in research and development. By sketching the essential elements of the internationalization strategies of Huawei, the chapter not only extends the academic literature on emerging market multinational enterprises (MNEs) but also enriches the knowledge of managers working in such MNEs.

Background

Huawei, the first China-headquartered multinational enterprise (MNE), whose overseas sales contribution to its global revenue is more than its home country sales, has become a role model for emerging market firms to enter the international market. Huawei has accomplished a remarkable achievement in the global markets with an unconventional internationalization process. In

Z. Deng • Y. Zou • J.-Y. Mao (✉)
Renmin Business School, Renmin University of China, Beijing, China
e-mail: maojiye@rmbs.ruc.edu.cn

© The Author(s) 2018
S. Iñiguez de Onzoño, K. Ichijo (eds.), *Business Despite Borders*,
https://doi.org/10.1007/978-3-319-76306-4_13

Table 13.1 Financial indicators of Huawei (CNY million)

	2010	2011	2012	2013	2014	2015	2016
Total revenue	**182,548**	**203,929**	**220,198**	**239,025**	**288,197**	**395,009**	**521,574**
By product							
Carrier business	145,800	150,145	160,093	164,947	192,073	235,113	290,561
Corporate business	5834	9164	11,530	15,238	19,391	27,610	40,666
Consumer business	30,914	44,620	48,376	56,618	75,100	125,194	179,808
Others	0	170	199	2222	1633	7092	10,539
By region							
China	62,143	65,565	73,579	82,785	108,881	167,690	236,512
Overseas	120,405	138,364	146,619	156,240	179,316	227,319	285,062
EMEA	n.a.	n.a.	77,414	84,006	100,990	127,719	156,509
Asia Pacific	n.a.	n.a.	37,359	38,691	42,424	49,403	67,500
America	n.a.	n.a.	31,846	29,346	30,852	38,910	44,082
Others	n.a.	n.a.	0	4197	5050	11,287	16,971
Net profit	**24,716**	**11,647**	**15,624**	**21,003**	**27,866**	**36,910**	**37,052**
Cash flow	**31,555**	**17,826**	**24,969**	**22,554**	**41,755**	**52,300**	**49,218**
Total assets	**178,984**	**193.283**	**210,006**	**231,532**	**309,773**	**372,155**	**443,634**
Owner's equity	**69,400**	**66,228**	**75,024**	**86,266**	**99,985**	**119,069**	**140,133**

Source: Annual reports of Huawei for various years. "EMEA" refers to Europe, the Middle East, and Africa

1987 a veteran engineer, Mr. Zhengfei Ren, founded Huawei with 21,000 yuan (approximately US$5000 at that time), importing Private Branch Exchange switches from Hong Kong and reselling them to the Mainland Chinese market. No one imagined that the company could compete head-to-head with the telecom giants such as Ericsson. In 2017, 30 years after the inception of the firm, Huawei has become a leading ICT solution provider with more than 180,000 employees, connecting a third of the world's population located in more than 170 countries and regions (Table 13.1).[1]

What are the indispensable elements in the internationalization strategies of Huawei as an evident latecomer in the global telecom industry full of strong incumbent brands? In the following sections, we explain how Huawei, as an emerging market MNE, has leveraged its core values and implemented a portfolio of internationalization strategies.[2]

Core Values

Staying Customer-Centric

The success of Huawei in internationalization lies in its unwavering adherence to its core values of "staying customer-centric, inspiring dedication".[3] Staying customer-centric sounds simple and plain, and is known to every entrepreneur or manager. However, probably no other enterprise has implemented it as resolutely and radically as Huawei.

Huawei employees wholeheartedly embraced that core value of staying customer-centric after a painful journey of fighting for potential clients with the global giants in the telecom equipment industry. When Huawei was founded in 1987, it was a tiny kayak in the massive ocean of telecoms and had no R&D team on telephone switches until four years later. Huawei after-sale managers had to respond quickly to clients to overcompensate for the imperfections of new products. Therefore, for a long time, Huawei was not known for its product quality but its superior maintenance services.

Relentlessly rapid response to customers has been key for the growth of Huawei's overseas businesses. In February 2008, the representative office of Huawei in Switzerland received a request for a proposal from Swisscom. Huawei submitted a business proposal with more than 1000 pages. The project manager, Aiguo Duan, worked more than 12 hours a day for more than 40 consecutive days and updated the implementation specification PowerPoint file with 300 pages after 28 revisions. By contrast, the rivals of Huawei only provided a PowerPoint file with 90 pages after 9 revisions. Finally, Huawei won the Swisscom bid, and its network products successfully entered the Swiss market (Duan 2017).

A senior manager in the European market stated that "several years ago, a Spanish telecom firm approached us for help. That firm had collaborated with Ericsson for 20 years and had asked Ericsson to improve the mobile phone signals along the high-speed railway between Madrid and Seville with innovative technologies for continuous signal coverage. Ericsson needed 16 months to develop the technologies and deliver the entire project. It happened that Huawei had just finished a similar project in Shanghai, China. Huawei only spent three months tackling the technological challenges and built 17 base stations along the 22-kilomoter railway between Shanghai city center and Shanghai Pudong Airport. Huawei invited the engineer team of the Spanish client to take the train in Shanghai and experience Huawei technology. The client was impressed by Huawei's innovation speed and complained that the major telecom giants had been spoiled and become slow in their response to clients' demands".

Inspiring Dedication

Staying customer-centric involves much more dedication to the global business. Huawei personnel have contributed remarkable efforts and delivered equipment and services to the Earth's forbidden zones. For example, Huawei has built base stations on Mount Everest at an altitude of 6500 meters, which is 1300 meters higher than Everest Base Camp (the highest point for non-athlete tourists). In February 2017, founder Zhengfei Ren, aged 73, personally visited Huawei employees working at the Base Camp (Ren 2017).

In April 2011, three weeks after the Japanese tsunami and nuclear accident, the affected regions urgently needed telecom networks to be restored. But most of the telecom equipment providers had withdrawn. While high risks of nuclear radiation still existed, Huawei manager Guangxie Yuan led a small team with three Japanese employees to the central area of the affected region and built dozens of new base stations to provide the victim shelters with coverage within four days (Yuan 2017).

In war zones and regions on high terrorist alerts, Huawei employees have also worked hard to satisfy customers' need. In April 2007, Hua Li was simultaneously in charge of projects in the Faisalabad and Multan regions of Pakistan. Li spent three days supervising the project in Faisalabad and three days in Multan. Li and his colleagues had to travel between these two cities overnight to save time. His bodyguard was a veteran captain, who coordinated with local police officers and police cars in five different regions to escort Li's trucks (Huawei People 2017).

Huawei has designed rigorous promotion institutions to ensure the implementation of internationalization strategies. More than half of Huawei's global sales are contributed by the overseas market; having a significant portion of experienced senior managers in the headquarters is important. Approximately 10 years ago, Huawei implemented a new policy regarding management promotion. Any manager who held a position at or above level three must have overseas experience with at least three consecutive years. If a manager does not have such an experience, he or she must resign within a year and gain international exposure abroad.

Behind international market exploration, Huawei has constructed highly dedicated support teams in finance and accounting, human resource management, and visa preparation. Take the visa department as an example. Huawei first sent market managers to overseas markets in 2000, sparking an exponential growth in the demand for visas. In 2016 alone, more than 40,000 Huawei employees visited overseas countries for short visits or long-term employment. Chinese passport holders must apply for visas in more than 80% of countries and regions in the world, even for a short-term visit. In response, Huawei set up a dedicated visa department. Qingzhi Tian, who set up the visa department, has been working for Huawei for 18 years, and her mobile phone has always been on 24/7. It has become the norm for Tian and her colleagues to work during weekends when urgent visa applications are sent in. Several years ago, a finance manager called from overseas for help on a Friday. The manager asked the visa team to provide detailed information, such as the entire history of entry into and exit from that country of each Huawei employee due to an urgent lawsuit from the local taxation office. Tian and her colleagues worked through the night, and carefully searched the visa database, ticket office, employee safeguard database, and HR database, and provided all of the information required on the Saturday morning. The visa information helped the overseas subsidiary in providing solid evidence and avoiding any taxation penalty.

Huawei has boldly dispersed its shares to its employees from an early stage to ensure their devotion. Huawei is a private enterprise whose shareholders include Zhengfei Ren (with 1.4% shares) and 81,144 employees (with a combined 98.6% shares) as of 31 December 2016. According to Huawei's 2016 Annual Report, total personnel expenses (including salaries, bonuses, and dividends) for all 180,000 employees in 2016 was 121,872 million CNY; thus, the expense per capita was 716,894 CNY (equivalent to 104,000 USD, approximately) (Huawei 2017). According to the Chinese National Bureau of Statistics 2017), the average annual income per employee in a private firm in the telecom and IT sectors in China was only 57,719 CNY in 2015. This extremely high income has provided strong incentives for Huawei employees to be fully engaged with the company's global business expansion.

Huawei's Internationalization Process

Local Immersion

Centered on its core values, Huawei has adopted unconventional internationalization strategies, featuring local immersion, dynamic location choices, and intensive demand-driven R&D. Huawei has been recruiting native employees in overseas markets from day one of its internationalization process. Driven by the customer-centric core value, Huawei learned the importance of understanding the local culture and public relationships through local employees. In countries and regions outside China, the localization rate of employees was more than 71% in 2016 (Huawei Annual Report 2016). The UK subsidiary has approximately 1500 employees in 2017, 70% of whom are locally recruited (C114 2015).

Huawei has encouraged its employees to enhance their local cultural awareness. A senior manager said: "When I was assigned to Hong Kong in 2000, I couldn't understand Cantonese Chinese at all. So I communicated with my clients in English. Soon, I realized that wasn't the way to do business – why should two Chinese speak with each other using English? Then I started to learn Cantonese. But I was too busy to attend language classes. So I grasped every opportunity to practice spoken Cantonese, with taxi drivers, with local employees, and with my clients. In the first three months, whenever my telephone rang, my colleagues all laughed at me before I picked up the phone, because I was about to speak my awfully pronounced Cantonese again. But after about nine months, I could understand about 70% and speak about 50%. After two years, after I communicated with a Hong Kong client in Cantonese, he actually thought I was a local as my pronunciation was so authentic. I firmly believe that my language practice helped me a lot in getting orders for Huawei".

Globalized knowledge sourcing has also been a powerful mechanism for Huawei to obtain exposure to the best local talent and most advanced technological teams for the local market. By 2016 Huawei had built 15 independent research centers and 36 joint research centers around the globe, including facilities in the USA, Finland, Colombia, India, Russia, and Turkey. In October 2015 Huawei signed a partnership with the University of Manchester to jointly develop graphene technologies for better performance in 5G technologies (University of Manchester 2015). By October 2016 Huawei had invested nearly 10 million pounds in academic research in the UK (Dai 2016). By 2017 Huawei has had 62,519 patents granted, approximately 35% of which are outside China (Huawei 2017). In 2010, Huawei launched the Huawei Innovation Research Program to sponsor novel research in universities and research institutions in the areas of information and communications technology. By the end of 2016, 100 fellows from the Institute of Electrical and Electronics Engineers and the Association of Computing Machinery have participated in the Program. In 2016, Huawei announced a long-term strategic partnership with a German premium lens brand, Leica Camera, to enhance the dual camera photography technologies of Huawei smartphones and to beat its major competitors, namely, Apple and Samsung (Leica Camera 2016).

Dynamic Location Choice: From Periphery to Core Countries

The internationalization of Huawei, as a latecomer, had to focus on markets that had been neglected or given up by strong incumbents (e.g., Lucent and Siemens), such as the "periphery" markets in emerging economies or less developed economies. Many of those markets are notorious for their low living standards, unstable institutional environment, and uncertain business prospects. Doing business in those markets tends to require the sacrifice of work-life balance and extreme patience from Huawei pioneer expatriates. One year after Huawei entered its first overseas market in Hong Kong in 1996, Huawei sent a sales team with approximately 100 members to Russia, at a time when the market involved huge uncertainties after the collapse of the Soviet Union. Huawei also invested 30 million USD to set up an international joint venture in Brazil. Along this international expansion path, Huawei entered more countries, such as Ecuador in 1999 and Venezuela in 2004. According to the 2015 Annual Report, major market growth was obtained from emerging markets, such as China, the Middle East, Africa, India, the Philippines, Thailand, Mexico, Argentina, and Peru (Huawei 2016).

Huawei started its business in Europe in 2001 when the European market had a strong demand for equipment and network upgrading to the 3G standard. Hence, a new window of opportunity was opened to Huawei, which usually offered its products at a lower price than its competitors. Having accumulated market experience and reputation in collaborating with small firms in the UK, France, and the Netherlands, Huawei became an approved global supplier of prestigious brands such as Vodafone, British Telecom, and Deutsche Telekom in 2004 and during subsequent years. Endorsed by those top brands, the overseas orders of Huawei boomed. In 2005, its international sales exceeded sales in its home market for the first time.

The experience in periphery markets provided a precious opportunity for Huawei to learn to transfer core values and best practices from its home market to overseas locations. According to a senior manager who has been in charge of the European market, "in the first 10 years of the internationalization journey, during the period 1997-2006, Huawei virtually made no profits at all form overseas markets. It was only after obtaining the halo effect of collaborating with top European brands that Huawei started to witness a rapid growth in overseas sales and profit. Our patience and perseverance in those less promising markets finally paid off. Our potential clients would easily build trust on Huawei's brand whenever they saw our contracts with top brands such as Vodafone and our sample projects for those top brands. The branding spillover effects were so strong that by around the year 2010, Huawei's market share in many countries had become the absolute leader. Typically, Huawei occupies more than 50% of the market share, leaving the rest to be shared by rivals such as Ericsson and Nokia. But we have to admit that emerging markets and less developed markets provided a learning platform to test the waters and cultivate internationalized talents at a relatively low cost in the early years of our internationalization journey. But solely relying on those markets will not help an emerging multinational fly high. I firmly believe that an emerging market MNE must build up a strong reputation and brands before thinking about expanding sales and profit growth".

A strong home market is the key to being able to sustain international market entries. According to an unnamed senior manager, setting up a representative office with ten employees in Germany entails an expense of approximately five million euros per year. However, setting up the same office in a less developed market involves a fraction of that cost. For any emerging market MNEs, to directly rush into the most developed markets would be a formidable challenge. The process model or stage model of internationalization (Johanson and Vahlne 1977) apparently applies to the Huawei case. Huawei's Nepal business took approximately 25 years to break even (Ren 2017). A former Western European manager stated that "An emerging market firm planning international expansion must have strong cash flow and deep pockets in its home market, so that it may tolerate losses in the international markets for an average of about 10 years. In the case of Huawei, home market profits subsidized overseas markets from 1997 to 2008".

The USA is the most difficult market for Huawei to enter due to cybersecurity concerns and ideological conflicts. In 2008 Huawei's attempt to team up with Bain Capital to acquire 3Com was terminated by an inter-agency watchdog, the Committee on Foreign Investment of the US (CFIUS). In 2010 Huawei and another Chinese telecom firm, ZTE, were excluded from the five-billion USD contract to construct a 4G network for Sprint Nextel. Several US senators even sent letters to President Obama to express their concerns regarding the potential threat caused by the penetration of Chinese firms into US telecom infrastructure (Lublin and Riace 2013). In 2011, CFIUS demanded that Huawei cancel its acquisition of an asset from an American computer company. The process had been completed in 2010 but was not disclosed to CFIUS on time. Finally, Huawei had to bow to CFIUS and exit the deal. After seven months of investigation, the Intelligence Committee of the US House of Representatives released a report on 8 October 2012, explicitly warning that "private-sector entities in the United States are strongly encouraged to consider the long-term security risks associated with doing business with either ZTE or Huawei for equipment or services. U.S. network providers and systems developers are strongly encouraged to seek other vendors for their projects" (US House of Representatives 2012).

Overcoming the debacle of these blocks in the US market will take a long time and will heavily depend on an improvement in US–China diplomatic ties. Huawei has had to bring its major business plan for that market to an indefinite halt. At the same time, Huawei has focused on exploring the

European market to improve its international image. Moreover, Huawei has been trying to enhance its consumer products (mainly smartphones) in the US market to revert its image of opaqueness. David Strehlow, the VP of Marketing of Huawei Digital Home Product, admitted at the CBSI Conference in Langfang, China, on 18 May 2017 that Huawei lacked stable and long-term collaboration with the major network carriers such as AT&T; for this reason, realizing the brand spillover from consumer business (mainly cell phones) to carrier and corporate businesses (e.g., telecom equipment) will take time.[4]

Intensive Customer-Driven R&D

Huawei has been investing more than 10% of its total sales in R&D facilities to satisfy customers' current and potential needs every year since the company specified its minimum R&D intensity at 10% in the 1998 Huawei Basic Law. The Law outlined the core values and essential strategies of Huawei after three years of discussion and revisions. Huawei's 2016 Annual Report states explicitly: "We do not decrease investment in innovation based on fluctuations in short-term business performance or short-term financial results". In 2016 its R&D expenditures reached an unprecedented level of CNY 76,391 million, which constitutes 14.6% of sales value, dwarfing most of the technologically leading multinationals in the world. The composition of Huawei employees appears to be "dumbbell-shaped". A total of 45% of the 18,000 Huawei employees are engaged in R&D activities, approximately 35% are engaged in the sales and marketing services, and approximately 20% are assigned to the manufacturing of core components and administrative services.

The R&D team, which is heavily driven by the international market demand and competition, responds by developing its own components and products with indigenous proprietary knowledge. For example, Huawei has been developing its own brand in smartphone chipset, Kirin, since 2010. In 2017, all of its high-end smartphones in the P series and Mate series (the mainstream Huawei series sold in the developed overseas markets) used its own Kirin chipsets. Moreover, "Huawei has employed Kirin chipsets in 80% of its system equipment", a senior manager of Huawei stated during our interview. "Despite the huge R&D sunk costs, the marginal cost of a Kirin chipset, which is outsourced to a Taiwanese manufacturer, is just a 10th of the counterpart designed and manufactured by a chipset firm". After Apple and Samsung, Huawei is the third major smartphone brand that has its own chipsets. The technological advantages enable Huawei to be more responsive by tailoring its chipsets for the fast-changing and internationally diverse market demand. When Huawei desperately explored the European market in 2003, the fourth and smallest Dutch telecom firm, Telfort, found that its server room was too small to accommodate sufficient 3G servers. Nokia and Ericsson refused to develop small-sized servers for Telfort. Huawei designed a distributed base station system for that company. This innovative system was adopted by Vodafone's Spanish subsidiary in 2006. The fourth generation of the system (Single RAN) fully unleashed its market potential after 2008 (C114 2014). The market share of Huawei in the European wireless market, which is supported by its technological leadership, rapidly increased from 9% in 2010 to 33% in 2012, becoming the unshakable market leader.

Enabled by intensive R&D investment, Huawei has endeavored to position itself as a company that offers products and equipment that are equivalent to the best brands but at a slightly lower price and with superior service. A former country representative of South Korea said during our interview in April 2017 that "we realized that Huawei could not compete purely on a price basis. In the Korean market back in 2001, the local clients were extremely picky on the equipment quality. They usually implemented a set of rigorous tests on all potential providers' products. If a firm's product quality couldn't meet their expectation, they wouldn't even bother inviting that firm to quote a price. That is so-called 'technology first, commerce second'. The same market rules apply to the European and North American markets". Only after convincing advanced clients in the major markets with the highest level of product quality, for example, Vodafone, BT, and Deutsche Telekom, did Huawei start to enjoy the magnificent halo effects of its prestigious business partners and witness an explosive boom in overseas orders.

Conclusions

As a China-headquartered leading information and communications technology solutions provider, Huawei has a unique internationalization experience to share with other emerging market firms that are enthusiastically eyeing dynamic international markets. Starting as a grassroots local sales company without any technology or brand in 1987, Huawei began to actively explore international opportunities after ten years of local operations in its home market (C114 2015). The internationalization process cannot be readily explained by any established internationalization theory alone. Instead, it calls for a new theory to support the internationalization strategies of emerging market MNEs. This case study sketched a framework with which to summarize the key elements

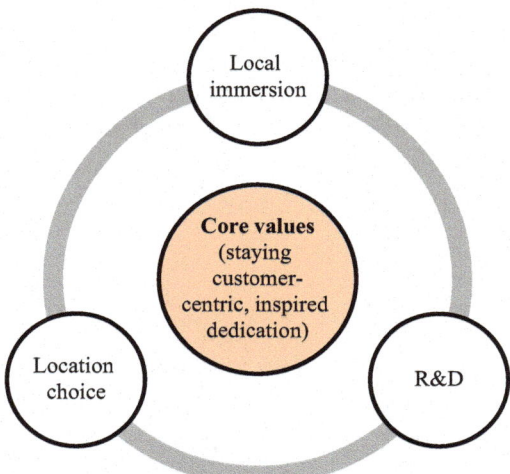

Fig. 13.1 Huawei's internationalization: core values and strategies. (Source: The authors)

that constitute the solid foundation of Huawei's exceptional internationalization performance (Fig. 13.1).

The core values of Huawei have undoubtedly played a crucial role in every major step along its internationalization journey. Particularly, always staying customer-centric, dedication, and perseverance are the most important factors underpinning Huawei's rapid growth in international markets with rather strong gatekeepers. Local immersion effectively helps an emerging market multinational enterprise understand local market demand and tailor its products. Location choice from periphery to core markets enables the infant emerging market multinational enterprise to avoid competing with strong rivals in their main battlefield early on. Instead, it helped Huawei to accumulate international experience beforehand. Finally, intensive customer-centric R&D input justifies the emergence of Huawei as a true technological leader and sustainable global player given that the ICT field has been dynamically changing almost on a daily basis.

Nonetheless, the sustainability and generalizability of Huawei's international success are still subject to many challenges. First, given that 71% of Huawei's overseas employees are localized, whether the local employees appreciate the core values of Huawei, especially dedication and perseverance, manifested by endless overtime and sufficient devotion to work in war zones and in the world's least developed regions, becomes a daunting challenge. Second, the consumer business (mainly smartphones) has increasingly contributed to Huawei's revenue (34.5% in 2016 compared to 16.9% in 2010), which might place the old Huawei model on a shaky ground. In its traditional carrier network area, only approximately 500 networks exist in the global market. However, several billion potential consumers are in the consumer business, which could overstretch the attention of Huawei's management team and divert their strategic focus from industrial leadership to short-term consumer market profitability.

Notes

1. Huawei's official website provides a full list of main milestones in its internationalization process (http://www.huawei.com/en/about-huawei/milestone). Accessed 12 June 2017.
2. We collected information from media reports, books, and public speeches of Zhengfei Ren and his colleagues, Huawei's annual reports, and Huawei Xinsheng's online community. Moreover, in April 2017, we visited the headquarters of Huawei in Shenzhen and interviewed three senior managers who had worked as overseas country-level managers in Asia, Europe, and Africa in the past 15 years. We have kept their names anonymous for privacy purposes.
3. "Staying customer-centric and inspiring dedication" has been the most frequently quoted value on the Huawei website and in its annual reports, although a more recent full expression of its core values is "staying customer-centric, inspiring dedication, persevering, and growing by self-reflection" (De Cremer and Tao 2015). This chapter will focus on these two values.
4. One of the authors communicated with David Strehlow during the meeting.

References

Huawei. 2017. "Corporate information: What do we stand for?" http://www.huawei.com/en/about-huawei. Accessed 14 June 2017.

D. De Cremer and T. Tao. 2015. Huawei's Culture Is the Key to Its Success. Harvard Business Review online. 11 June. https://hbr.org/2015/06/huaweis-culture-is-the-key-to-its-success. Accessed on 28 May 2017.

A. Duan. 2017. "See the opportunities" (in Chinese). http://app.huawei.com/paper/newspaper/newsPaperPage.do?method=showNewHwrPaperInfo&newsInfo=34994&sortId=1&commentLanguage=. Accessed 23 May 2017.

Z. Ren, 2017. "The speeches of Zhengfei Ren in Thailand and Nepal". http://xinsheng.huawei.com/cn/index.php?app=forum&mod=Detail&act=index&id=3384225&search_result =. Accessed 28 May 2017.

G. Yuan. 2017. "The unforgettable earthquake". http://app.huawei.com/paper/newspaper/newsPaperPage.do?method=showNewHwrPaperInfo&newsInfo=35254&sortId=1&commentLanguage=1. Accessed 23 May 2017.

Huawei People. 2017. "Career World", huawei.com http://xinsheng.huawei.com/cn/index.php?app=forum&mod=Detail&act=index&id=3378621&search_result=1. Accessed 23 May 2017.

Huawei. 2017. 2016 Annual Report. 30 March.

National Bureau of Statistics of China. 2017. http://data.stats.gov.cn/easyquery.htm?cn=C01. Accessed 28 May 2017.

C114. 2015. "President Xi Jinping visits Huawei UK". 22 October. http://www.c114.net/news/126/a924022.html. Accessed 28 May 2017.

University of Manchester. 2015. "Huawei signs partnership with University to develop graphene-based technologies". http://www.manchester.ac.uk/discover/news/huawei-signs-partnership-with-university-to-develop-graphene-based-technologies/. Accessed 27 May 2017.

T. Dai. 2016. "University tie-ups unleash innovation". China Daily. 25 October. http://www.chinadaily.com.cn/business/tech/2016-10/25/content_27162750.htm. Accessed 28 May 2017.

Huawei. 2017. "Research & Development". http://www.huawei.com/en/about-huawei/research-development. Accessed 27 May 2017.

Leica Camera. 2016. "Huawei and Leica Camera announce long-term technology partnership for the reinvention of smartphone photography". https://en.leica-camera.com/Company/Press-Centre/Press-Releases/Press-Releases-2016/Press-Release-HUAWEI-and-Leica-Camera-announcelong-term-technology-partnership-for-the-reinvention-of-smartphone-photography. Accessed 27 May 2017.

Huawei. 2016. 2015 Annual Report. 22 March.

J. Johanson & J.-E. Vahlne. 1977. "The internationalization process of the firm-a model of knowledge development and increasing foreign market commitments". *Journal of International Business Studies*, 8(1): 23.

J. Lublin & S. Riace. 2013. "Security Fear Kills Huawei Bid in U.S." Wall Street Journal. https://www.wsj.com/articles/SB10001424052748704353504575596611547810220. Accessed 25 May 2017.

US House of Representatives. 2012. Investigative Report on the U.S. National Security Issues Posed by Chinese Telecommunications Companies Huawei and ZTE.

C114. 2014. "Huawei enters the European market". http://www.c114.net/news/16/a852173.html. Accessed 25 May 2017.

14

People, Purpose, and Performance at Barry-Wehmiller: Business as a Powerful Force for Good

Nick Van Dam and Eileen M. Rogers

Abstract Bob Chapman, Chairman of the Board and CEO of Barry-Wehmiller, looked out over the Rocky Mountains from the deck of his home in Aspen, reflecting on all that he and his team members had accomplished over the past decades. By adopting a unique set of value-creating strategies over the past 30 years and, more recently, embracing a culture of 'Truly Human Leadership,' Barry-Wehmiller had created a robust organization that delivered value to all of its stakeholders—from its almost 12,000 global team members and their families, to their customers, shareholders, vendors, and suppliers, and to the communities in which they conduct business. While proud of achieving more than 14% compound annual return for its shareholders over three decades, Chapman and his team had come to see that true success should be measured by the way they touch the lives of people.

Along their journey to create a sustainable business grounded in people-centric practices, Chapman and his team realized their profound responsibility for the lives entrusted to them as leaders and how their leadership significantly impacted not only the time people spent at work but also their health and

Chapter based on an interview with Bob Chapman (June 21, 2017); existing articles and videos; website Barry-Wehmiller; and the book *Everybody Matters* (New York, NY: Penguin, 2015)

N. Van Dam (✉)
Nyenrode Business University, Breukelen, the Netherlands
e-mail: N.vDam@nyenrode.nl

E. M. Rogers
LeadershipSigma, Madrid, Spain

© The Author(s) 2018
S. Iñiguez de Onzoño, K. Ichijo (eds.), *Business Despite Borders*,
https://doi.org/10.1007/978-3-319-76306-4_14

193

family life. After testing and refining ground-breaking leadership practices on the 90-plus companies Barry-Wehmiller has acquired through the years, their challenge is to ensure that Truly Human Leadership becomes firmly integrated into the DNA of the Barry-Wehmiller global leadership practices. In addition, they wanted to inspire other organizations to adopt their approach—ensuring that business becomes a powerful force for good in the world by letting people know that who they are and what they do matters!

Truly Human Leadership

In 1969, Bob Chapman joined his father Bill Chapman, owner and CEO of Barry-Wehmiller, in an 84-year-old company that produced machinery primarily for the beer industry. The company was in a precarious financial position, with $20 million in revenues and a rapid decline in demand for its products. Prior to this, during Bob's traditional business education, he had earned his degree in accounting at Indiana University, gained his CPA, received an MBA from Michigan, and then joined Price Waterhouse as an auditor. In other words, he studied typical business practices, as taught at most business schools, where they prepare students for a very traditional business journey focused on creating shareholder value.

After the unexpected death of his father in 1975, Bob became CEO of the 90-year-old company and described the situation as: "I assumed the leadership of a company that was struggling to define and create its future. In reaction to my father's death, I was deeply motivated to make something of the company for the sake of my father's legacy."

For the first 20 years in this role, Bob pursued the traditional management practices that he had learned from his business school education to address the challenges, resulting in an increase in organic revenues from $20 million to $70 million in a span of 5 years. This dramatic growth led to significant unexpected difficulties, resulting in a financial crisis in 1983. Then, following a tough refinancing of the business, a new strategy—to grow through acquisition despite the lack of financial resources or experience—was embraced in 1984. In 1987, an initial series of acquisitions was spun off on the London Stock Exchange. The offering was 31 times oversubscribed—overcoming the continued lack of financial resources that impeded the acquisition strategy and providing the solid funding and credibility to enhance the acquisition strategy going forward.

In 1988, starting again with its original base business of brewery equipment that was not part of the London IPO, the team created a vision of an ideal packaging equipment company, shaped by the experiences under his leadership. Barry-Wehmiller began acquiring companies that had experienced similar challenges to those that they had faced and overcome. After 10 years of pursuing this unique strategy, the company had grown from $20 million to $200 million. Around this time, Bob began to see and appreciate the profound impact he could have on the lives of the Barry-Wehmiller associates (the employees). He had never been taught, or heard, or been made aware, that the way we lead our businesses has a profound impact on the lives of our associates and their families. He had thought that professional lives and personal lives were totally separate. Therefore, his management practices were focused on creating value for the shareholders. He believed that his ultimate 'success' was defined by traditional measures of money, power, and position.

However, Bob came to the realization that 'leadership' is quite different from 'management.' Gradually, the difference became more and more apparent. Through careful observation and practice, posing serious questions, gathering teams to consider new ways of defining leadership, Bob developed an awareness of his responsibility for the people in his care. This discovery came parallel to his initiatives to embrace the profound responsibility of parenting his blended family of six children. These parallel learnings evolved over the late 1980s and 1990s when he realized that what he was learning about parenting was really about 'leadership,' or as he defined leadership—caring for those lives entrusted to him. These parallel experiences of how to genuinely care for others provided the foundation for Truly Human Leadership.

This new understanding of the role of leadership and the impact that leadership has on the lives of his company associates made him realize that what he had been taught—management—was the 'manipulation of others for my success' and that in businesses, people who were 'managed' this way were simply 'functions' for achieving traditional success. His thinking was evolving rapidly and he came to the realization that leadership is the stewardship of those whom we have the privilege of leading. He believes that leadership success is not defined by money, power, and position, but by 'the impact we have on others' lives for good.' But Bob was clearly not prepared by his traditional business education to be a good steward of those lives in the organization. The journey to master this new perspective was a deliberate, intense, and ultimately transformative journey for Bob, his team, and his company.

Generally all over the world in organizations today, most people go home from work stressed, enduring the grind of their job, feeling they are not cared for, but just seen as a number—not as a human being. The Barry-Wehmiller team learned that when people are treated this way in organizations for 40 hours a week, it impacts the way they treat their families when they get home. The health and societal costs of this are enormous. According to

Gallup—a staggering 87% of employees worldwide are not engaged. This means they are not happy, and there is a significant relationship between work, stress, health, and family relationships. If people are in an ongoing work situation that is negative, they have a higher potential for negative health consequences. About 80% of people experience stress on the job and this is far and away the single major source of stress for adults. Sadly, it has escalated progressively over the past few decades, as layoffs become more common in overcoming business strategy shortcomings and/or meeting short-term financial targets.

It may not be a surprise that there is a 20% increase in heart attacks on Monday mornings as an 'outpouring' of stress hormones, such as cortisol and adrenaline, occurs within working people on Monday (Sinatra). Less than 50% of employees trust the company they work for, which is extremely demotivating and very costly for organizations (Myers 2016). Finally, according to NetScape, the #1 reason people quit their jobs is a bad boss or negative immediate supervisor. Therefore according to the Mayo Clinic, "Your supervisor is more important to your health than your primary care physician".

Much of this stress is the result of the standard business practice of cutting costs to meet financial targets, with routine layoffs and frequent 'right sizing,' 'restructurings,' 'delayering,' or 'digital transformation'—all euphemisms for eliminating jobs in a bid to survive. The outcome of these practices, graphically on view in the 'rust belt' of the United States, includes communities hollowed out, factories failing, stores and restaurants boarded up, school registrations below capacity, and young people leaving in search of opportunity and jobs—a race to the bottom. Chapman saw that conventional management practices were actually suppressing the creative gifts of people and hindering the contributions they were both willing and able to make. Bob stated: "My business education ignored the question of how my leadership would impact the lives of other people; instead, it was mostly about how to use people to further my own financial success" (Chapman and Sisodia 2015).

An insightful comment is made by Simon Sinek (author of *Leaders Eat Last*): "In the military, they give medals to those who are willing to sacrifice themselves, so that others might gain. In business, we give bonuses to those that are willing to sacrifice others so that they may gain." In addition, Rogers and Van Dam state that the new discoveries in cognitive neuroscience and positive psychology prove that the way we organize, manage, motivate, and reward work in our traditional hierarchical organizations is diametrically opposed to the way the human brain works (Rogers and van Dam 2015). Thus, the results we see today—disengagement and ill-health caused by stress and discouragement at work.

Many companies espouse the value that "Our people are our most important asset." However, most decisions in these organizations are made without truly considering the impact on people's lives, or on the communities and the businesses who serve them. This pretense creates a culture of self-interest, fear, cynicism, and paranoia. That is why leadership matters, because leaders set and *are* the culture!

Many CEOs and leaders question how they might embrace a culture of People, Purpose, and Performance:

- How can I change my profit-driven, product-focused, management-heavy, low-engagement business into one where everybody matters? One that sends people home fulfilled, knowing that what they do and who they are matters?
- What are the culture and practices of a business where:
  - Success is measured by the impact on the lives of people whose lives we touch.
  - Everyone's potential for leadership is recognized, and these leaders are actively embraced and developed.
  - People are inspired to discover their gifts, share their gifts, and be appreciated for doing so.
  - Leadership looks for the goodness in the organization every day and holds it up to encourage others.
  - Everybody comes in every day committed to continuous improvement and helping others realize their gifts!

The Journey Toward Truly Human Leadership at Barry-Wehmiller

Bob Chapman's pattern was established early in his life, with a habit of asking probing questions of others, listening carefully to their response …, and then quickly taking appropriate and positive action toward the newly understood goal. Another of Bob's resources has been his insightful observation of human activity and an ability to interpret what he sees into positive and inspiring real business practices that benefit his company's associates and ultimately have a positive impact on business performance. As a result, led by Bob Chapman and his team, Barry-Wehmiller has gone through a vibrant transformation, *from business as usual* to *business as a 'driver for human achievement and fulfillment.'*

With this combination of a curious mind, deep listening skills, and a series of epiphanies (or flashes of insight), Bob began a transformative journey from 'management to leadership,' which created a new paradigm of leadership and ultimately led to new business models, especially related to global mergers and acquisitions.

Epiphany #1—It was 1997, and it was 'March Madness' in the United States …, which is a playoff series of the best college basketball teams. Bob was observing the people of a new acquisition who would soon gather for his introductory remarks. Everyone was talking about the latest games, with lots of laughter, camaraderie, and positive energy. As the time drew closer to 8:00 am when the work was to begin, he could see and hear the joy leave the room and their bodies.

Immediately, Bob asked himself the question "Why can't work be fun?" In the moment, simply in the spirit of fun, he proposed a game: Whoever sold the most parts in a week would win a small cash award, and if the team made its goal for the week, everybody on the team would get a monetary team award. Although there were many objections and potential problems expressed, Chapman had ready, thoughtful answers. The result—within the first quarter, sales were up more that 20%. Chapman states: "When people started having fun in their roles, we saw an enhancement in their customer service skills, and they went home each night knowing how they had done and how the team was doing … they could <u>see</u> the score and know when they were winning!." Thus the journey began.

Soon thereafter, Chapman drove another innovation in sales, working with his team in the development of a new sales system. Of course, it began with another question: "What should our ideal approach to the market look like?" so Bob prepared a list of the ideal behaviors of a sales executive. Then in his standard approach, he brought together a diverse group of team members to refine this list. They came up with statements such as: "We will operate from a foundation of trust. Shared information and open communication create competitive advantage. Participate when you can add value." They then put in a whole system solution: reorganizing the sales organization; sharing through a new communication medium; putting in place an incentive structure to inspire/reward the right behavior; and developing a recognition and celebration program for those who embraced the change. The program was named E3—*Efficient*-to serve the market, *Enhance*-the sales experience, *Empower*-the sales executives.

Epiphany #2—Chapman was in church listening in awe to his mentor, Ed Salmon. With sudden insight, he appreciated that he was inspired by someone who had only one hour a week with him. Then he thought about his business and recognized that his organization had people in its care for at least 40 hours a week. His realization was: "Business <u>can</u> be one of the most powerful forces for good in our society!" But this would be possible only if everyone in the organization accepted the profound responsibility they have as leaders for positively impacting the people whose lives they touch.

One early result was the development of the Guiding Principles of Leadership (GPL) in 2002. The goal was to articulate ideal leadership behaviors so that, based on their experiences at work, Barry-Wehmiller team members could lead richer, and more fulfilling lives. To begin this journey, Chapman brought together a team of thoughtful leaders. Prior to their discussion, they were sent materials to prepare their thinking about the true nature and role of leadership. The result of the collaborative gathering was a profound statement that stands as the cornerstone of Barry-Wehmiller's culture, its GPL. Chapman stated, and the team leaders aligned with the touchstone, that "Everything we do in the future needs to be in harmony with these principles" (Table 14.1).

Table 14.1 The Guiding Principles of Leadership at Barry-Wehmiller

The guiding principles of leadership
We measure success by the way we touch the lives of people.
A clear and compelling vision, embodied with a sustainable business model, which fosters personal growth.
Leadership creates a dynamic environment that:
Is based on **trust**
Brings out and **celebrates** the best in each individual
Allows for teams and individuals to have a **meaningful role**
Inspires a sense of **pride**
Challenges individuals and teams
Liberates everyone to realize 'true success'
Positive, insightful communication empowers individuals and teams along the journey.
Measurables allow individuals and teams to relate to their contribution to the realization of the vision.
Treat people **superbly** and compensate them fairly.
Leaders are called to be visionaries, coaches, mentors, teachers, and students.
As your sphere of influence grows, so grows your responsibility for **stewardship** of the guiding principles.
We are committed to our employees' personal growth.
Barry-Wehmiller
Building A **better world** through business

Chapman B., & Sisodia, R. *Everybody Matters* (New York, NY: Penguin, 2015) pg. 53

Today, every decision that impacts peoples' lives is weighed against these principles.

In 2005, a next step was taken to ensure that this ideal culture was increasingly understood and embraced by all in the organization. A new reward and recognition program enabled all to begin to act on these principles. This was named GPL (Guiding Principles of Leadership)—SSR and it came again from Chapman's wish to embed this focus on goodness into the organizational culture and his desire to instill fun and appreciation into the associates' lives. In this process, colleagues were to nominate peers for the award, and a committee of their peers chose the winner, based on what their colleagues had written about their behavior and actions exemplifying the principles of the GPL. The winner received the opportunity to drive a bright yellow Chevrolet SSR for a week, a very public way of recognizing the associate for their goodness. Anyone nominated, whether they win or not, receives a document showing what their colleagues wrote about them…encouraging them to ever higher levels of engagement and performance.

Of course the impact on the culture was profound … all were now looking for the goodness in their co-workers, not what is wrong, failing, or disappointing. This let people know that the organization believes in them and that they are together going to build a better future. In fact, Rogers & van Dam note that a brain process has been uncovered that demonstrates that whatever a person pays attention to builds new gray matter in the brain, at any age. This is termed 'attention density.' So if the entire organization is focused on the goodness in others, individually and collectively the people are growing new brain capacity to recognize goodness in more diverse and deeper ways (Rogers and van Dam 2015).

This approach has expanded into a new 'recognize, reward, and celebrate' culture through another epiphany of Chapman's. Watching a Green Bay Packers football game, he saw the quarterback throw a long pass into the end zone. The receiver caught the ball, and this was then followed by a big celebration of his accomplishment. Once again, Chapman reflected on the fact that the receiver was aided by many people to be in a position to make that successful catch. And he contemplated about how such gratitude to the team members, who made an individual success possible, could be recognized at Barry-Wehmiller. That became the basis for the Barry-Wehmiller High Five award, which celebrates a team member's contribution to any given achievement. Anyone can be nominated. Those nominated for recognition receive a small gift, such as a certificate for a dinner for two, but what they appreciate more than the gift is that a letter is sent to their family citing their goodness that has been recognized by their peers.

A major test of their commitment to the GPL came in the crucible of the economic collapse of 2007–2009. The company faced a 35% downturn in new equipment orders and the backlog declined rapidly as customers canceled or put orders on hold. Layoffs seemed inevitable.

However, the moral compass of the GPL gave the leadership team a vision that they didn't have before. It equipped them to face the crisis with a much deeper sense of responsibility for the lives in their care. Chapman posed a question: "What would a caring family do when faced with such a crisis?" He and his team came to the conclusion that all family members would pull together and each take a bit of the sacrifice for the survival of the whole family.

Thus, the leadership team identified several initiatives to act on this principle in harmony with their vision. The initiatives included, among others:

- Voluntary unpaid furlough—four weeks for all associates. According to Bill Ury, author of '*Getting to Yes,*' "It was a moment of creativity. It was a moment of confidence. People felt a moment of security and realized, 'OK people really do count in this company!'" (Chapman and Sisodia 2015).
- Suspension of the 401 K match and executive bonuses.
- Deployment of a vigorous communication strategy through messages delivered by video.
- Chapman reduced his own salary from $875,000 to $10,500.
- Offers of generous voluntary separations were made to those associates close to retirement.

The idea of shared sacrifice was widely accepted and the implementation throughout the global organization was quick and smooth. These practices generated almost $20 million in cost-savings, and everybody's livelihood was protected. Fear of the future was eliminated, replaced by positive feelings of safety, gratitude, and togetherness. Aligning their leadership practices with the GPL, it was affirmed that the associates were valued and that the leadership team was acting to preserve their future. Interestingly, this crisis allowed them to demonstrate that this vision statement was not just a paper on a wall, but that the company was going to 'walk the talk' even in tough times.

Another result, amazingly: fiscal 2010 was a record year in earnings! Operating profits recovered strongly and they felt ethically compelled to make a decision on how to financially reward all of the associates. The first suggestion was to give everyone a check, but it made more sense to the leadership team and the union to reimburse everyone the lost 401K match, proving that the focus was still on an investment in the associates' future.

Epiphany #3—While attending a wedding of his friend's daughter, Chapman watched him walk his daughter down the aisle. At the front of the church, he was asked: "Who gives this woman to be married to this man?" And of course his answer was the traditional, "Her mother and I do." In Chapman's mind came the thought of what his friend might want to say ... "Listen, young man, her mother and I have brought this precious child into the world and have done everything in our power to protect and support her growth as the human she was meant to be. This is a sacred trust you are taking on ... do you accept it?" Reflecting on this, Chapman realized that every team member working for Barry-Wehmiller was someone's precious child, and his immediate desire was to ensure that all would be acknowledged, respected, and given the opportunity to flourish as they would in a loving family.

Again for Chapman, this led to immediate action. His thinking about each associate as a precious child, with the need to grow and develop into the best human being they could be, gave rise to the concept that the full responsibility of leaders is to be a good steward of others in their care. Chapman and the leadership team believe that stewardship means to truly care and have a deep sense of responsibility for the lives they touch. It goes beyond ethical behavior, although that is critical too, to taking action from a deep sense of what is right. Another important facet of their description of leadership as stewardship is that it implies trust and freedom of choice. Our role as leaders is not to command and control, but to inspire and guide. It is an opportunity to serve others and the greater good, aligned with the vision and purpose of Barry-Wehmiller.

The team realized that it was going to be a monumental challenge to transform its 'managers into leaders' and the only way this could be realized was by creating a University to teach 'leadership' in harmony with their vision. The challenge was how do you teach 'leadership' when all the traditional Universities taught 'management.' The ensuing action Chapman took was the development of a Leadership Checklist that would become the concepts that would be 'taught' in the leadership development classes at Barry-Wehmiller University (BWU).

Of course, a similar approach of applying a thorough check list prior to taking action is utilized in several industries. For example, before taking off, an airline pilot and co-pilot go through a standard checklist to ensure that the plane is safe and ready to fly. Also, in some hospitals, surgeons in the operating theater go through a checklist with their team to ensure that there are no errors. So this process has ensured thousands of safe flights and many lives saved, sparing patients needless suffering and prolonged hospital stays. In the same way, Barry-Wehmiller determined that to be truly aligned with their vision, they needed a standard of leader performance, expressed in a checklist,

Table 14.2 Leadership Checklist at Barry-Wehmiller

Leadership checklist
I accept the awesome responsibility of leadership. The following statements describe my essential actions as a leader.
I practice stewardship of the guiding principles of leadership through my time, conversations, and personal development.
I advocate safety and wellness through my actions and words.
I reflect to lead my team in achieving principled results on purpose.
I inspire passion, optimism, and purpose.
My personal communication cultivates fulfilling relationships.
I foster a team community in which we are committed to each other and to the pursuit of a common goal.
I exercise freedom, empowering each of us to achieve our potential.
I proactively engage in the personal growth of individuals on my team.
I facilitate meaningful group interactions.
I set, coach to, and measure goals that define winning.
I recognize and celebrate the greatness in others.
I commit to daily continuous improvement.
When we engage our heads, hearts, and hands around these habits, extraordinary levels of trust and fulfillment will result.

Source: Chapman and Sisodia (2015)
Chapman, B. and Sisodia, R., Everybody Matters (NY, NY, Penguin, 2015) pg 140–141

which would guide their leaders to exemplify the 'stewardship' standard of leadership.

The process to develop this checklist again involved many in the organization. From more than 250 leadership traits and characteristics, a checklist of leadership behaviors was defined, which could be taught and that would ultimately impact those in the organization, through the stewardship of their leaders (Table 14.2).

Processes and Initiatives to Engage Everyone in Creating the Future: Everybody Matters

We can bring humanity and dignity back to the workplace by inviting people to own the process. (Chapman and Sisodia 2015)

Barry-Wehmiller accomplished this by launching a customized 'lean' initiative. This initiative was very different from the traditional experience. In most companies, a lean process is intended to reduce costs and improve quality and profitability. However, companies with this goal in mind generally miss the opportunity to genuinely listen deeply to their associates and hear how the process might be completely transformed not only to achieve excellence, but to inspire their associates by engaging not just their hands, but their heads and hearts as well. Inspiration comes when people are truly listened to and engaged in offering their insights and ideas into improving the entire process … again a holistic approach to organizational transformation, engaging *all* the capabilities of the people in designing and achieving compelling goals at work. "We have paid people for their hands for years, and they would have given us their heads and hearts if we had only know how to ask them!"

Barry-Wehmiller developed a 7S system for continuous improvement, building on the widely renowned and adopted 5S Toyota process. Those identified by Toyota in this model (roughly translated):

- Seiri=Sort
- Seiton=Straighten
- Seiso=Shine
- Seiketsu=Standardize
- Shitsuke=Sustain

And recognizing that people are the ones who actually create value, Barry-Wehmiller added:

- Safety (which actually takes the first place on their list)
- Satisfaction

Thus, this process defines the 'good' in the Japanese expression, kaizen "change for good," as the good is created for the individual actually doing the work, not just as an improvement in measurable business results. This process earned the name L3 (Living Legacy of Leadership) because of the effort made in this process to enable people to see the connection to Truly Human Leadership at every level in the organization. The focus was on the individual who was actually doing the work, empowering them to take positive action. This sanctioned their contributions and accelerated the time to experience actual positive changes on the job, because they could take appropriate, responsible action. This process proved its value and gave many divisions and functions in Barry-Wehmiller greater autonomy to align their behavior to the vision and positively 'touch' the lives of their stakeholders (Table 14.3).

It is clear that a unique and critical component of this approach to Lean involves extensive, deep listening and understanding of the perspective of the speaker … in this case, the person doing the work. An extension of this is that Barry-Wehmiller, as a key feature of its culture, has recognized the impact of asking the right thought-provoking questions and fostering a culture where

Table 14.3 Comparison between Traditional Lean and the Living Legacy of Leadership

Comparisons between Lean and L3			
Category	Traditional lean	Barry-Wehmiller	Why
What is it called?	Lean	L3-Living Legacy of Leadership	What you call something matters. L3 is a way of leading and a more human way of living, not a cost-reduction process.
What is the focus in finding areas of improvement?	Waste	Frustration	Waste is about things; focusing on frustration makes it human.
How do we engage people for continuous improvement?	Mandating	Listening	Some traditional Lean leaders come in like dictators, saying, "This is how we are going to do things." And they impose tired approaches that worked in other businesses, building followers not thinkers. We create 'pull' for change in our people. That starts with inviting people to participate, listening with vulnerability and helping people let go of baggage.
How do we think about the process?	Process vs. people	People and process	Some Lean leaders see the process focus as a way to drive out human error and human engagement; our approach is about bringing greater humanity to the process. The process must serve the people, not the other way around.

Source: (Chapman and Sisodia 2015)
Chapman, B. and Sisodia, R., Everybody Matters, (NY, NY, Penguin, 2015)

questions are encouraged and accepted in both directions. The most impactful question has been: "How does this make you feel?"

In fact, frequently, the GPL sessions ask the group for responses to significant questions that have the potential to foster leadership behaviors aligned with the vision and that grow the culture. Questions asked in these sessions include:

- Where are we not living up to our vision?
- Where are the gaps?
- Where are the opportunities?
- What part of this is unclear?

Openness and transparency are not just acceptable but required so that the organization can learn and be inspired to change.

The Barry-Wehmiller Culture

Epiphany #4—"My greatest concern is that what we develop here won't live beyond my years. We could build something great that is too dependent upon me. If something happened to me it would fall apart." Bob Chapman (Chapman and Sisoda 2015).

Since Bob Chapman recognized this dilemma, the leadership team at Barry-Wehmiller has taken a holistic view of embedding Truly Human Leadership and a vibrant culture into the DNA of the organization. This has been a deliberate pursuit, as culture does not happen by accident. At this point, this leadership team can actually state that the people have taken ownership of the culture and that it no longer needs to be driven from the top. When they began this journey, this was the end game. But how did it begin and what tools and methods did they use frequently to accomplish such a BHAG (Big, Hairy, Audacious, Goal)—to embed Truly Human Leadership in the cultural DNA of every one of their associates?

The year 1997 was the beginning of their cultural journey. This was the year that they realized that work could be fun! Their commitment grew to building a sustainable business model, one that would be resilient in shifting times. Business became an enduring engine that could drive a truly human leadership approach and support an organization dedicated to the compelling vision of each human realizing their full potential.

At an early point in the journey, the leadership team realized that they could not let this happen by serendipity, but that they needed to be very intentional and holistic in their approach to building the new organizational values, vision, processes, and methods. These needed to be visible and pervasive so that all could embrace the creation of an institution that will endure and generate value for all its stakeholders.

One powerful process that was used frequently during this journey was a *visioning* process. It was first employed in the development of the GPL but then became a frequent and productive method at all levels of the organization to solve problems, innovate, and refine the direction of the group. It is used to describe what it would look and feel like to achieve the goals of the vision. It communicates purpose and values to everyone in the organization, and then they can take action in harmony with the vision. The visioning process asks the big questions:

- Where are we going?
- Why are we going there?
- How will each of our stakeholders be in a better place when we get there?

And it is used in two ways at Barry-Wehmiller:

- Business visioning—primarily an opportunity to dream about what the business future could be and creating a road map to get there. Definitely a leap and not incremental improvement of the status quo.
- Cultural visioning—about the 'why' in defining the values and behaviors. A disciplined process applied internally not just in the organizational culture, but also in areas such as safety, continuous improvement, and well-being.

Elements derived from the successful development of the GPL cultural visioning experience include:

- Purposeful preparation
- Gathering a wide variety of participants
- Focusing on the people first
- Describing the ideal state

And once the vision is in place, then 'listening' becomes critical. It is important to conduct small group discussions, to identify gaps between the experienced reality and the stated vision. Then leaders must take immediate action to close these gaps.

Of course, during this journey, Bob Chapman asked the question: "How can we ensure that these initiatives to embed a Truly Human Leadership culture in the organization, so that it lives well beyond our tenure?" This is the question he was reflecting on at the beginning of this account.

One step that was undertaken in response to this question was the establishment of the BWU launched in 2008. Again, embracing an approach to leadership development that is ground breaking in its intent and also in its methods, the visioning process for BWU resulted in a very short mission declaration:

- The purpose of the BWU is to develop an integrated, inspirational, and sustainable way of *living our vision.*
- We believe that we can use the power of business to *dramatically impact the world in a positive way.*
- We exist to enhance participants' ability *to touch people's lives* and equip them to be successful with others both inside and outside BWU.

What was different were expressed in three statements:

- We will teach no content from other sources, but what we develop will be distinctively Barry-Wehmiller evocative or express our unique world view.

- Every professor will be a team member of Barry-Wehmiller, rather than someone we hired from the outside.
- Our teaching will be inspirational and transformational (Chapman and Sisodia 2015).

The courses offered were attended voluntarily, and there was and still is a waiting list to take part in the courses. The original Leadership Fundamentals course is a transformative experience that inspires people to truly embrace the awesome responsibility of leadership. It is not restricted to people with titles. In fact peoples' titles, functions, and roles in the organization are not stated during the program. People set aside their professional identity for the duration of the course.

It offers a deeply interactive experience with frequent storytelling to engage the emotions and create connection. The professor's style is to impart insight not information, to create the perfect environment for learning by paying attention to every detail, such as the room configuration; the room dynamic; and the personal disclosures they offer to the participants.

Participants are selected based upon the following considerations:

- What is your sphere of influence?
- Can you make immediate changes?
- Do we think that you personally have the capacity to do that?
- Do we have the right mix of roles in the class?
- Do we have the right balance between office and manufacturing?
- Do we have the right mix between the front line and leadership?
- Do we have good gender balance?
- Do we have good divisional balance?

Another initiative that has spread the Barry-Wehmiller culture globally has been their approach to *acquisitions*. Chapman listened to his mentor Chuck Knight and determined that the best business strategy for Barry-Wehmiller was a combination of organic growth and strategic acquisitions. Barry-Wehmiller went into acquisitions looking for challenged companies where the difficulties they were experiencing would obscure their value to others. Many of the companies had been family businesses with a large installed base of buyers who were in frequent contact with customer service for after-market parts and service. Barry-Wehmiller realized that this was a very good, diversified business strategy for them.

In spreading and embedding the Barry-Wehmiller culture of a Truly Human Leadership model, the first step in a merger was always to visit the acquired company, and rather than a message of "Hello, 30% of you are going to be laid-off," the message was "Hello, welcome to the Barry-Wehmiller family of companies. We value all of your contributions and want to introduce you to our 'Everybody Matters' culture." As a result, the mergers of the acquired companies with Barry-Wehmiller, globally, have been successful. This is amazing, since according to an article by KPMG ('Why Mergers Fail,' April 2012) mergers have a failure rate of anywhere between 50% and 85%. One KPMG study found that 83% of these deals hadn't boosted shareholder returns. Unlike others, Chapman believes that the key for unlocking the potential lies in getting these businesses to change the way they think about value creation and the way they treat their people. During the first meeting with an acquired company, Barry-Wehmiller starts by sharing their GPL and letting people know that the leadership believes in them and that together they would build a vibrant future.

It turns out that once people in various cultures come to understand it, the human value expressed in the Barry-Wehmiller Truly Human Leadership approach is a universally accepted standard. It is universal truth that there is a shared human longing to be valued, supported, to be in charge of the scope and methods in work, and to develop and learn things that motivate and excite us. Everyone wants to know that what they do and who they are matters, whether they are in France, Italy, Germany, the UK, or Spain. Also, the Barry-Wehmiller team works hard to embrace the unique culture of each acquisition and to respect the history of each organization. The team members are proud of their history whether they are in Phillips, Wisconsin, or Lucca, Italy. As stated by the Chief People Officer, Rhonda Spencer: "Implementing organizational change is always a balance between allowing for the uniqueness of each business, and challenging people to move outside their comfort zone to embrace the new and different organizational culture."

Other initiatives that further spread and embed the cultural vision and values across the Barry-Wehmiller business platform include their selection of new hires and performance management processes. According to Rhonda Spencer, hiring is taken very seriously, because their standard is that the new hire will be with the company for life. She states: "We are committed to help them (new hires) grow, use their gifts and talents to the fullest, and help them to become what they are meant to be in this world." Actually by this point the awareness of the Barry-Wehmiller culture is growing, so people are attracted to the organization and want to work there. They have also identified a key set of competencies that are aligned with thriving in their culture and they interview for those competencies generally, but especially for those in leadership roles.

The Barry-Wehmiller Impact

The results are in, and Barry-Wehmiller is now a $2.8 billion company, with 12,000 team members around the world. Its compounded growth rate since 1987, when Chapman began to implement this new approach, has been 18% and its share price has gone up on average 14% a year. All of which reinforces Chapman's insistence that "It's not people over profit, its people in harmony with profit" (Holmes 2017). If businesses don't create sustainable business value, they cannot create a vibrant future for their people and give them opportunities to grow.

The people-centric culture created at Barry-Wehmiller accelerates business performance by enabling all people to realize their full potential. All associates are given respect and dignity in their roles and for their contributions to the business. They believe business performance is the result of maximizing people performance. People growth and business growth are complementary pieces in creating value.

They also that believe that if you can make Truly Human Leadership work in an old-world industrial business like theirs, then you can certainly make it work in all types of businesses.

Their approach is simple, powerful, transformative, and it is a testable idea: "Every one of your team members is important and worthy of care. Every one of them is instrumental in the future of your business, and your business should be instrumental in their lives" states Bob Chapman, "This offers a sustainable human solution, to bring everybody up, not just remove those at the bottom" (Chapman and Sisodia 2015).

A sought after speaker about how to build a thriving people-centric organization, Chapman shares these key takeaways from Barry-Wehmiller's journey to Truly Human Leadership:

- **Management is the manipulation** of others for your success; **leadership** is the **stewardship** of the lives entrusted to you.
- Everybody wants to know that **who they are and what they do matters!**
- **Listening** is a critical leadership skill and the most powerful act of **caring.**

- How we **lead** has a profound impact on how those entrusted to us **live—and their health**!
- The truest measure of success is **by the way you touch the lives** of people!

The desire of Barry-Wehmiller is to inspire other companies and organizations to embrace Truly Human Leadership. They have pioneered the way and are totally generous in sharing their processes, methods, and tools with others to customize to fit their business, industry, and vision. As we consider the learnings out of the Barry-Wehmiller journey, some questions to consider include:

- Do your education and organizational experiences align with the fundamentals of Truly Human Leadership and what are the major differences from your experience?
- Do you feel that business organizations should be focused on shareholder value or stakeholder value?
- Can you identify which of these ideas, processes, and/or methods might be implemented in your organization? And then find answers to the following:
  - What is the opportunity?
  - What are the challenges?
  - What is the vision?
  - What first steps do you need to take?

As Bob Chapman emphasizes, you don't need to wait for a memo from corporate to begin being a good steward of the lives in your care. His advice is to "Embark on your journey now. No executive order is required to allow you to pause each day to have a thoughtful conversation with someone in your organization. Listen to them. Show them that what they do and who they are really matters" (Chapman and Sisodia 2015). The fundamentals are People, Purpose, and Performance. You must embrace the profound responsibility of leadership, inspire your people around a purpose that unleashes human potential, and work together to create value.

References

Myers, J., "Why Don't Employees Trust Their Bosses?", World Economic Forum, 2016. https://www.weforum.org/agenda/2016/04/why-dont-employees-trust-their-bosses /

Netscape editors, "No. 1 Reason People Quit Their Jobs", CompuServe. http://web-centers.netscape.compuserve.com/whatsnew/package.jsp?name=fte/quitjobs/quitjobs

Barry-Wehmiller website. www.barry-wehmiller.com

Rogers, E., & Van Dam, N. *YOU! The Positive Force in Change* (Raleigh, NC: LULU, 2015) p.18

Holmes, P. *Caring and Courage are the Keys to Leadership,* presentations at the Aspen Idea Festival, 2017

Chapman B., & Sisodia, R. *Everybody Matters* (New York, NY: Penguin, 2015) p.6

Gallup Workplace, "Drive Employee Engagement", Gallup. http://www.gallup.com/services/190118/engaged-workplace.aspx?utm_source=gbj&utm_campaign=20161221-gbj&utm_medium=copy

Sinatra, S., "Heart Attack Risk Factors Rise on Mondays", Dr. Sinatra. https://www.drsinatra.com/heart-attack-risk-factors-rise-on-mondays

15

Management After Acquisition Inside Multinational Companies from Emerging Economies: The Haier Experience

Lin Zhou and Runtian Jing

Abstract Post-M&A integration is a highly challenging issue for both buyer and seller companies in international M&A. For buyers from emerging economies, they might face even more difficulties due to the problem of "liability of origin". In this chapter, we first review Haier's acquisition of Sanyo's home appliance business and compare the management philosophies of Chinese and Japanese companies, as well as their solutions to overcome the problem of "big company disease". Then, we recount how Haier has implanted its model of "Individual-Goal Combination" into Sanyo's management system after acquisition, and how it has helped the company to realize employees' potential and to improve market performance. Next, we compare this case with two other M&A cases concerning Haier in Thailand and New Zealand, and illustrate how the "liability of origin" affects post-M&A integration in different cultural contexts. We conclude by giving suggestions to guide future management practices in this area.

The authors would like to thank Jingguo Du, Stuart Broadhurst, Yong Wu, and Xiaoming Yan for their support on this research project.

L. Zhou (✉) • R. Jing
Antai College of Economics and Management, Shanghai Jiao Tong University, Shanghai, China
e-mail: zhoulin@sjtu.edu.cn; rtjing@sjtu.edu.cn

© The Author(s) 2018
S. Iñiguez de Onzoño, K. Ichijo (eds.), *Business Despite Borders*,
https://doi.org/10.1007/978-3-319-76306-4_15

Introduction

Most studies on international management are conducted from the developed economy's point of view. When a multinational company decides to acquire a company in an emerging economy, an important source of disadvantages is the "liability of foreignness", which emphasizes the legitimacy disadvantage of multinational companies in foreign markets due to insufficient information on local networks and institutions (Zaheer 1995).

Companies from emerging economies must face the additional "liability of origin", which might be more troublesome than the "liability of foreignness" when they want to acquire competitors in developed economies (Amankwah-Amoah and Debrah 2017). Liability of origin is a legitimacy disadvantage borne with respect to a specific host country as a consequence of companies' national origins. While "liability of foreignness" causes discrimination against firms for where they are not from (not local), "liability of origin" emphasizes the discrimination against firms for where they are from (the specific countries of origin).

As a result, companies in emerging markets must overcome more of an obstacle while working with acquired companies in developed countries. CEO Zhang Ruimin of Haier Group developed a management model called "Individual-Goal Combination" in 2005 in order to combat big company disease (BCD). It became a success within all Haier subsidiaries across China. The company did not stop there, exporting the model to its international subsidiaries after it acquired a factory in Thailand in 2007, the Sanyo appliance business in Japan in 2011, and Fisher & Paykel in New Zealand in 2012. In the end, the Individual-Goal Combination Model helped these acquired foreign companies overcome their own management problems with different degrees of success.

Haier's "Individual-Goal Combination" Model

Founded in 1984, Haier has rapidly grown from a small refrigerator plant in Qingdao, China, to a global leader in home appliances. Currently, Haier designs, manufactures, and sells various home appliances including refrigerators, air conditioners, and washing machines in over 100 countries.

Under the visionary leadership of Zhang Ruimin, Haier has developed its unique management philosophy and models. For example, to guide the M&A practices, Haier has elaborated a so-called eating shocked-fish approach (Paine and Crawford 1998). In this instance, "eating shocked-fish" means a strategy to acquire companies with good resources and hardware conditions but poor management. In market competition, strong fish cannot be eaten alive, and dead fish may lead to stomachache after being eaten; therefore, the best choice is to eat shocked-fish. After each acquisition, Haier will not lay off the top management team or rank-and-file employees, nor will it provide additional investment. Instead it will export its organizational culture and management model to the acquired firm.

Haier has created a learning culture within the organization, by which it attempts to overcome management challenges in different stages by self-driven organizational transformation. Ten years after being founded, Haier began to feel the symptoms of BCD, which threatens the survival and growth of any multinational company in later development stages. "Big Company Disease is a game played between employees and the various departments. Everyone may damage the interests of the company or other colleagues in order to maximize his or her own interest. Firewalls are built up between departments" (Zhang 2009: 18).

To overcome the BCD problem, Haier undertook various organizational changes to stimulate employees' initiatives and potential. In 1998 Haier introduced an internal market mechanism in an attempt to attach market values to work units and employees. As a further step, in 2005, Zhang invented the management model of "Individual-Goal Combination", in which individual refers to employees, and goal refers to market orders but includes the needs and value of resources of both internal and external users. Unlike employees in most companies who wait for their leaders to assign their work, employees at Haier set their own goals to develop innovative products or services by interacting with internal or external users (mostly through the web), and their compensations are calculated based on the user values they create. Thus, the "Individual-Goal Combination Model" is essentially an incentive system to motivate employees to become user-orientated.

This model has become more mature as it is being continuously improved and refined. At present, approximately 76,000 employees are grouped into over 200 micro-enterprises (MEs), which continuously design and develop innovative products in response to users' demand. An ME is a self-managing team that has the authority to determine its own goals, team members, business model, and rules. An early version of ME in the company's history was called a *Strategy Business Unit* (SBU) or *Zhi Zu Gong Tong Ti* (ZZJYT). Such organizational transformation has proved crucial for Haier to adapt itself in the highly turbulent Internet Age.

Acquisition of Sanyo's Home Appliance Business

Background

The Sanyo Electric Company was founded in February 1947. Starting from the dynamo-powered lamp, Sanyo later entered such fields as speakers, information communication, home appliances, commercial machinery, electronic components, and batteries. At the end of 2002, it owned 158 overseas affiliates, and sales totaled 15.2 billion USD. Meanwhile, BCD problems began to slow down the speed of its market response, and the company started to skid downward. On March 26, 2001, Sanyo initiated a so-called Challenge 21 plan to improve the control function of headquarter operations and the management of consolidated subsidiaries inside the group.

On September 25, 2001, Satoshi Iue, the president of Sanyo, led his management team to Haier to learn how to manage SBUs. In April 2003, Sanyo reformed the company structure based on four business groups (consumer, commercial, component, and service) and 271 SBUs, and the number of employees in company headquarters decreased from 900 to 370.

Unfortunately, the reform aiming to improve resource allocations failed badly. The planned operating income and ROE in 2003 were 165 billion yen and 9.3%, respectively, whereas the actual numbers were 95.5 billion and 2.7%. The 2004 Chūetsu earthquake made things even worse. It severely

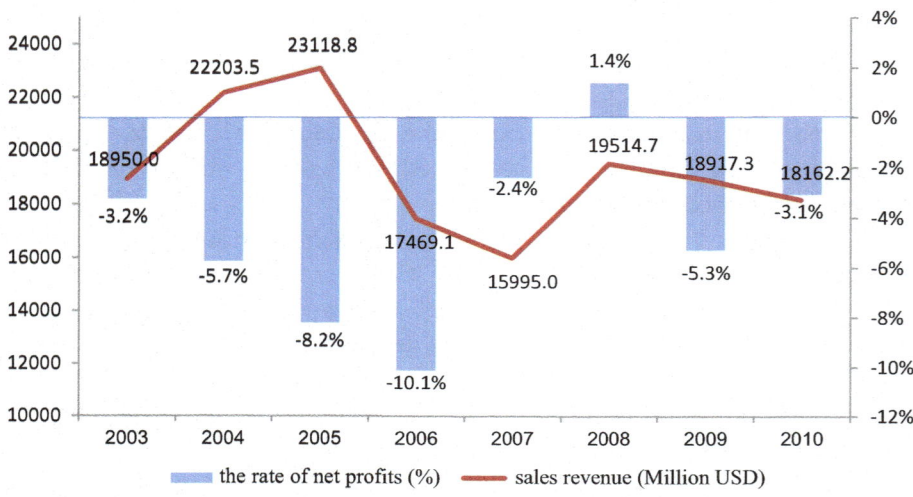

Fig. 15.1 Financial performance of Sanyo before Haier's acquisition

damaged the company's semiconductor plant. Sanyo recorded huge financial losses in the following years (see Fig. 15.1).

In December 2009 Sanyo was acquired by Panasonic. In the M&A process, Panasonic put its emphasis on the battery business of Sanyo, which was then the biggest manufacturer of lithium batteries in the world. But Panasonic did not pay sufficient attention to the home appliance business that Sanyo managed painstakingly because it overlapped with Panasonic's business. The acquisition by Panasonic failed to change Sanyo's management predicament.

Haier's Acquisition of Sanyo Home Appliance Business

In 2001 Haier and Sanyo established an overarching competitive/cooperative relationship before Haier acquired Sanyo's refrigerator business in 2007. In October 2011 Haier acquired Sanyo's white goods business in Japan, Vietnam, Indonesia, the Philippines, and Malaysia, as well as Sanyo's AQUA brand. Mr. Jingguo Du, a long-serving Haier executive, was appointed as CEO to take charge of the new company's transition.

New Organizational Structure

Haier implemented a system-wide M&A approach to maximize synergy among the various functional teams at Sanyo and Haier in different countries, and it rearranged resources in technology, manufacturing, marketing and sales, and the service network from a global perspective. A trinity structure of R&D, manufacturing, and sales was established. Products are sold under both Haier and Sanyo brands in Southeast Asia, and under Haier and Aqua brands in Japan, targeting different market segments. "Haier should definitely capitalize on the Sanyo brand equity to succeed in Japan", said Cristina Baus, a Euromonitor consumer appliance analyst. "Sanyo is perceived as a technologically savvy brand with a strong focus on producing energy-efficient appliances. This should be Haier's main focus".

As the architecture supporting the above business development, Haier Asia International Company was established in Osaka in 2012 to take charge of the development, manufacture, and sale of white goods in Japan and the rest of Asia. The acquired Sanyo AQUA Corporation was officially renamed Haier Aqua Sales Co Ltd.; refrigerator businesses were added, and the company mainly took charge of the marketing of the new brand Aqua in Japan (Fig. 15.2).

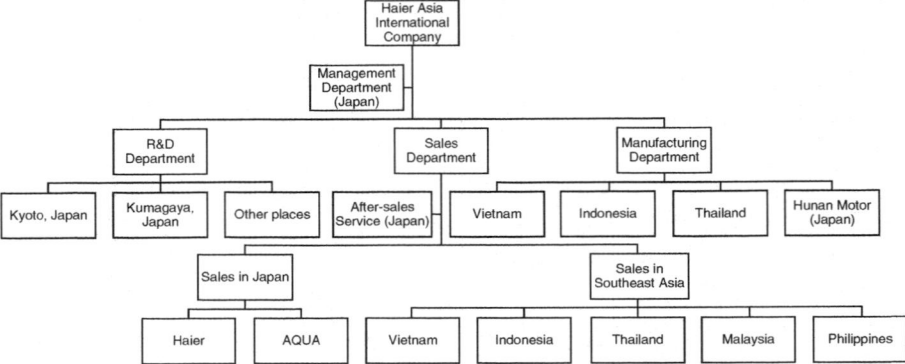

Fig. 15.2 Organizational structure of Haier Asia International

Implementing the "Individual-Goal Combination Model"

Clearly, the performance-oriented culture at Haier runs contrary to Japanese cultural values, as demonstrated by the remarks of a Japanese employee: "I do not want my salary to be much higher than my colleagues; I hope that the design of the income system is based on the achievement of our team, not on that of individuals".

With astute cultural awareness, Du implemented the "Individual-Goal Combination Model" in Sanyo incrementally. First, he decided to give more bonuses to R&D employees who could develop better products. He let the team decide how to distribute bonuses, but on the condition that there must be individual differences to reflect personal contributions. At first, Japanese employees did not accept such an idea and thought it went against team spirit. The conflict lasted for six months before the bonuses were finally distributed after individual contributions were recognized. After this breakthrough, Du began to apply the "two-stage incentive plan" to the R&D team: in the product design stage, designers who could satisfy the requirements from the market department would obtain a performance premium; in the product commercialization stage, designers of products of high market revenues would share the bonus from product sales.

The "Individual-Goal Combination Model" was also applied to set the goals of Haier Aqua. The Aqua team was facing various difficulties after Haier's acquisition. As Haier was a Chinese company and not well-known to Japanese consumers, without the support of the "Sanyo" brand, marketing had to start from scratch. Japanese employees were unstable since they could choose to join Haier Aqua or to work for Sanyo, now part of the Panasonic Group, according to the M&A agreement (Sanchez-Runde et al. 2012). Facing such high levels of uncertainty, the Aqua team proposed a sales goal of seven billion yen for 2012. To the Aqua team, this was already very demanding. However, it was unsatisfactory to Du. He intended to encourage the team to change the goal by themselves.

He first introduced the ongoing "inverted triangle" structural management from Haier headquarters to his Japanese colleagues. In Haier's "inverted triangle" structure, employees (at the top of the inverted triangle) set the sales goal based on their direct interaction with users, while the management (at the bottom) should provide support and resources for the fulfillment of the goals. Du listed the advantages for the employees in pursuing higher goals and suggested ways to overcome some of the difficulties. For example, aided by the financial support from Haier group, the company invited the famous Japanese star Koizumi Kyoko to do the celebrity endorsement. Instead of just imposing a higher goal, Mr. Du asked his Japanese colleagues to "think like CEOs"—in other words, work out how to overcome the obstacles they had identified. The team came up with many creative answers that included starting the design and manufacture of new products before the takeover officially took place. Through candid discussion, Japanese employees learnt how Haier wanted them to rely on their own initiatives. In the end, the president of Haier Aqua Company, Mr. Nakagawa, dramatically changed the original annual sales goal from seven billion yen to 35 billion (accounting for 10% of the Japanese market share). "At first I thought it would be OK if we could accomplish five billion yen, but later we adjusted it to seven billion yen. However, at the end of 2012, we ended up at 34.8 billion yen!" Nakagawa stated.

Result of the Implementation

Sanyo returned to profitability eight months after Haier's acquisition. In 2014, the total sales of Haier Asia International Company reached 35.6 billion yen with a profit of 2.6 billion yen. More importantly, the Japanese employees began to accept Haier management and show a positive working morale. "In that year, we created a special record. At that time, it was expected by Sanyo and the industry that after the acquisition, 30% to 40% of the Japanese employees would resign because most of them are technicians, who take charge of a certain aspect of the entire technology system. In addition, the integrity of the system is very important. I was also very worried. In fact, in that year, only one employee resigned, for family reasons. After several years, apart from retirements, the rate of resignations among technicians is nearly zero, something which was beyond our expectations" (Jingguo Du).

After acquisition, most companies would operate their foreign subsidiaries with expatriate managers from headquarters, such as in the cases of Lenovo's acquisition of IBM PC business and Suning's acquisition of Japan's LAOX Company. Haier, on other hand, usually employs experienced local employees to manage foreign subsidiaries. It respects local managers and believes in their capability and professionalism. Currently, only six Haier employees have been sent to Haier Asia in Japan. In total, the company has over 700 employees in Japan and 6700 employees in other Southeast Asian countries.

For Haier, the acquisition of Sanyo helped to realize its strategic objective. Haier had only a 0.2% share of Japan's major electric appliances market in 2010, according to Euromonitor. Now, with the dual brand strategy, the refrigerators, freezers, and washing machines of Haier and AQUA capture 12% of the Japanese market (2016.4.1–2017.3.31, GFK[1]).

Two Other Cases of Overseas Acquisition by Haier

Acquisition of the Thailand Factory

The history of cooperation between Haier and Sanyo could be dated back to many years ago, when both took advantage of each other's sales network to sell products in the same market.

In 2007, Haier acquired a refrigerator factory owned by Sanyo in Thailand, which had suffered financial losses for several years. The factory was one of the production bases of Sanyo in Southeast Asia, and its products were sold in Southeast Asia. Given its strategic position, the organization structure of the factory was very simple. There were 1500 local employees working in manufacturing positions, and there were no independent R&D and sales functions, only managers in charge of contacting Japanese headquarters on orders and technology.

There were five Japanese managers at the top management level: president, general manager of the factory, and directors of technology, purchasing, and quality. The Japanese managers' wages were based on seniority, and the local employees were paid according to the incentive system of "daily wage" plus "annual bonus". While the daily wage was fixed, the annual bonus was negotiated by the labor union and the Japanese managers each year in November. Since the annual bonus of the Thai managers were tied to employees' wage level (between 0.5 and 6 months of wages), they would secretly support employees to push for higher annual bonus. The system above, on one hand, provided a low incentive to work, and, on the other hand, made it hard to reach a negotiated settlement. The negotiation always lasted 10 rounds over two months and often required the intervention of the local government. The problem was that employees had no sense of accountability for poor performance. The factory never made a profit under Sanyo's management.

Before Haier acquired Sanyo's entire appliances unit, acquiring its Thailand factory was the first step for Haier to enter Southeast Asia. On August 6, 2009, Mr. Yong Wu alone was appointed as the general manager tasked with undertaking a strategic transformation of the factory. "Haier was very confident to give a young person like me an enterprise with annual sales of 300 million dollars". At that time, Wu was just 31 years old, while the Japanese president was 63 years old, and many of the other managers were over 50 years old; the strategic transformation really was a huge challenge for Wu.

"At that time, I had nothing to rely on, except the Individual-Goal Combination Model, which was the management tool that I was mostly familiar with". Wu adjusted the organizational structure at first, establishing R&D and market departments, while seeking other market opportunities beyond Sanyo orders. He planned to promote the incentive system of "Individual-Goal Combination" in Thailand through four stages.

In the first stage, through meetings and information dissemination, all employees knew that everyone should have a market goal. The reward level of the employees was lower than the average level of local firms due to the company's poor financial performance. In the second stage, the focus was on how to accomplish a strategic transformation in three years. Wu had discussions with over 20 managers from different departments: "What should you do if we want to accomplish the strategic transformation?" With this as the operational goal, the performance of goal fulfillment would become the basis for the annual bonuses. In the third and the fourth stages, goals were set for all managers and for all ordinary employees.

It was difficult to convince all employees in the last stage as many were accustomed to income appreciation through negotiations conducted by the labor union. The management team explained to all employees how their bonuses would be linked to their individual goals and to the realization of the company's goals (within Haier, this is called "Valuation Adjustment Contract").

The turnaround was immediate as the Thailand factory became profitable for the first time at the end of 2009. It has never looked back since. Employees also saw their incomes rise as they were linked to the firm's objectives. The mean bonus of all employees was 2.5 months' salary in 2010, and it climbed up to four months' salary in 2013.

Acquisition of Fisher & Paykel

Founded in 1934, New Zealand's Fisher & Paykel designs and manufactures premium brand kitchen and laundry appliances. Its products, best known for their creative designs, are available in over 80 countries. The company ran into financial difficulties after it launched a major expansion in 2007. Haier came to the rescue when it purchased a 20% share of Fisher & Paykel that allowed the company to refinance its debts. Haier took complete control of Fisher & Paykel when it acquired the company for 766 million USD.

After the acquisition, Haier and Fisher & Paykel integrated resources and developed many creative products together. Direct-current dynamo is a technology developed by Fisher and Paykel. It makes washing machines quieter and more stable, and it promises 30% in energy savings. Haier installed the direct-current dynamo in many washing machines sold in China, which brought significant revenue to Fisher & Paykel. It also helped Haier keep its leading position in the washing machine market.

While Haier kept on the senior management team of Fisher & Paykel, it applied the "Individual-Goal Combination" model to the acquired company. In the early days at Fisher & Paykel, employees were offered shares in the company as part of their compensation package. But the compensation policy was completely undistinguished at the time of Haier's acquisition. For service employees, 100% of their compensation was fixed; for salesmen, 90%; and for senior leaders, 100%. This was in line with prevailing business practices in New Zealand and Australia. Inspired by Haier's practices, the company restructured its organization and the compensation policy. Individual compensations were linked to performance. Currently, the fixed part of the salary of service employees stands at 85%, sales 80%, and senior leaders 70%. "It has been moving over there during the period of four years, leading to this significant move" (Stuart Broadhurst, CEO of Fisher & Paykel).

Fisher & Paykel also learned from Haier's innovative approach toward ME and platform-style organization (Jing et al. 2016), and decided to reconfigure its organizational structure. The company first identified 10 products and functional fields. A virtual ME would be set up at the cross point of each product with functional field and regional market, such as Cooking Australia or Commercial Sales China. Fisher & Paykel currently has about 500 virtual MEs. Each virtual ME must have leaders who are in charge and provide business updates on a weekly and monthly basis. At the same time, ten platform departments have been set up, such as Quality, Product development, Product Management, Procurement, HR, and IT, to provide the necessary support to MEs. Thus, previously isolated functional departments became MEs that had responsibility for the entire business operations, and their employees began to be challenged to create their own market values.

Fisher & Paykel has fully recovered from its worst days in the aftermath of the financial crisis. The ratio of net profit reached its highest level since the financial crisis, from 3.9% in 2008 to 7.9% in 2016. Haier and Fisher & Paykel together account for 42% of sales in the home appliance market in New Zealand. It won first prize in a vote among New Zealand consumers to choose "the most respectable home appliances brands".

Conclusions

After the acquisition cases covered in this chapter, Haier also completed a mega-deal to buy GE appliances for $5.6 billion in 2016, which catapulted Haier to the position of number one home appliance maker in the world. It is a tantalizing prospect to see whether Haier can repeat its success with this latest acquisition.

When going global, companies from emerging market countries must confront the "liability of origin" problem in addition to those common to all multinational firms. Many companies based in economic giants (such as Sanyo and GE) might have built up over the years "a culture of intolerance" that resists different ideas that are not born within, particularly those of newer players from emerging market countries. What can emerging market companies learn from Haier's experiences?

First, be confident in your own management knowledge. Many firms like Haier have developed business models and ideas that are battle-tested in response to fierce competition in emerging markets. They are highly entrepreneurial and focus on creating maximal values for consumers, which can serve as a base of cultural changes in guiding companies in developed economies to overcome BCD problems. Many people are surprised that three giant US companies, that is, Budweiser, Burger King, and Heinz, are doing well after they were acquired by 3G Capital, a relatively unknown Brazilian investment company. The secret to 3G's success is simple: it improves the efficiency of these giant firms by eliminating bureaucracy and excess costs (Correa 2014), an approach deriving from the same creed as that of Haier's Individual-Goal Combination Model.

Second, make sure the two sides know each other well and build mutual trust. It is important to have open communication on management philosophy, as well as changes to be implemented as a result of the acquisition, so that there are no biases and mistrust between the two sides. In the three cases considered, Haier simply sought to acquire companies with which it had already had a long-term cooperative relationship. They already had joint subsidiaries, or strategic alliances, or stock-holding, and so on. In fact, Haier has never carried out a hostile takeover. Then, after each acquisition, Haier usually forms joint taskforce teams to develop new business models or new products, through which the acquired firms gain opportunities to learn about Haier's ideas and ways of doing business under the stewardship of Haier's management.

Notes

1. Here, GFK stands for Gesellschaft für Konsumforschung (Society for Consumer Research), one of the largest global market research institutes, which was established in 1934. Sic passim.

References

J. Amankwah-Amoah, and Y.A. Debrah, "Toward a Construct of Liability of Origin", *Industrial and Corporate Change*, 26, 2017.

C. Correa, *Dream Big: How the Brazilian Trio behind 3G Capital – Jorge Paulo Lemann, Marcel Telles and Beto Sicupira – acquired Anheuser-Busch, Burger King and Heinz*. (Primeira Pessoa Press, 2014).

R. Jing, Y.N. Zhao, and Y. Teng, "Platform Organization, Mechanism Design, and Intrapreneurship: Case Study on Platform Transformation of Haier Group" (In Chinese). *Management Journal Quarterly*, 4, 2016.

L.S. Paine and R.J. Crawford, "Haier Group, The (A)." *Harvard Business School Case* 398–101, March 1998.

C. Sanchez-Runde, Y.T. Lee, and S. Reiche, "Hailing a New Era: Haier in Japan", *IESE Business School Case* DPO-264-E, November 2012.

S. Zaheer, "Overcoming the Liability of Foreignness". *Academy of Management Journal*, 38, 1995.

R.M. Zhang, "Put Leader in the Bottom of Pyramid Structure" (In Chinese). *IT Time Weekly*, 7, 2009.

Index[1]

---

[1] Note: Page numbers followed by 'n' refer to notes.

© The Author(s) 2018
S. Iñiguez de Onzoño, K. Ichijo (eds.), *Business Despite Borders*,
https://doi.org/10.1007/978-3-319-76306-4

Printed by Printforce, the Netherlands